ict

for

you

Stephen Doyle

Published in 2003 by:
Nelson Thornes Ltd
Delta Place
27 Bath Road
CHELTENHAM
GL53 7TH
United Kingdom

05 06 07 / 10 9 8 7 6 5 4 3

A catalogue record for this book is available from the British Library.

0 7487 7416 5

Illustrations by John Fowler, Derek Griffin, Alex Machin and Mark Ruffle

Design and page make-up by GreenGate Publishing Services

Printed and bound in Spain by Graficas Estella

Contents

Acknowledgements

The author would like to thank the following people for their valuable advice and assistance in the development of this resource:

Rick Jackman and Sarah Robertson at Nelson Thornes; Louise Watson; and Katie Chester and Dave Mackin at GreenGate Publishing Services.

AQA (NEAB) (SEG) / AQA examination questions are reproduced by permission of the Assessment and Qualifications Alliance.

The publishers would also like to thank the following for their permission to reproduce copyright material:

ActivCard (Figure 3.5); Age Concern England (www.ageconcern. org.uk) (Figure 9.9); Amazon.co.uk (Figure 8.1); AOL (Figure 9.4); BAS/ P. Bucktrout (Figure 3.15); DRS Data & Research Services plc (Figures 2.10 top left and 3.9); easyjet airline company limited (Figures 8.2 and 8.7); ebay (Figure 8.4); Environmental Images (Figure 1.13); GNC (Figure 1.15); Google Inc (Figure 8.3); HSBC Bank plc (Figure 8.5); Experimental GPS Buoy River Level Monitoring System (Figure 1.14) courtesy of the IESSG, University of Nottingham; Liverpool Echo (page 229); Steve Jebson, Information Officer and Visual Aids Manager, Met Office (Figure 3.14); Modus (Figures 11.1 and 11.2); Quadrant Systems Limited (Figures 11.3 and 11.4); Royal Caribbean Cruise Lines AS (Figure 3.2); Thomas Cook 2003 (Figure 8.6); © Wolfgang Kaehler/CORBIS (Figure 9.7).

Microsoft Office screenshots are reproduced with permission from Microsoft Corporation. Microsoft and its products are registered trademarks or trademarks of Microsoft Corporation in the United States and/or other countries.

Introduction

Welcome to the AQA GCSE in Information and Communication Technology (called ICT for short). On starting this course, you will have already had plenty of exposure to ICT and ICT systems. All the information that you will need to do well on the course is presented here in an easy-to-understand way. Where a term is used for the first time, it is clearly explained.

All of the examples for the practical work are based on Microsoft applications. Microsoft Office XP has been used throughout. If you have a previous version of Office, then most of the instructions in the practical activities will still work. Microsoft Word XP and Excel XP are very similar to the previous versions, but the database Access differs more.

If you do not use one of these Microsoft products, do not worry as similar tools and facilities are available in other applications, although the techniques in using them will be different.

Specification coverage

Specifications are documents produced by the assessment board, AQA, which tell the teacher what they have to teach and also how the assessment is made. There are two different specifications for AQA; Specification A and Specification B. This book covers both of these specifications for both the full and short courses.

The full course and the short course

You can approach Information Communication Technology by taking either:

- GCSE Information Technology full course, or
- GCSE Information Technology short course.

The differences between the full and the short course

The short course involves less work than the full course and when passed, you will have the equivalent of half a GCSE. At a later date, you can do some further work to convert this into a full GCSE. Completing the short course GCSE shows that you are a skilled user of ICT but you have not studied the subject to the depth of the full course.

The full course includes all the requirements of the short course but requires you to extend your knowledge of ICT.

Tiers of entry

As well as the two types of course (full and short) there are two tiers of entry for each course. For both AQA specifications (A and B), the tiers and grades are summarised in the table below.

Tier	Grade range
Foundation	C to G
Higher	A* to D

Activities

There are plenty of activities in this book to help build up your skills in using software and also to build up your knowledge of the subject. The different types of activity included in the book are outlined here.

Paper-based activities

This type of activity is indicated by the following icon.

Paper-based activities are activities that are completed away from the computer and on paper.

Computer-based activities

This type of activity is indicated by the following icon.

Computer-based activities are activities performed using the computer. Some of these activities will be research-type activities where you have to find out further information using the Internet.

Find it out yourself

'Find it out yourself' is an activity where you have to do your own research and investigation about a subject or topic.

Case studies

The case studies outline how real businesses and organisations use ICT in a way that is covered by the material in the chapter. The case studies are followed by some questions designed to reinforce the points made in the case study.

Build your notes

'Build your notes' is a feature included at the end of each chapter. You have to insert words from a list to complete a number of sentences. When you have copied out and added the correct words, you will be left with a set of notes that you can use for revision.

Multiple-choice questions

Multiple-choice questions are not part of the assessment used by your assessment board, AQA, but they are included here as a way of testing how well you have understood the material in the chapter. Your teacher/lecturer will go through the answers with you.

Examination questions

The first set of examination questions has been structured so that the questions get harder the further you work through it. These questions have been written in a style similar to the actual examination questions which follow.

F questions

F questions are those examination questions set at the foundation tier. If you are taking the foundation tier then you should answer these questions. Many of these questions are actual examination questions.

H questions

H questions are those examination questions set at the higher tier. If you are taking the higher tier then you should answer these questions. Many of these questions are actual examination questions.

Key jargons

Key jargons in each chapter define terms and words that you may be unfamiliar with and that are important for you to understand.

Glossary

The glossary, which is at the end of the book, contains all the words defined in the key jargons. If you find a term that you do not understand you can do one of two things to help you find out what it means. First, you could turn to the glossary and look it up. Here you will find a brief explanation of what it means. However, if you want a fuller explanation, use the index to find the relevant chapters. When a key term is used for the first time, its definition is included on the page in the 'key jargon' feature.

Looking up words in the glossary will reinforce your knowledge of the subject. You will find that several of the shorter examination questions will ask you what is meant by certain computer terms. It is a good idea to try to learn some of the words in the glossary along with their meanings.

How will your work be assessed?

There is a mixture of examination and coursework with the coursework component representing 60% of the total marks.

Advice on coursework and exam preparation

Chapter 16 provides information on what you have to do for your coursework. There are also some useful tips that will enable you to get the best mark for your work.

Also included in this chapter is a section on examination preparation.

Getting data into a computer

Input devices

Hardware and software: what is the difference?

An information system consists of two main parts, the hardware and the software.

Hardware is those parts of the computer you can touch. Here are some questions to help you decide whether something is hardware or software.

Is it a piece of computer equipment?　　　YES
Can you touch it?　　　YES

Then it is **hardware**.

Is it a piece of computer equipment?　　　YES
Can you touch it?　　　NO

Then it is **software**.

A blank floppy disk or a blank CD is classed as hardware. If a computer program is placed on either of them then the program itself is called software. You can see that it is hard to separate the two, although if you sent the program over the Internet then it would no longer need a disk until it was stored at the other end of the line.

Key Jargon

hardware – the parts of the computer that you can touch and handle.

software – the actual programs that allow the hardware to do a useful job.

Activity 1

1　There are two parts to a useful computer system: hardware and software. Explain the differences between hardware and software.

2　Use your definition in the first part of this activity to decide whether each of the following items is hardware, software or something else. Copy the table out and put a tick in the appropriate box.

continued over page

Name of item	Hardware	Software	Something else
Screen			
Keyboard			
Operating system			
Wordprocessing program			
Printer			
Blank DVD			
Game for a Sony Playstation			
Toaster			

Types of computer

There are a number of options available when buying a computer. Here are some of the options.

Mainframe computer

A mainframe computer is a large, powerful computer which is capable of supporting a large network with 500+ terminals. These computers are used by large organisations such as banks, building societies and insurance companies.

Personal computer

A personal computer (or PC) is the type of computer that you are most likely to encounter at home or at school.

Desktop computers are computers where the screen sits on top of the processing unit. Tower and mini-tower systems usually have the processing unit at the side, out of the way of the screen and keyboard.

Laptop computer

Laptop computers are designed to be portable and used while you are on the move. They usually include a touch pad instead of a mouse for moving the cursor and making selections. Laptops make use of LCDs (liquid crystal displays) which use less power than a normal screen. This is important because laptops require rechargeable batteries when used away from a power supply. Because laptops are often used in public places, there is a greater likelihood of their being stolen than other types of computer.

Personal digital assistants (PDAs)

PDAs are much smaller than laptops and are around the size of a calculator. PDAs allow you to:

- keep track of appointments
- store details (names, addresses, e-mail addresses, etc.) of contacts
- exchange data with PCs
- check your e-mail.

Mobile telephones

Many mobile phones come with features that you would also find on a PDA or computer. Mobile phones that have computer features are generally larger than other mobile phones because they have to include a small keyboard to allow the user to type in information. Some mobile phones now incorporate a digital camera which means that you can take pictures and e-mail them to your friends.

Activity 2

Use the Internet to find out more about the following:

- mainframe computers
- desktop computers
- tower/mini-tower computers
- laptop computers
- personal digital assistants (PDAs)
- the latest mobile telephones with computing facilities.

For each one:

1 Copy a diagram of the computer/device, or download a diagram from the Internet.

2 Write a few sentences to describe the main uses of the computer/device.

What is a peripheral device?

A peripheral device is:

- a device connected to a computer
- a device that can be controlled by a computer (it could for example, be switched on and off by it)
- situated outside the computer (the computer being the processor and the memory).

Peripheral devices include devices to:

- input data to the computer
- output information from the computer
- store data and programs.

Activity 3

Draw a diagram of a cut-open computer. Mark on the diagram the computer processor and the memory chips. Show wires going to other devices (i.e. the peripheral devices).

Figure 1.1

Can you name each of these peripheral devices?

Input peripherals

Input peripherals are used to get data from the outside world into a computer. For example, you may want to store and then send a story that you are writing to someone in another country.

A keyboard can be used to type in the story. Your story will then be converted into a code (a series of 1s and 0s), stored on disk and then sent along a wire.

Keyboard

- Keyboards are the most popular input peripheral.
- Most computer systems come with one.
- Inputting large amounts of data using a keyboard can be slow.
- It is easy to make mistakes when you are using a keyboard.
- You need special training to be able to type quickly and accurately.
- If you are not used to using a keyboard, they can be frustrating.

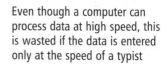

Even though a computer can process data at high speed, this is wasted if the data is entered only at the speed of a typist

There are some specialist keyboards which do not look like an ordinary keyboard. One type of keyboard has raised dots on the keys and is used by people with a visual impairment.

Figure 1.2

Notice the raised dots on this keyboard, which is specially designed for visually impaired people

A simpler Braille keyboard has fewer keys. It is used by people who have severe visual impairment.

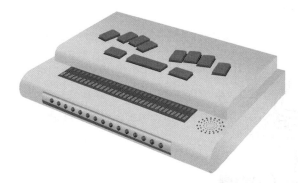

Figure 1.3

This Braille keyboard has fewer keys than a standard keyboard

Some keyboards, like the one in Figure 1.4, have been redesigned to make them easier or more comfortable to use.

Figure 1.4

This keyboard is in three sections. This is intended to make it more comfortable to use

Hunt

Press

If you are a 'hunt and peck' typist, then a keyboard can be very frustrating to use

Mouse

This input device is small (like a mouse) and has a 'tail' in the form of a wire connecting it to the computer.

- When the mouse is moved, a pointer or cursor moves on the screen.
- The movement of the mouse is mirrored by the pointer.

- Selections can be made by pressing the mouse buttons.
- Some mice have a scroll wheel for scrolling through long documents.
- A mouse can also be used for drawing lines and sizing graphic objects such as photos or clip art.

Figure 1.5

Wireless mice use infra-red rather than a wire to send signals to the computer. Notice the scroll wheel between the two mouse buttons

Touch pad

Like a mouse, a touch pad controls the position of the cursor on the screen.

- A touch pad is used instead of a mouse on a laptop computer.
- The movement of your fingers on the touch pad is mirrored by the pointer on the screen.
- There are buttons next to the touch pad to make selections.

Figure 1.6

Most laptop computers do not come with a mouse because there is not always the space to use one. You can still connect a mouse to a laptop if you find it easier to use than a touch pad

Tracker ball

- A tracker ball can be used instead of a mouse.
- A tracker ball is like an upside-down mouse.
- The 'mouse' part is stationary and the 'ball' part moves.
- The user rotates the ball with their thumb or the palm of their hand.
- The movement of the ball is mirrored by the cursor on the screen.

Joystick

You have probably used a joystick for playing games, such as those in amusement arcades.

Figure 1.7

A tracker ball. By moving the ball you move the pointer/cursor on the screen

- They are ideal for moving and making selections quickly.
- This is why they are an ideal input device for playing games.
- They can be used to move the cursor on a screen.
- Specially designed joysticks that can be operated by the foot or mouth are used by disabled people.

Microphone

A microphone allows you to speak into a computer, and for the sound to be converted into data. Special software, called **voice recognition** software, is used to interpret the sounds.

- A microphone lets you tell the computer what to do.
- You can dictate letters and other documents directly into your wordprocessor or e-mail package.
- A microphone lets you send voice mail or take part in videoconferencing.
- You can issue instructions to your computer verbally instead of typing them in.

Scanner

- **Scanners** are used to scan photographs and other images so they can be put into documents or web pages.
- Scanners can also be used to scan text into a wordprocessing or other package. This saves having to retype it.

Figure 1.8

A joystick is ideal for moving around and firing in a fast-moving computer game

digital camera – a camera that can be used to take a picture and store it digitally.

scanner – a hardware device used to scan pictures or text into a computer system.

voice recognition – the ability of a computer to 'understand' spoken words by comparing them with stored data.

Figure 1.9

A scanner

Digital still camera

A **digital camera** looks like an ordinary camera except there is no film and there is usually a screen on which you can view the picture (called the image) you are taking.

- Digital cameras have a memory where the image is stored.
- The more memory a camera has, the more pictures you can store.
- There are no developing costs (unlike an ordinary camera).
- You can take as many pictures as you want, depending on the amount of memory the camera has.
- You can transfer the images to a computer where you can store and edit them.
- Digital cameras are more expensive than ordinary cameras.

Digital cameras produce an image made up of millions of dots. The greater the number of dots in the same-sized space, the clearer the picture will appear. This is called the resolution of the image. High-resolution images use more dots and take up more storage space on the computer.

A

Buy the film

Take the pictures

Wait until you have used all the film

Pay and wait for film to be developed. Pay for extra copies

B

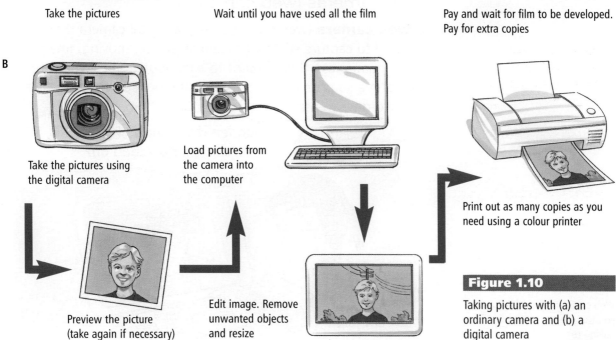

Take the pictures using the digital camera

Load pictures from the camera into the computer

Print out as many copies as you need using a colour printer

Preview the picture (take again if necessary)

Edit image. Remove unwanted objects and resize

Figure 1.10

Taking pictures with (a) an ordinary camera and (b) a digital camera

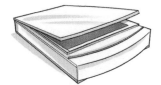

A

To store on a computer or send using email, each photo has to be scanned in

Photo albums take up so much space

Photo can come out wrong – or not at all!

B

You can attach the pictures to e-mails and send to friends

You can put the pictures on your website without the need to scan them in

You can store thousands of photos on your hard disk or on CD-RW

Figure 1.11

(a) Some of the problems with conventional photography
(b) The advantages of digital photography

Digital video camera

Digital video cameras look like ordinary video cameras, except that they store images digitally.

- Most digital video cameras can capture still as well as moving images.
- Images can be stored and edited on a computer.
- You can use video in web pages.

Web cameras (web cams)

A **web camera** (web cam) is simply a digital camera that can be used to capture still images and video (i.e. moving) images. These images can then be sent to a computer where they are stored in a suitable graphics format. If required, the images can be used on a website.

I wonder if he knows he has his web cam switched on?

Web cams are good fun because you can see the person you are talking to

If you buy a computer system, a web cam might be included with it. The camera is placed on top of the monitor. Such a system can be used for **videoconferencing**.

Web cams are not restricted to the tops of computer monitors. They have many different uses.

Advertising

Cruise companies place web cams on their ships so that potential customers can see what is going on aboard the ship and where the ship is at a particular time.

Childcare

All parents worry about their children. When they leave their children in nurseries or playgroups, they want to be sure that they are looked after properly. Some childcare centres have web cams so that parents can view their children on the computer while they're not there.

Weather checks

There are web cams just about everywhere, so you can see what the weather is like virtually anywhere in the world. This might be useful if you were planning a trip and needed to know what the weather conditions were likely to be when you arrive.

Digitiser

A digitiser is a pen-like device that you use to draw or write on a tablet, which looks a bit like a flat board. The image or text then appears on a computer screen.

- You can use a digitiser to design your own graphics.
- Digitiser tablets include special buttons for selecting particular shapes or pictures.

Sensors

Sensors are able to detect and measure physical quantities such as temperature, pressure and amount of light. The signals picked up by the sensors can be sent to and then analysed by a computer. (There is more about sensors in Chapter 3.)

- Sensors can be connected directly to a computer.
- Sensors can record data over a period of time, and then the data can be transferred to a computer (this is called **data logging**).
- Sensors can be found in lots of devices such as burglar alarms, central heating systems and washing machines. As

videoconferencing – using computer equipment to conduct a virtual face-to-face meeting.

web camera – a digital camera used to capture still and video images.

Figure 1.12

Using a digitiser tablet

data logger – a sensor that automatically collects data over a certain period of time.

sensors – devices which measure physical quantities such as temperature and pressure.

well as taking measurements they are also used to control the device in some way.

Figure 1.13

A sensor being used to monitor air pollution in a busy city

Case study

Noisy neighbours

Jane has a problem with her neighbours. They play their music too loud, right through until the early hours of the morning. Jane has rung up the council to complain. They have supplied her with a data logger that records the loudness of the sound and the time. The data collected will be used by the council as evidence to prosecute Jane's neighbours.

1 Here are some sensors the council can choose from.

- heat sensor
- light sensor
- pressure sensor
- sound sensor.

Which sensor would be used to measure the loudness of the music?

2 Why is the time recorded at the same time as the sound is measured?

Flood warnings

The water levels in rivers are continually monitored by sensors. The data from the sensors is sent directly to a computer, which uses weather data and data about the tides to predict when and where flooding could take place. The use of sandbags and other measures can be taken to minimise any damage caused by the flooding.

Red light cameras

Have you ever seen anyone go through a red light at traffic lights or at a pedestrian crossing? You can see how dangerous it is and it causes many accidents. Red light cameras are used to photograph automatically any vehicle going through a red light. There is a sensor buried in the road which detects vehicles travelling over it once the lights are on red. When the sensor detects a vehicle going through a red light, a photograph is taken to identify the vehicle. Another photograph is then taken showing the vehicle in the intersection. The time, date and speed of the vehicle are also recorded. A letter is sent to the owner of the vehicle who then has to pay a fine.

Touchscreen (touch-sensitive screen)

To operate a **touchscreen** you simply touch the item on the screen you wish to select. Touchscreens are ideal input devices in certain situations because they are so easy to use.

- They are used in restaurants and shops because the staff need little training to use them, and they reduce the risk of errors.
- Touchscreens are ideal for use in public information systems such as tourist information displays and timetables.

Figure 1.14

Water levels in rivers are continually monitored to assess the danger of flooding during heavy rainfall

Key Jargon

touchscreen – a special type of computer screen that is sensitive to touch. A selection is made from a menu on the screen by touching it.

Figure 1.15

A touchscreen being used in a health-food shop to find information on products

13

A light pen enables you to draw directly on the screen. This is very useful if you are a designer or artist

Light pen

Using a light pen, you can select items on a computer screen by touching them with the point of a pen. You can also draw lines by using the screen like a piece of paper.

Getting data out of a computer

Output devices

After data entered into a computer has been processed, the resulting information needs to be output. There are many different output devices. The screen (monitor) and printer are the most popular.

Output peripherals

Output peripherals are devices that allow you to view information produced after data has been processed.

Screen (VDU or monitor)

Screens are sometimes called monitors or VDUs (visual display units).

- Screens come in many different sizes.
- They are usually in colour.
- They are useful for displaying the results of enquiries (When is the next train to ...?, Do you have a holiday on this date ...?).

If you are doing design work or desktop publishing, the screen needs to be as large as possible.

Laptop computers use TFT LCD (thin film transistor liquid crystal display), flat panel display screens. This is because they are very thin and flat. TFT LCD screens are also becoming popular in desktop computer systems because they take up much less space on the desk than an ordinary screen and they generate less heat.

Printer

Printers are used to produce a printed copy of the output (called a hard copy). There are several different types of printer and which one you choose depends on the type of document you want.

Dot matrix printer

You may not have seen this type of printer as they are not very common. They work like a typewriter and use small pins that hit an inked ribbon to form the characters on the page.

Figure 1.17

A flat-screen monitor

- Dot matrix printers are noisy.
- They are normally used with continuous stationery (a long piece of paper with holes down the side and perforations between the pages).
- They are useful for printing multi-part stationery (stationery that needs to be printed through several sheets).
- The characters are not printed clearly – they appear to be made of many tiny dots.
- Dot matrix printers are cheap.
- They are not suitable for wordprocessing or desktop publishing work.

Ink-jet printer

An ink-jet printer can be used to print in colour as well as black and white. The ink is sprayed onto the paper.

- The output from ink-jet printers is of high quality.
- They are quiet.
- They are cheap to buy although the ink cartridges are quite expensive.
- The ink can smudge on the paper.

Laser printer

Laser printers produce the highest quality output and are the most expensive type of printer. Laser printers are capable of printing in colour, as well as black and white.

- Laser printers produce very high quality text and graphics.
- They are fast.
- They use a toner cartridge as well as ink.

Plotter

Plotters are ideal for printing out graphs, designs, plans and maps. They produce very precise drawings.

- Colour plotters use a series of different-coloured pens.
- There are two types of plotter: flatbed or drum.
- Drum plotters use large sheets of paper and flatbed plotters use small sheets of paper.
- In a drum plotter the paper moves.
- In a flatbed plotter the paper does not move.

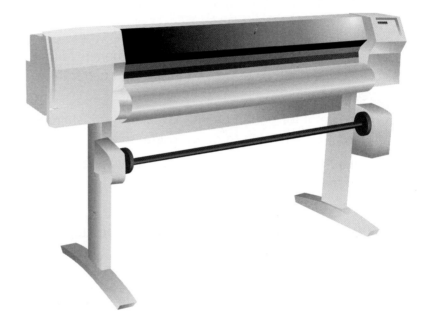

Figure 1.18

Drum plotters are used by pattern makers, architects and engineers for printing their designs and plans

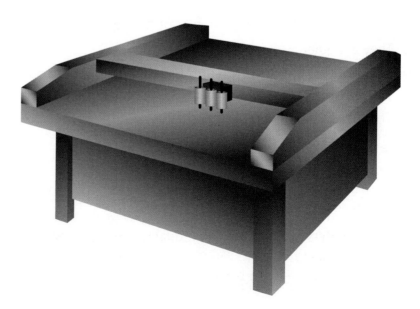

Figure 1.19

Flatbed plotters can be very big and take up a large amount of space

Activity 4

There are many different types of printer, for example:

laser printer   ink-jet printer   dot matrix printer

1 Which one of the printers listed above would be used with continuous stationery?

2 Which one is likely to be the most noisy?

3 Which printer from the list produces the lowest quality text?

4 Which printer from the list would use a toner cartridge?

Speakers

If you want to hear sound or speech from your computer system, then you need speakers as an output device. Here are some of the things that you can do if your computer system includes speakers:

- You can listen to messages left on the computer in voicemail systems (a voicemail system is like a telephone answering machine except the voice messages are digitised and stored on the computer).

- You can listen to radio stations anywhere in the world using the Internet.

- You can listen to downloaded music from the Internet or on CD.

- You can make use of multimedia programs (encyclopaedias, games, learning resources, etc.).

Using a computer to operate switches

Switches can be turned on and off using a computer. A computer can be used to control a central heating system. A temperature sensor is used to measure the temperature in a room. The signal is sent to the computer where it compares the temperature with the desired temperature of the room. If the room is cooler than the desired temperature, the computer turns the heating on using a switch. If the room becomes too hot, then the computer turns the heating off.

Key Jargon

actuator – a hardware device, such as a motor, which reacts to signals given to it by a computer.

Using a computer to operate an electric motor

Electric motors can be controlled by computers. For example, a computer can be used to control a motor that opens and closes a window in a greenhouse. A computer can also be used to switch a pump on or off.

A device which responds to a signal from a computer is called an **actuator**. The electric motor and pump in this example are therefore actuators.

Where data is stored in a computer
Storage devices and media

Once data is in a computer, where is it stored? For example, when you type in a letter using your wordprocessor, where is it stored? If you haven't saved it, it is stored in the memory. The memory of the computer consists of a number of computer chips. Data held in memory is available immediately it is needed.

There are two types of storage:

- main store (memory storage in chips in the computer)
- backing storage (storage on magnetic disks, magnetic tape, CD, etc.).

Memory

Memory can be **volatile** or **non-volatile**. With volatile memory, the data is lost when the power is turned off. Non-volatile memory does not lose data when the power is switched off.

There are two types of memory:

RAM (random access memory)

- **RAM** is held on a computer chip.
- You can write data into RAM and also read data from RAM.
- RAM is volatile memory.
- RAM needs power. If the power is switched off the data in RAM disappears.
- RAM holds data and programs.

ROM (read-only memory)

- **ROM** is held on a computer chip.
- ROM cannot be altered by the user.
- You cannot store your own data on ROM.
- ROM is used to hold the instructions for starting up the computer.
- ROM is non-volatile memory.

Cache

Cache is pronounced 'cash'. It is a very fast part of a computer's memory which allows instructions to be carried out at very high speeds.

Printer buffer

When jobs are sent to the printer by a computer they cannot be printed all in one go. Instead a printer buffer is used where the print jobs wait until the printer can deal with them. The printer buffer acts as a 'waiting room' for jobs sent to the printer, and frees the computer to get on with other tasks.

Units of memory and storage

The amount of data and instructions a computer can store in its memory are measured in bytes. One byte contains eight bits (a bit is a binary digit – 0 or 1). A single character (a letter, number or symbol on the keyboard) can be stored in one byte. This means that one byte is an extremely small unit of storage. We normally measure storage/memory in terms of kilobytes (kB), megabytes (MB) or gigabytes (GB).

Approximately:
1000 bytes = 1 kilobyte; 1000 kilobytes = 1 megabyte; 1000 megabytes = 1 gigabyte

Key Jargon

non-volatile memory – memory which does not lose programs or data when the power is switched off.

RAM – random access memory. A fast, temporary memory area where programs and data are stored only while a computer is switched on.

ROM – read-only memory. Computer memory whose contents can be read but not altered.

volatile memory – memory which loses data and programs when the power is switched off.

Activity 5

1 A floppy disk has a storage capacity of 1.44 MB.
   What is this approximately in
   a   bytes
   b   gigabytes?
2 A program is distributed on floppy disks. If the size of the whole program is 10 MB, what is the minimum number of floppy disks (1.44 MB capacity) that it can be distributed on?

Backing storage

Hard disks

All computers come with a hard disk drive. It is on the hard disk that programs and data are stored.

- On hard disks, the data is represented as a magnetic pattern.
- Reading data onto and off a hard disk is much faster than using a floppy disk.
- Hard disk drives are more reliable than floppy disk drives.
- Hard disks can have a huge storage capacity.

Floppy disks

Floppy disks consist of a floppy (i.e. flexible) disk inside a hard case.

- On floppy disks, the data is stored digitally as a magnetic pattern on the surface of the disk.
- Floppy disks are portable and are ideal for moving data from place to place.
- Floppy disk drives are slower than hard disk drives.
- You have to look after floppy disks carefully – they are easily damaged.
- Floppy disks are very cheap.
- Most computers come with a floppy disk drive.
- Floppy disks hold 1.44 MB (megabytes) of data.

CD-ROM

CD-ROM means compact disk read-only memory. CD-ROM disks store data as an optical pattern on a plastic disk. They use the same method of storage as music CDs.

- You can only read data off a CD-ROM disk. Users cannot write data to the disk.
- CD-ROM disks have a large storage capacity (typically 600 MB).
- They are used to distribute software (just one or two CD-ROM disks can hold as much software as lots of floppies).
- CD-ROM disks are ideal storage for multimedia (encyclopaedias, clip art collections, etc.).

CD-recordable (CD-R)

CD-R allows you to store your own data on a CD, but only once.

- Once data is recorded onto a CD-R, it cannot be altered.
- CD-R disks can be used to back up files on a hard drive.

CD-rewriteable (CD-RW)

A **CD-RW** disk allows data to be put onto a disk and altered over and over again.

- You can treat a CD-RW disk just like a floppy or hard disk. You can write data onto the disk many times.
- CD-RW disks are more expensive than CD-R disks.

DVD (digital versatile disk)

DVDs will be familiar to most of you as they are used to distribute the latest films. DVD has a much higher storage capacity than CD-ROM.

- CD-ROM typically stores 600 MB whereas DVD can store 4.7 GB.
- DVDs are now available with a storage capacity of 17 GB.
- DVD drives are replacing CD-ROM drives on the latest computers.
- They are being used in an identical way to CD-ROM for the storage of data.
- There are two types of DVD, called DVD-ROM and DVD-RAM.

DVD-ROM

This is just like CD-ROM except with greater storage capacity.

- You can only read the data off the disk – you can't alter it.
- It is used mainly for films, software, multimedia, games programs, etc.

DVD-RAM

This is just like CD-RW because you can store data on the disk over and over again.

Special drives are needed and these are more expensive than CD drives. DVD-RAM will eventually take over from the video cassette recorder (i.e. video recorder) for recording television programmes.

Key Jargon

CD-ROM – a compact disk containing data and programs that can only be read.

CD-RW – a CD that can be used in a similar way to a floppy disk.

DVD – digital versatile disk. A disk with a larger storage capacity than a CD-ROM. Set to replace CD-ROMs, recent models allow the user to write data to the disk.

Magnetic tape

Magnetic tape stores data on a plastic magnetic-coated tape. The tape is similar to the tapes used to store music.

- Magnetic tape has a huge storage capacity.
- Magnetic tape is used to back up the data stored on hard disks.
- Because it takes time to move the tape to the position where the data is stored, tape storage is much less common than disk storage.

Backing up your data and programs

Backing up your programs and data means keeping copies in case the originals are lost or damaged. Here are some reasons why you should back up your programs and data.

Programs crash

Computer hardware can be stolen

Power cuts can happen

You can write over an important file

Computer hardware can go wrong

Disasters!

Figure 1.20

Things that can happen, causing you to lose programs or data

Activity 6

Computer people use many different terms when talking about computers. This makes it difficult for beginners to understand them.

Here are some terms. You have to explain them in easy-to-understand language. Try not to use any new computer terms when you explain them.

1 hardware

2 software

3 hard copy

4 peripheral

5 input device

6 output device

7 storage device

Activity 7

Here are some places where data can be stored:

RAM   ROM   DVD   magnetic hard disk   magnetic floppy disk

Choose one of these places to answer each of the following questions.

1 Which of the above lose data when the power is turned off?

2 Which one of the above looks just like a music CD?

3 There are two parts to computer memory. Which one in the list above is non-volatile?

4 Where would data and programs normally be stored?

5 Which one of the above is ideal for the distribution of films?

6 Which one of the above would be the best for transferring data between computers?

Find it out yourself

1 Take a look at a recent advert for a complete computer system. You can find these adverts in newspapers and computer magazines. Cut the advert out or photocopy it.

Here is what you have to do next.

a Make a list of the components included in the computer system. (You need to list these because all computers look the same on the outside.)

b For each item in your list, write a few sentences to explain its importance.

If there are any items that you have not come across before, you will need to look them up in a computer dictionary. A good place to look for a computer dictionary is the Internet. Here are two sites to get you started.

A good dictionary that makes use of 3D graphics to explain the terms:

http://207.136.90.76/dictionary/

You can always Ask Jeeves (the kids' version):

http://www.ajkids.com/

2 If you look in a computer magazine such as 'Computer Shopper', you will see that there are many computer peripherals that have not been mentioned in this chapter. Each of them has a specific use.

Find out:

a The name of a peripheral.

b How it can be used.

c A typical job/application to which it is well suited.

Activity 8

You will be using a lot of computer hardware as part of your GCSE work at school. It is important for you to know what hardware you will be using.

For this activity you have to find out what hardware is available in your school. Copy and fill in the following form to help you.

Input devices

....

....

Output devices

....

....

Storage devices (backing store only)

....

....

Build your notes

Here are some notes that summarise this chapter. The notes are incomplete because they have words missing.

Using the words in the list below, copy out and complete the sentences A to S, underlining the words that you have inserted. Each word may be used more than once.

> peripheral   volatile   DVD   touch pad   joystick   digital
> ink-jet   output   keyboard   software   programs   mouse
> hardware   input   laser   scanner   sensors   ROM
> microphone   non-volatile   RAM   digitiser

A   A computer system consists of two parts: _____ and _____.

B   Software is the name given to the _____ which enable the computer to do a useful task.

C   Devices used to get data from the outside world into the computer are called _____ devices.

D   _____ devices are devices that are connected to the computer and under the control of the computer.

E   The commonest input device, which comes with all computers, is the _____.

continued over page

F A _____ is used to move a pointer or cursor around the screen and to make selections.

G Where space is restricted, such as on a laptop, a _____ _____ is used instead of a mouse.

H A _____ is used primarily with games software.

I With a voice recognition system a _____ is used as the input device.

J The input device used to scan in text and images is called a _____.

K Cameras that can transfer an image directly to the computer are called _____ cameras.

L A pen-like device used to draw or write on a tablet is called a _____.

M Quantities such as temperature and pressure can be detected and measured using _____.

N Printers and plotters are examples of _____ devices.

O The type of printer that produces the highest print quality print and uses a toner cartridge is called a _____ printer.

P A cheaper printer, which squirts a jet of ink at the paper is called an _____-_____ printer.

Q There are two types of memory: one retains data when the power is removed and is called _____; the other loses data when the power is turned off and is called _____.

R ROM is classed as _____ whilst RAM is classed as _____.

S _____ can store more data than a CD-ROM and is used to store films as well as data.

1 An ink-jet printer is best described as:

a an input device
b an output device
c a storage device
d computer memory.

2 Which two of the following are input devices?

a mouse
b laser printer
c monitor
d scanner

3 Which one of the following is a storage device?

a scanner
b disk drive
c microphone
d central processing unit

4 Which one of the following is an important feature of RAM (random access memory)?

a It is an input device that only allows data to be entered slowly.
b Its contents will not be lost when the computer is switched off.
c Its contents will be lost when the computer is switched off.
d It is an input device that only allows data to be entered quickly.

5 Smoke alarms are often fitted in homes. Which one of the following devices can be used to detect smoke?

a an OCR reader
b a mouse
c a thermometer
d a sensor

(NEAB Tier F, June 2000, p1, q1 to 5)

6 **Which three of the following are input devices?**

a scanner
b laser printer
c monitor
d OCR reader
e mouse
f database

7 **Which three of the following are output devices?**

a OMR reader
b ink-jet printer
c light pen
d VDU
e CD-ROM
f motor

8 **Which three of the following are storage devices?**

a disk drive
b CD-ROM drive
c modem
d plotter
e ROM
f speaker

9 **A computer peripheral is best described as:**

a an off-line device
b a device which is part of a computer's operating system
c a device which is part of the CPU
d a device which is attached to and under the control of a computer. *(NEAB Tier F, June 2000, p1, q1 to 4)*

1 Suggest, with a reason, the printer that is most suitable in each of the following situations.

   a A printer that will print invoices on multi-part stationery.
   b An inexpensive printer that can print colour posters.
   c A very fast printer for printing hundreds of personalised letters for a mail shot.
   d A printer capable of producing a very high quality colour image.

2 Give the names of **two** input devices that you might find on a laptop computer.

3 Liquid crystal displays are used with laptop computers. They are also becoming very popular with desktop computers. Give **one** reason why they are chosen for desktop systems.

4 All computer systems can be split into three main components. They are shown in the following diagram.

Copy and complete the diagram below by adding the names of **four** different input devices and **four** different output devices.

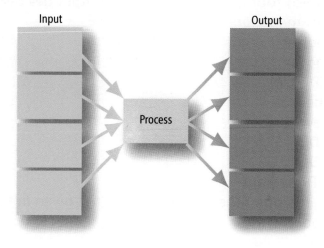

5 The keyboard is the most popular input device.

a Give **one** advantage of using a keyboard as an input device.

b Give **one** disadvantage of using a keyboard as an input device.

F | Questions

1 a RAM is a type of volatile memory used by computers.
  (i) What do the letters RAM stand for?
  (ii) Explain what is meant by the term 'volatile memory'.
  (iii) Why is RAM needed in a personal computer?

b ROM is a type of non-volatile memory used by computers.
  (i) What do the letters ROM stand for?
  (ii) Explain what ROM would be used for in a personal computer.

c Give **two** uses for each of the following devices in a personal computer:
  (i) hard disk drive
  (ii) floppy disk drive
  (iii) CD-ROM drive

(NEAB Tier F, June 2000, p2, q6)

2 a Which **four** of the following are output devices?
dot matrix printer
plotter
mouse
CD-ROM
speaker
keyboard
VDU
ROM
DTP package

b Name **one** other output device, not given in the list above.

c   Name **two** input devices, given in the list above.
d   Name **one** input device, not given in the list above.

(AQA Specification A Tier F short course, specimen paper, q1)

3 RAM and ROM are both types of computer memory.

a   (i)   What do the letters RAM stand for?
    (ii) What do the letters ROM stand for?

b   Which statements below are correct about RAM and which are correct about ROM?
    (i)   Contents are lost when the computer is turned off.
    (ii) Contents are not lost when the computer is turned off.
    (iii) Stores the programs needed to start up the computer.
    (iv) Stores application programs and data when they are being used.

(AQA Tier F, June 2001, p2, q1)

H Questions

1 Which **five** of the following are input devices?

touch-sensitive screen
plotter
motor
CD-ROM
speakers
graphics digitiser
VDU
ROM
DTP package
light pen
microphone
sensor
RAM

(AQA Specification A Tier H full course, specimen paper, q1)

2 Keyboards are the commonest input device.

    a Explain why the keyboard is the most popular input device used with computers.

    b Keyboards are unsuitable as input devices for large volumes of data. Give **three** reasons why this is so.

    c Here is a list of situations. Choose which input device would be the most suitable for inputting the data into the computer.

      (i)   Taking a photograph to input directly into a document without the need to develop the film.

      (ii) Including a video clip in a website.

      (iii) Accepting instructions from people who are accessing information about their building society accounts by touching the screen of a special monitor.

      (iv) Including a diagram in a document that has already been drawn on a piece of paper.

      (v) Issuing instructions to a computer's operating system by using your voice.

      (vi) Used with a laptop computer as an alternative to a mouse for moving the cursor on the screen and making selections.

      (vii) Taking temperature readings automatically at a weather station.

3 a Copy and complete the table below.

Application	Most suitable output device
Producing a large plan of a house	
Producing a colour picture taken with a digital camera	
Producing a series of invoices with several copies that can be sent to different departments	
Producing a warning when a barcode is read incorrectly	
For listening to messages from a voicemail system	
Displaying the results of a quick search on the availability of a holiday	

b Memory can be classed as volatile or non-volatile. Explain briefly what this means.

c ROM and RAM are both types of memory.

   (i) Explain the meaning of the terms ROM and RAM.

   (ii) Why are both types of memory needed?

d Explain the purpose of the following:

   (i) cache

   (ii) printer buffer.

Software

Key Jargon

program – the set of step-by-step instructions that tells the computer hardware what to do.

software – the programs used in a computer.

virus checker – a program that detects and gets rid of computer viruses which can do damage to a computer system.

What is software?

Software is the general name given to all the **programs** that can be run on computer hardware. Games, wordprocessors, databases, **virus checkers** and Microsoft Windows are all examples of software.

The two types of software

Operating systems and applications

Operating systems

There are two types of **operating system**: operating systems (usually meaning single-user operating systems) and network operating systems. Network operating systems are more complicated because they have to deal with more than one user at a time. This means that:

- security needs to be greater
- users need to have access to a central pool of data
- users need to be restricted to certain files.

What does an operating system do?

An operating system is a program (i.e. a piece of software). A computer is useless without an operating system.

The main purpose of the operating system is to allow the **applications software** (i.e. the programs, such as games, wordprocessors, etc.) to interact with the computer hardware. Basically, the operating system tells the computer hardware what to do.

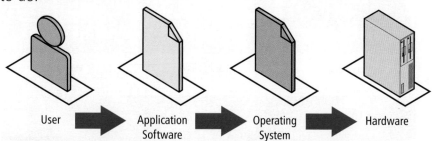

User → Application Software → Operating System → Hardware

Here are some things the operating system does:

- It allows the application being run to do things such as print a file, save a file and open a file.
- It sorts out where to store the data on the disk drives.
- It deals with security by allowing users to create user names and **passwords**.
- It allows you to organise your files by creating folders (places to put similar files together), and to copy and delete files.
- It manages the data travelling between the peripherals (printers, scanners, etc.).

User interface

When you turn on a computer you see a **user interface**. This consists of the cursors, prompts, icons, menus, etc. that allow you to do things with your computer. A user interface can make your computer either hard or easy to use. You will probably have experienced software that is frustrating to use. This could be because the user interface has been badly designed.

Key Jargon

applications software – software designed to do a particular job.

operating system – the software that controls the hardware and runs the programs.

password – a group of characters (i.e. letters, numbers and punctuation marks) that needs to be entered to gain access to a program or a computer system.

user interface – the way that a user interacts with a computer system.

I see Perkins in Human Resources is having problems using the new software again!

Command driven   Menu driven   Graphical

Very hard   Fairly easy   Very easy

Figure 2.2

Different types of user interface

Figure 2.3

Here is the more familiar (and modern) type of interface, the GUI (graphical user interface)

Figure 2.4

Here you have to accurately construct commands. This is a command-driven interface

Figure 2.5

Factors to consider when designing a user interface

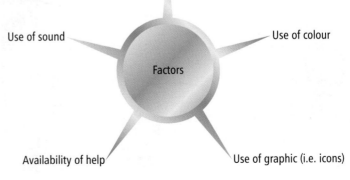

Position of items on screen

Use of sound

Use of colour

Factors

Availability of help

Use of graphic (i.e. icons)

Utility programs

Utility programs are provided as part of the operating system but they can also be bought separately. A utility program is a program that performs a common task (e.g. copying files or listing the files on a disk).

Tasks carried out by utility programs that are provided as part of an operating system include:

- formatting disks (preparing disks for use)
- listing files
- copying files
- copying disks
- renaming files
- backing up files
- searching for particular files.

Here are some tasks which are sometimes provided as part of an operating system or bought as a separate utility program:

- repairing damaged files
- detecting and removing computer viruses (a virus checker).

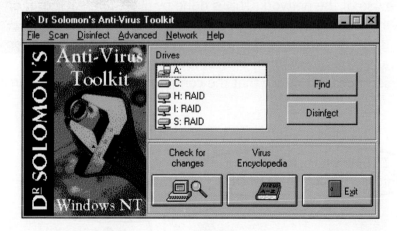

Figure 2.6

Probably the most widely used and essential utility program that is bought separately is the virus checker. Nobody should be without one!

Multi-tasking and multi-user operating systems

Multi-tasking

It is possible to have several windows open at the same time. For example, you might be printing a very long document and want to type in another document at the same time. This is an example of multi-tasking.

No need to wait until you have printed one document before starting the next

Here the computer has lots to do – it is playing a music CD and accessing the Internet at the same time

Figure 2.7

Multi-tasking allows the computer to do more than one job at the same time

Multi-user

A multi-user operating system allows several users to access the same data at the same time. Multi-user operating systems are used with networks. Each person on the network appears to have sole use of the network. This is done by allocating each user on the network a time slice of the computer's time. Once they have used up this time slice the next person is given a go, and so on. Because the processor of the computer works so fast, each person does not notice that the computer's time is being shared.

Where is the operating system stored?

The operating system is usually stored on the computer's hard disk drive. Part of it will also be in ROM (read-only memory).

Here is what happens when you first switch the computer on:

As soon as the power goes on, part of the operating system residing in ROM starts to work. These 'built-in' instructions contained in ROM are automatically obeyed as soon as you press the power start-up button. This process is often called 'booting-up' the computer. The instructions tell the computer where the rest of the operating system is located. They also tell the computer to load these instructions and start obeying them.

Applications software

Applications software is software that is capable of doing a specific job. A job is also called an application.

When you buy applications software you need to make sure of the following:

- that it will work with the hardware that you are using
- that it will work with the operating system that you are using.

Some software can be used in any type of business and is called general purpose software. General purpose software includes:

- wordprocessing
- spreadsheets
- databases
- desktop publishing
- presentation.

Some software is developed for a particular application. For example, there is software that helps in the running of a school. It keeps details of staff, students, timetables, etc. It can only be used to help run a school – it cannot be used for any other purpose.

Printer drivers

A printer driver is software that is needed to convert a printing request from the applications software into a language that the printer understands.

Integrated packages

Most people have some use for wordprocessing, spreadsheet and presentation software. These software packages often come as part of an integrated package. An integrated package is easier to use than separate software packages. This is because all the pieces of software in the integrated package look similar and are used in a similar way. Also, it is much easier to pass data from one package to another if the whole package is integrated. For example, you might want to put a copy of a spreadsheet into a wordprocessed report and this is easier using an integrated package.

Microsoft Office is an example of an integrated package.

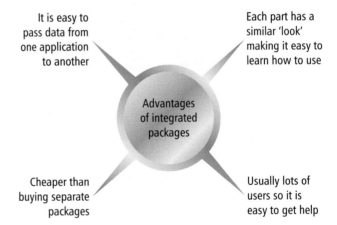

It is easy to pass data from one application to another

Each part has a similar 'look' making it easy to learn how to use

Advantages of integrated packages

Cheaper than buying separate packages

Usually lots of users so it is easy to get help

Figure 2.8

The advantages of buying integrated packages rather than separate packages

Activity 1

Find out the names of the individual software packages in the integrated package called Microsoft Office.

For each of the packages named, write a short paragraph explaining the purpose of the package.

The development of applications software

Applications software is written in a programming language by a person called a programmer. The programmer designs and then puts together the step-by-step instructions that tell a computer what to do. The whole set of instructions to do a particular task is called the program code.

Just as there are a lot of spoken languages in the world, there are many computer languages. Which one you use to write a program depends on the type of task you want the program to carry out.

Here is a table giving the names of some popular computer programming languages. Also included in this table is the type of task that each language is ideally suited to.

Language	Application
C++	A general-purpose programming language
Visual Basic	Ideal for creating windows-style programs
Java	Ideal for public websites and intranets
HTML	Used for developing web pages and websites
LOGO	Used for teaching children about programming and computers. Children are taught to write instructions that move a turtle on the screen

Developing software is like buying clothes ...

If you buy some clothes you will probably buy them 'off the peg'. In other words you just choose clothes (the size, colour, style, etc.) that are already made. If they are not quite what you want or they don't fit correctly you can either put up with them, or return them to the shop.

This is like packaged software. You simply buy it over the counter at a computer shop or via mail order.

Another option is to buy the clothes and then have them altered slightly to fit you (for example, by taking up a hem). This costs a lot less than having clothes made specially for you.

Some software is like this because it is possible to configure it (alter it slightly) to suit the user.

You also have the option of making more extensive alterations to your clothes. You could have coloured patches added to your jeans. This makes them look different from other people's jeans.

Software is made up of program code. It is possible to alter this code. This is called customising the program to meet the needs of the user.

If you had the money and the time, you could get clothes specially designed and then made specifically for you. They would fit you perfectly and the design would be exactly as you wanted.

Customising means that slight alterations can be made!

Large companies sometimes choose to design and then write their applications software from scratch. The advantage of this is that the software fits their needs perfectly.

The software fits the company, rather than the company having to alter the way it works to fit the software.

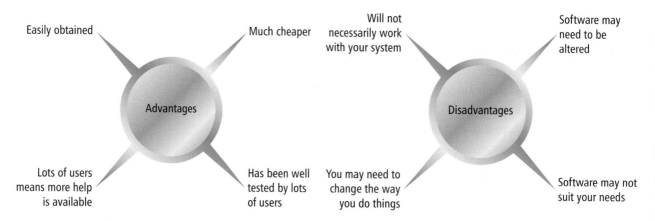

Easily obtained

Much cheaper

Will not necessarily work with your system

Software may need to be altered

Advantages

Disadvantages

Lots of users means more help is available

Has been well tested by lots of users

You may need to change the way you do things

Software may not suit your needs

Figure 2.9

The advantages and disadvantages of buying packaged software compared with having software specially written

Macros

Macros allow you to record automatically a series of keystrokes so that you can simply press a combination of keys to repeat them when required. For example, you could write a macro that allows you to simply press two keys and get your name and address printed at the top of the page when you are writing a letter using your wordprocessor. Macros are very useful for repeating tasks that need to be done over and over again.

Running applications software

Here are some terms you will need to be familiar with when talking about applications software.

On-line

On-line means available for immediate use. It can also mean that you are connected to the Internet or another network service. A peripheral device, such as a printer or scanner, that is turned on and connected to a computer for immediate use, is also said to be on-line.

Processing

Processing data can be done a bit at a time (**real-time processing**) or the work can be saved up over a period of time and done all in one go (**batch processing**).

To understand the difference between real-time and batch processing we can look at the similarity with washing your clothes.

Real-time processing would be similar to wearing each item and as it became dirty, washing it. You would be washing clothes one or two items at a time. It would be wasteful in terms of time and resources (electricity, washing powder, etc.). However, there might be a situation where you would want to do this. Say you had a favourite shirt or dress and needed it for a night out but it was dirty. It would be important to get the item clean, there and then, so the washing would be real time.

Most people, on the other hand, would keep the dirty clothes until they had a batch. They would then put the batch of clothes along with the washing powder (i.e. the inputs) into the machine, select the program and leave the machine to get on with it. The outputs (i.e. the clean, dry washing) are all produced in one go.

Batch processing

Batch processing is used when a particular job needs to be done in one go rather than being broken down into a number of parts. All the relevant data is collected and processed together. It has the advantage that once all the inputs are ready and the program has been selected, the computer can just get on with the job without any human intervention.

Key Jargon

batch processing – all the inputs needed are batched together and processed in one go.

macro – a program written using applications software to automate a collection of keystrokes or events to save time.

real-time processing – the input data is processed as it arrives. The results have a direct effect on the next set of available data.

Batch processing is ideal for:

- producing attendance statistics from attendances recorded on special forms that are read automatically by the computer (called OMR, see page 65)
- producing bills for water, gas, telephone and electricity companies
- producing monthly bank or credit card statements
- marking multiple-choice examination papers.

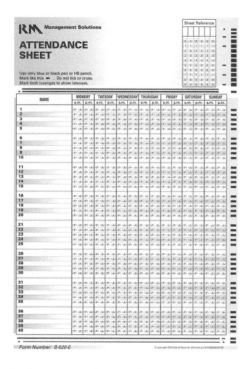

Once a job is started, you can relax and watch the match, and make sure the paper doesn't jam the printer!

Registers on OMR forms can be read by a computer. The data is processed and attendance figures for each pupil are printed

Scripts for multiple-choice tests can be marked and processed by a computer. It is quicker, cheaper and more accurate to do it this way

Figure 2.10

Examples of batch processing

Real-time processing

With real-time processing, the system is automatically updated every time a change is made. This means that the system always contains up-to-date information. An airline booking system would use real-time processing so that as seats are sold the number of seats available would automatically be reduced. This would prevent double booking. Because terminals need to be connected to the computer all the time, a real-time system is also an on-line system.

Real-time processing is ideal for:

- flood warning systems
- booking systems (for airline, holiday, concert or theatre tickets)
- autopilots for aircraft
- computer games
- traffic light control systems
- process control systems in factories (e.g. steel making or chemical plants)
- controlling robots.

Activity 2

Here are some situations. Which ones are suited to batch processing and which are suited to real-time processing?

1 Producing quarterly bills for a utility company (gas, electricity, telephone or water).
2 Dealing with payments made by customers towards their credit card bills at the end of the month.
3 Checking the availability of seats on a certain flight.
4 Marking multiple-choice answer sheets for a GCSE examination, making use of OMR (see page 65).
5 Monitoring the snow conditions in an alpine resort so that an avalanche alert can be issued if necessary.
6 Controlling the automatic pilot in an aircraft.
7 Booking a ticket for a pop concert.

Transaction processing

Transactions are bits of business; an order arrives, a customer changes their details, a customer makes a payment and so on. They can occur at any time and need to be dealt with quickly. Transaction processing takes place when needed, rather than at set times like batch processing.

Background processing

This type of processing occurs 'in the background' when the user is not interacting with the program. For example, you could be typing in a letter while the computer is checking for viruses between keystrokes.

Interactive

This describes a two-way conversation between a computer and a user. The computer asks a question and the user gives the answer, and then the process is repeated. It is a bit like a question and answer session.

Activity 3

Software is either applications software or operating system software.

For each of the following, say which of these two types of software it is.

1 software that decides where to put the data on a disk drive
2 wordprocessing software
3 kitchen design software
4 software that allows users to design leaflets and printed material
5 software that controls the hardware directly
6 an accounts package
7 software that allows you to organise your files in folders
8 software that allows files to be copied
9 database software

Activity 4

A book containing a list of computer terms and their meanings is called a computer dictionary. A shorter list is called a glossary and there is one at the back of this book.

There are many good dictionaries and glossaries of computer terms on the Internet. If you do not understand what something means then you can look it up. Sometimes it is useful to look up several definitions of the same term.

It is important to find sites on the Internet where computer terms can be looked up.

1 Here is a good site where a computer dictionary can be found:
www.maran.com/dictionary/index.html
Access this website on the Internet.

2 Use the computer dictionary on this website to access definitions for each of the following terms. Write down each term and what it means.

a   applications software

b   operating system

c   icon

d   integrated package

e   interface

f   GUI

g   multi-tasking

h   window

i   pull-down menu

Find it out yourself

If you look in any computer magazine (*Computer Shopper* is a good one to choose), you will see a lot of different software for sale in the advertisements. Choose ten different types of software.

For each type of software, find out:

1 the name of the software

2 how the software can be used

3 a typical job/application to which it is specifically suited.

Activity 5

You are now going to produce a picture of the screen (called a screenshot) of the graphical user interface you are using (either at home or at school).

Here are the steps that you will need to take:

1 Load your operating system in the normal way.

2 Press the Prt Sc button on your keyboard. This will make a copy of the screen and store it on the clipboard (an area of memory). At this stage, nothing happens that you can see.

continued over page

3 Now load your wordprocessing software.

4 Start a new document.

5 Press Enter a couple of times to leave a few blank lines at the start of the document. This is to make room for a title to be inserted.

6 Click on Edit and then Paste. This copies the contents of the clipboard (i.e. the screenshot of your GUI) into the document (see Figure 2.11).

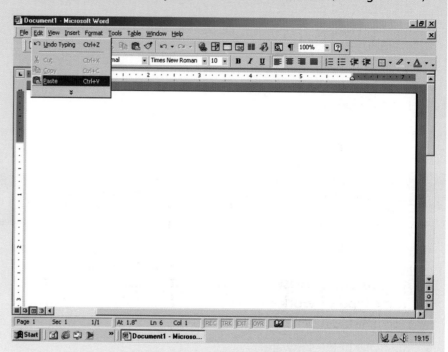

Figure 2.11

Your document, with Paste selected

Your screen should now look something like Figure 2.12.

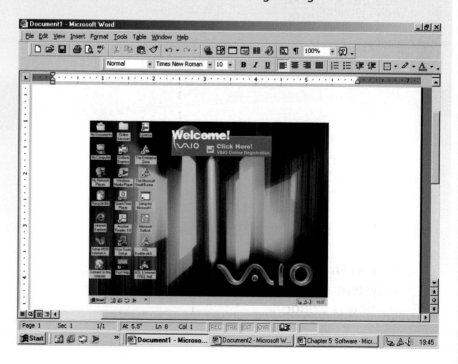

Figure 2.12

Your document, with your screenshot copied into it.

7 If you click on the screenshot, little black squares called handles will appear around it. If you move the cursor over one of them, the cursor will turn into a double-headed arrow. You can use the handles to adjust the size of your screenshot. Experiment with these.

8 Now put the name of your user interface or operating system at the top of your document.

Case study

Choosing software

Snagsby, Tulkinghorn and Krook are a firm of solicitors and they are planning to buy new hardware and software for their practice.

They have been advised that the best applications package for their type of work is Microsoft Office XP. This is the latest version of Microsoft Office.

They have been told by their supplier that Microsoft Office is an integrated package and that this will make transferring data from one program to another much easier. Mr Snagsby priced the individual packages and it is much cheaper to buy the integrated package.

Before they buy the integrated package they have been told that this applications software must be capable of working with both the hardware and the operating system they have. To check what the hardware and software requirements are to run Office XP, they use the Internet to access the Microsoft site at:

www.microsoft.com

They type in Office XP in the Search window and then look for the system requirements. The operating system they will be using is Windows XP, and the requirements for this are:

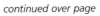
continued over page

Figure 2.13

Microsoft Windows is the name of the operating system the firm will be using.

- Computer/processor: Pentium III or above.
- Memory: 128 MB of RAM + 8 MB of RAM for each Office application (e.g. Word) running at the same time.
- Hard disk: 245 MB of available hard disk space.
- Peripherals needed: CD-ROM drive (to be able to install the software off the CDs supplied), Microsoft-compatible mouse.

Miss Krook has heard that it is possible to use speech recognition with the system. To do this the firm will need to use a microphone as the input device. Speech recognition will be a big help to them as they will be able to dictate letters straight into the wordprocessing package. They will then be able to check the grammar and the spelling and edit the work themselves before printing and sending it to clients.

Windows XP is capable of background processing. When you are connected to the Internet and not actively using it, the system will detect this. It will then use the spare time to automatically download any updates to the operating system. As soon as you start using the Internet again, the system will detect this and stop the background processing. It will then re-start when there is another period of inactivity.

1 Microsoft Windows XP is an example of an operating system. Write down three things that an operating system does.

2 Software can be divided into applications software and operating system software. Give a definition of:
  a applications software
  b operating system software.

3 All the software the solicitors have chosen use a GUI.
  a What does the abbreviation GUI stand for?
  b Why do you think the solicitors have chosen software that makes use of a GUI? Give one reason.
  c Give the names of two other types of interface the solicitors could have chosen.

4 The operating system Windows XP is capable of multi-tasking. This means that more than one application can be run simultaneously.
  a Give the names of two applications that the solicitors might want to run at the same time.
  b Explain how running the two applications in (a) would benefit the solicitors.

5 Give two advantages of using integrated software rather than separate packages.

6 The solicitors could have had applications software specifically written for them by a computer programmer. Why didn't they consider this option?

7 Why is it important to choose the applications software before the hardware?

8 The version of Office XP the firm has chosen contains the modules shown in Figure 2.14.
Here are some of the tasks the solicitors have to do:

a Set up files to contain letters and documents for clients.

b Write letters to clients.

c Send bills to clients.

d Prepare accounts.

e Keep a database of clients' names and addresses.

f Book appointments for clients.

g Keep a diary of events, court appearances, meetings, appointments, etc.

h Send, receive and store e-mails.

i Train staff in the workings of the practice.

For each of the tasks above, suggest which of the modules in Office XP would be most suitable. You can use the Microsoft website to find out about the separate packages and what they do. The web address is: **www.microsoft.com**

 Word
The Office word processor

 Excel
The Office spreadsheet

 Outlook
The Office personal information manager and communication solution

 PowerPoint
The Office presentation graphics program

 Access
The Office database solution

Figure 2.14

The modules in the Office XP integrated package

Activity 6

You will be using a lot of computer software as part of your GCSE work at school. It is important to know what items of software are available.

For this activity you have to find out what computer software is available. Copy and fill in the following table to help you.

Wordprocessing
Spreadsheet
Database
Desktop publishing
Operating system

Build your notes

Here are some notes that summarise this chapter. The notes are incomplete because they have words missing.

Using the words in the list below, copy out and complete the sentences A to L, underlining the words that you have inserted. Each word may be used more than once.

macro   interactive   files   batch   operating   utility   multi-tasking
software   user interfaces   application   multi-user   real-time

A   Programs that can be run on a computer are called _____.

B   Software may be classed into two groups: _____ systems and applications software.

C   The operating system decides where to store _____ and deals with security.

D   The software to do a particular job is called _____ software.

E   Command driven, menu driven and GUI are examples of _____ _____.

F   Programs for formatting a disk, copying a disk, searching for files, etc. are called _____ programs.

G   Printing a document out whilst typing in another document at the same time is an example of _____.

H   An example of an operating system used by networks where several users can access the same data is a _____ system.

I   A _____ is a small program written using applications software to automate a set of keystrokes to save time.

J   The type of processing where changes are immediately acted upon and any files are immediately updated, is called a _____ system.

K   _____ processing is used where a job is all done at one time rather than in parts.

L   The type of system where the computer conducts a 'conversation' with the user, is called a _____ system.

1 Which one of the following is an example of software?

a hard disk
b CD-ROM
c wordprocessor
d DVD drive

2 Which one of the following is an example of an applications package?

a the operating system
b wordprocessing software
c a network operating system
d a hard disk

3 Which one of these is an advantage of getting someone to write software for a company instead of using a mass-produced package?

a it is cheaper
b it does not take as long
c the company will get software that fits their needs perfectly
d it saves having to wait

4 Which one of the following is not performed by an operating system?

a allocating space for files on a disk
b issuing an instruction to a printer to start printing
c managing the flow of data from a keyboard
d searching for a record in a database

5 An airline seat booking system is an example of:

a a real-time system
b an off-line system
c a single-user system
d an operating system.

6 One of these is not an example of software. Which one is it?

a operating system
b utility program
c applications program
d laser toner cartridge

7 Software is available for performing routine tasks such as renaming files, backing up files, copying files, deleting files, etc. Such software is called:

a applications software
b integrated software
c utility programs
d programming languages.

8 The system where the computer conducts a two-way conversation with the user is called a:

a batch-processing system
b conversational system
c interactive system
d tape system.

9 Using the Windows operating system, you can print out a large amount of material while you are doing some wordprocessing. This is called:

a transaction processing
b batch processing
c multi-tasking
d spellchecking.

10 GUI stands for:

a geographical user information
b great user interface
c graphical user interface
d graphical user input.

1   a   Give the name of the operating system that you use
        at school or at home.
    b   Write down two tasks that your operating system
        performs.
    c   Where in the computer is the operating system
        normally stored when the power to the computer is
        off?
    d   Where is part of the operating system stored when
        the power is on and the computer is being used to
        produce a spreadsheet?

2   A user buys a new computer system. Included with the
    system are the operating system and an integrated
    package.

    a   What is meant by an integrated package?
    b   Give **one** advantage of using an integrated package.
    c   Give **one** disadvantage of using an integrated
        package.

3   The three screens shown in Diagrams 1 to 3 show three
    types of user interface. You have to say which screen
    goes with each of the following types of interface.

      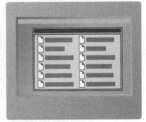

         1   2   3

    a   command-driven interface
    b   graphical user interface
    c   menu-driven interface

4   When an airline ticket is purchased over the Internet,
    the airline's computer needs to be capable of real-time
    processing.

    a   Write a sentence to explain the term 'real time'.
    b   Give one reason why the plane booking system must
        operate in real time.

c Give the name of a different application where real-time processing must be used.

F Questions

1 A company which designs and fits bedrooms is planning to buy a graphics package to produce designs that can be printed and given to its customers. Outline **five** features (other than saving and printing) that you would expect the package to have.

(AQA Specification A Tier F short course, specimen paper, q3)

2 Which **four** tasks below are carried out by an operating system?

Task
a storing records in a database
b managing memory space
c controlling the transfer of data to a printer
d managing system security
e changing the size of text in a wordprocessing package
f accepting input from a mouse
g data logging

(NEAB Tier F, June 2000, p2, q7)

3 a Give **three** types of user interface.
  b Give **four** factors that should be considered when designing a new user interface.

(NEAB Tier F, June 2000, p2, q8)

4 Choose **three** tasks from the list below that are carried out by all operating systems.

a underlining text in a wordprocessing program
b controlling peripheral devices
c storing data in alphabetical order
d transferring data between memory and a disk
e managing a system's security
f changing the size of a picture

(AQA Tier F, June 2001, p2, q4)

5 Graphical user interfaces (GUIs) are found on many computers.

  a Why do computers need a user interface?
  b Give **one** input device, other than a keyboard, that can be used with a graphical user interface.
  c Give **four** features of a graphical user interface.
  d (i) Give **one** other type of user interface.
     (ii) Give **two** benefits to an inexperienced user offered by a graphical user interface compared with this type of interface.

(NEAB Tier F, June 2000, p2, q5)

6 The owner of a riding stables with 25 horses wants to use a computer system to carry out the following tasks:

Task 1 Produce a price list to give to the customers.
Task 2 Send special offer advertisements to all customers.
Task 3 Store the upkeep costs such as feed and vet's bills for each horse.
Task 4 Keep a record of bookings for all the horses.

To carry out these tasks the owner could buy an integrated package or buy separate software packages.

  a Give **two** advantages of buying an integrated package.
  b Give **two** advantages of buying separate software packages.

(AQA Tier F, June 2001, p1, q10)

7 a Give **two** advantages to a company of buying an existing software package, rather than having one specially written.
  b Give **one** disadvantage to a company of buying an existing software package, rather than having one specially written.

(AQA Specification A Tier F full course, specimen paper, q6)

8 For each of the tasks listed below, say which **one** is the most suitable type of processing: batch processing, real-time processing or transaction processing.

a controlling the autopilot on an aeroplane
b producing electricity bills
c booking seats in a cinema
d processing cheques in a bank
e buying a CD on the Internet

(AQA Tier F, June 2001, p2, q6)

 Questions

1 Windows is an example of an operating system which has a GUI.

  a State **three** tasks that are performed by an operating system.
  b (i) What is meant by the abbreviations GUI?
    (ii) A GUI is one type of user interface. Give the names of **two** other types of interface.
    (iii) Give **two** advantages of the GUI over the other two interfaces you have named in part (ii).

2 All computer systems need an operating system.

  a Give **three** tasks performed by an operating system.
  b There is a difference between the operating system used by a multi-user system and that used by a stand-alone system.
    (i) Explain the difference between a stand-alone system and a multi-user system.
    (ii) Describe **one** task that would be performed by the operating system of a multi-user system that would **not** be performed by the operating system of a stand-alone system.

3 A kitchen design company would like some software to help them design bedrooms for their customers. They have the choice of buying a package or getting a company to write the software from scratch.

  a Give **one** advantage of buying a software package.
  b Give **one** disadvantage of buying a software package.
  c Give **one** advantage of writing the software from scratch.

Gathering Data

What is meant by data?

Data is the raw facts and figures that are used to produce **information**.

For example, here is some data:

69, 72, 71, 76, 81, 76, 75

If these numbers have meaning attached, then they become information. For example they could be the highest temperature for each day over a week in July. They could also be the ages of pensioners in a care home.

Processing data also results in information. We could enter the data into a spreadsheet to work out the average of these numbers. We could simply put the data into some order such as number order (highest to lowest).

The two types of data:
quantitative and qualitative

Quantitative data can be measured using a number. Here are some examples of quantitative data:

- age
- temperature in a room
- your school attendance for the year (this could be a fraction or a percentage)
- how well a product is selling (the number actually sold).

Qualitative data is usually difficult or impossible to measure using numbers. Here are some examples of qualitative data:

- the level of satisfaction of a customer with a product or service
- the morale of a group of employees
- customer loyalty.

Qualitative data is usually concerned with opinions. This means the data depends on the experience and judgement of the person supplying the data.

Where does data come from?

Data capture

Gathering data so that it can be used by the computer is called **data capture**. Data capture needs to be done quickly and accurately.

If there are large volumes of data to capture, then automatic data capture methods are used.

Here are some places where we can get data for processing:

- questionnaires
- surveys
- application forms (for school, college, university, jobs, loans, insurance, etc.)
- order forms
- sensors.

Hospitals have a lot of patients. They all need feeding and some have special dietary requirements. Not everyone likes the same food so patients need to be given a choice. Hospitals have a form that is used by patients to mark the meals that they would like for the day. This is entered automatically into the computer and it tells the kitchen what food to make.

The data for this system comes from the patients themselves when they mark the special cards.

```
         COLBY CITY HOSPITAL
            MENU CHOICE
     Shade one box in each section

              STARTERS
Mushroom soup                    □
Salad                            □
Orange Juice                     □

            MAIN COURSES
Lasagne (vegetable)              □
Chicken, chips & peas            □
Liver, onion & mashed potato     □

              SWEETS
Fresh fruit salad                □
Treacle pudding & custard        □
```

Figure 3.1

A card used for recording patient meal choices in a hospital

Documents filled in and then entered into a computer system are called data capture forms. Some data capture forms are capable of being read automatically by the computer system. These types of data capture forms are said to use direct data capture. Another type of data capture uses forms that have been filled in. The data on the forms is keyed into the system using a keyboard. Using the keyboard makes the system slow and prone to errors. If there is a lot of data to be entered, then it is best to use direct data capture.

Questionnaires

Go along any busy high street during the day and you will see people with clipboards collecting data from members of the public. These people are asking questions and are recording the answers on a card that is later read automatically by a computer. The data is used to provide important market research information about goods and services.

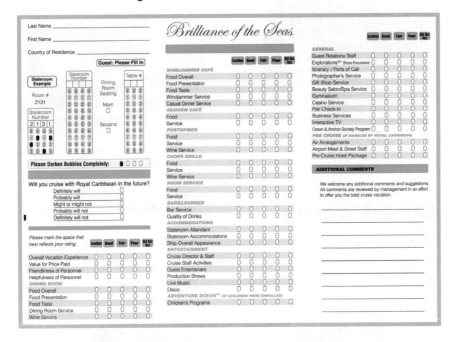

Magnetic stripes

Magnetic stripes are the black strips that you see on credit/debit cards, store loyalty cards, tickets (rail, plane, etc.) and so on. Information is stored in the magnetic stripe.

The information is read off the card using a **magnetic stripe reader**. Magnetic stripe readers can be found next to computerised tills, for example in shops and petrol stations. They are also part of a cash dispenser.

Key Jargon

magnetic stripe reader – a device that reads the data contained in magnetic stripes, such as those on the backs of credit cards.

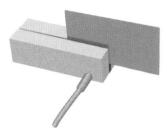

A magnetic stripe reader reads the information off the magnetic stripe on the card

Using a card on a cruise ship – for entry to your cabin and to buy trips, goods and services

Credit card – you can buy goods and services on credit. A credit card is essential if you want to buy things over the Internet

Some of the uses of magnetic stripes on cards

Debit card – different from a credit card because the money comes out of your bank account immediately

Airline tickets – used to capture flight and passenger information

Smart cards

Smart cards are 'smart' because they have their own chip inside them. The chip is like a small computer that holds important information about the owner of the card.

This smart card can be used like a credit card. You have to put money into your account before you can use it. You can then use the card to spend up to the amount you have put in

Here are some uses of smart cards:

● You can use them as an electronic purse. You simply transfer money to the card and then use the card to spend the money up to the amount you have put on it. This means you cannot spend more money than you have.

● They are used in mobile phones so that a user can identify him/herself and their payment details. These are called SIM cards.

● They can be used to store medical information about a person, such as their blood group, any allergies, medication taken, etc.

Barcodes

Barcodes can be seen on the labels of goods sold in supermarkets. You will also find them on the back of books such as this one.

Barcodes consist of bars with different widths. They have a number underneath which is the number represented by the bars. If the barcode is damaged, then the number can be typed in instead. Scanning the barcode takes less time and is more accurate than typing in the number.

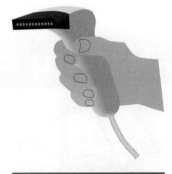

Figure 3.6

A hand-held barcode reader

This barcode is printed on the back of this book:

ISBN 0-7487-7416-5

9 780748 774166

This barcode is used on Royal Mail parcels:

Figure 3.7

Can you think of any other places where you have seen a barcode?

All goods sold in supermarkets have barcodes. The barcode contains numbers which can be used to find out the following information:

● the country where the good was manufactured

● the name of the manufacturer

● a code so that the item can be looked up in a database for its description, price, etc.

Note: The price is not coded in the barcode.

Activity 1

Obtain a label from a tin of food bought in a supermarket and stick it onto a sheet of paper. Label the following parts of the number which is printed below the barcode.

- first two numbers – the country of origin of the item (the UK is 50)
- the next five numbers – the manufacturer of the item
- the next six numbers – the code number of the product. This number is used to look up the item's name and its price held in a database in the store
- the very last number (which is also part of the product number) is a check digit to make sure that the barcode has been read correctly.

Activity 2

Use the Internet to find out about barcodes.

Then write a short description covering some or all of the following points using a wordprocessor.

- What applications use barcodes?
- Why are barcodes used?
- On a typical barcode on the label of an item bought in a supermarket, what do the numbers mean?

Magnetic ink character recognition (MICR)

You may have noticed the odd-shaped letters and numbers (called characters) printed on the bottom of bank cheques (see Figure 3.8).

These numbers:

- are printed in magnetic ink
- can be read at very high speed by a machine called a magnetic ink character reader
- are read with 100 per cent accuracy
- are hard to forge.

Key Jargon

magnetic ink character recognition (MICR) – a method of data input that involves reading magnetic ink characters on certain documents. MICR is used by banks to read information off cheques.

They are used by banks for reading bank account details in order to process cheques.

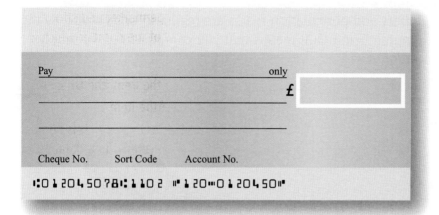

Pay _____ only

£ [   ]

Cheque No.   Sort Code   Account No.

:012045078: 1102 120 0120450

Figure 3.8

Characters printed in magnetic ink at the bottom of a cheque

Key Jargon

optical mark recognition (OMR) – the process of reading marks (such as shaded boxes) made on a specially prepared document. The marks are read by an optical mark reader.

Optical mark recognition (OMR)

There are special kinds of documents that are filled in by shading boxes using a pencil. The documents are then read by a machine called an optical mark reader.

Optical mark recognition is ideal for:

- recording lottery numbers
- marking multiple-choice examinations
- analysing the results of questionnaires/surveys
- recording attendances for students in a school or college.

Figure 3.9

A school attendance sheet. Tutors record pupil attendances by shading boxes and the sheets are read automatically by an optical mark reader

1420711983
Mr M. Philips
10 Waterside Drive
Anytown

Previous reading	12000
Expected high	20000
Expected low	14000
Present reading	14378

Customer account number	Previous reading	Present reading
0 0 0 0 0 0 0 0 0 0	0 0 0 0 0	0 0 0 0 0
1 1 1 1 1 1 1 1 1 1	1 1 1 1 1	1 1 1 1 1
2 2 2 2 2 2 2 2 2 2	2 2 2 2 2	2 2 2 2 2
3 3 3 3 3 3 3 3 3 3	3 3 3 3 3	3 3 3 3 3
4 4 4 4 4 4 4 4 4 4	4 4 4 4 4	4 4 4 4 4
5 5 5 5 5 5 5 5 5 5	5 5 5 5 5	5 5 5 5 5
6 6 6 6 6 6 6 6 6 6	6 6 6 6 6	6 6 6 6 6
7 7 7 7 7 7 7 7 7 7	7 7 7 7 7	7 7 7 7 7
8 8 8 8 8 8 8 8 8 8	8 8 8 8 8	8 8 8 8 8
9 9 9 9 9 9 9 9 9 9	9 9 9 9 9	9 9 9 9 9

Figure 3.10

OMR can be used to record meter readings

Key Jargon

optical character recognition (OCR) – uses a combination of software and a scanner to read characters (letters, numbers and punctuation marks) into a computer.

voice recognition – the ability of a computer to 'understand' spoken words by comparing them with stored data.

Figure 3.11

This is a pen-sized optical character reader (OCR), used for reading text from books. The text can then be put into a wordprocessor and edited

Optical character recognition (OCR)

Optical character recognition is where actual letters, numbers and punctuation marks are read and understood by the computer. Using OCR means that you can input text by simply scanning it.

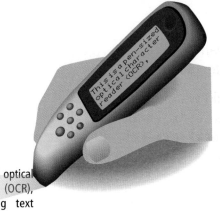

This is a pen-sized optical character reader (OCR), used for reading text from books.

A scanner is used to scan a printed page of text. Once the page has been scanned and read using special software, the text is put into an applications package such as a wordprocessor, desktop publisher, spreadsheet or database package. Once in one of these packages, the text can be edited (i.e. changed in some way).

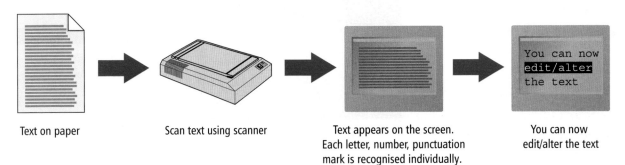

| Text on paper | Scan text using scanner | Text appears on the screen. Each letter, number, punctuation mark is recognised individually. | You can now edit/alter the text |

Figure 3.12

The processes involved in scanning text into an applications package, such as a wordprocessor or spreadsheet

Voice recognition

Voice recognition is the ability of a computer to understand spoken words by comparing them with stored data.

Voice recognition can be used to issue commands to a computer without having to type them in. It can also be used to enter data into applications software such as a wordprocessor. This means that you can simply speak into a microphone and the words will appear on the screen. It takes some time for the computer to get used to your voice, and it is not always as easy as it sounds.

Collecting data automatically
Data logging

Global warming is a hot topic at the moment. Basically, the average temperature of the globe is thought to be rising.

How could we test whether this is true? One way would be to look at past temperature records. These temperatures would have been taken regularly, over a period of time at a weather station. The temperatures would have been taken at the same times every day throughout the year.

In the past, these temperatures would have been measured by a person at the weather station. Modern temperature readings are taken automatically using **sensors**.

Sensors

Sensors are used to detect and measure physical quantities such as temperature, pressure, sound and light. There are many different types of sensor. Here are some of the more common ones.

Light sensors

Light sensors can detect the brightness of light. They can be used to detect low light levels so that a light can be turned on automatically. Light sensors can be used to turn street lights on automatically when it gets dark, and then turn them off when it gets light.

Temperature/heat sensors

Temperature/heat sensors are used to detect and measure heat. These can be used as part of a central heating system which switches a heater on when it gets cool. It can then be used to turn the heater off when the temperature has risen above a certain value.

Key Jargon

sensors – devices which measure physical quantities such as temperature, pressure, etc.

An infra-red sensor used to detect movement in a room

Passive infra-red sensors (PIRs)

These are used to detect movement in a room. These are the sensors you see in the corners of rooms that are part of a burglar alarm system (see Figure 3.13). Infra-red sensors can also be used to turn security lights on when someone approaches a house at night.

Sound sensors

Sound sensors detect the loudness of a sound. If you complained to the council about a noisy neighbour, the council would probably use a sound sensor to measure the amount of noise the neighbour made. If this was above a certain level, the neighbour could be prosecuted.

Push switches

Push switches can be used to sense whether a door is open or closed. The interior light in a car has a push switch to turn on the light when the door is opened.

Humidity sensors

A humidity sensor measures how much moisture there is in the air or the soil. They are used in greenhouses, where it is important for the air and soil not to become too dry.

Pressure sensors

Pressure sensors can be found on roads to detect cars approaching a set of traffic lights. They can also be used to measure the depth of water in rivers (the deeper the water, the higher the pressure).

data logging – a system that collects data automatically over a certain period of time. Remote weather stations use data logging.

Data logging

Collecting readings (i.e. data) regularly over a period of time is called **data logging**.

Data logging involves:

- collecting readings automatically using sensors
- storing and processing the readings using a computer.

Advantages of data logging

- There are no missed readings because they are taken automatically.
- The readings taken are accurate, i.e. no human errors are introduced.
- The data is processed faster.
- It is cheaper, as no-one needs to be paid to take the readings.
- Readings can be taken at exactly the right time.

Disadvantages of data logging

- Data-logging equipment could break down or give false readings.
- The cost of communicating the data from remote places can be high.

What quantities can be logged?

Basically, if a quantity can be measured, then it can be logged.

All of these quantities can be logged:

- temperature
- air pressure
- liquid pressure
- rainfall
- hours of sunshine
- pollutants such as sulphur dioxide or carbon monoxide.

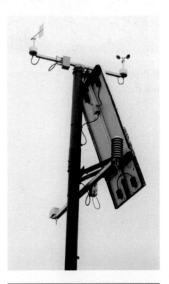

Figure 3.14

An automatic weather station like this one logs data such as air pressure, temperature, humidity, etc.

Monitoring traffic

Have you ever noticed a thin strip of rubber lying across a road? Have you also noticed that it is connected to a metal box placed on the pavement? Each time a vehicle travels over the strip a pulse is sent to the **data logger** in the metal box.

Perhaps the residents of the road have complained that the road is being used by motorists as a shortcut. The data logger is put there by the council to measure the actual volume of traffic on the road.

Key Jargon

data logger – a device which collects readings from a sensor at a certain rate over a certain period of time.

How many cars have passed since we started chatting?

Unlike humans, data loggers are not distracted

What happens to the data in the data logger?

Some data loggers store the data themselves. To enter the data into a computer, you connect the logger to the computer and the data is transferred through a cable. The readings are then stored and processed by the computer.

Many data loggers send the readings direct to the computer using either phone lines or even a radio link.

Logging rate and logging period

There are two main things that need to be set on a data logger:

- logging rate, also called the logging interval – how often the readings are taken (every minute, every hour, every day, etc.)
- logging period – the total period of time that the readings will be taken for. For example, if you wanted to find out about traffic flow along a road, then a logging period of a week would probably be enough.

Logging rates can be long or short depending on the application. Short logging rates include measurements taken every second, minute or hour. Longer logging rates are measurements taken every day or month.

Logging periods can also be long or short, with a short logging period typically being hours or days and a long logging period being months, years or even longer.

Calibrating sensors before use

Before a sensor can be used for data logging it needs to be calibrated. To measure the water level in a river, a pressure sensor could be used. As the river level rises, the pressure (as measured by the sensor at the bottom of the river) would increase. Calibrating the sensor would involve finding what pressure corresponded to different water levels. When a pressure reading is taken, the data logger would then know what is the corresponding water level.

Such a system could be used to issue a flood warning if the water level rose beyond a certain level.

Collecting data over large and small distances

Sensors or data loggers can be connected to a computer using a wire, if the distance between them is small. Sometimes the data logger can use a modem and a telephone wire to send data to the main computer for processing.

If the data needs to be logged somewhere that is remote, then radio signals can be used.

Figure 3.15

A weather station at the Antarctic

Simple data loggers store the data in the logger as it is collected. After the logging period, the data logger is attached to the computer and the data is downloaded from the logger to the computer.

The stages of data logging

These are the stages involved in data logging:

1   Set up the logging equipment (i.e. choose the sensors and connect them to the computer).

2   Set the logging period (i.e. how long the data is to be logged for).

3   Set the logging rate (i.e. how often a reading is to be taken – every second, every minute, etc.).

4   Collect the data.

5   Transfer the data to the computer for processing. The data can be transferred immediately as each reading is taken, or stored inside the data logger for downloading into the computer later.

6   Process/analyse the data. This involves using software. Sometimes the data can be transferred to an applications package such as a spreadsheet to calculate statistics such as mean, mode and median and to produce graphs and charts.

Activity 3

A manufacturer of polystyrene cups wants to know how well different thicknesses of cup allow hot drinks to hold their heat. They need to log how the temperature of the drink changes from about 100°C to 20°C.

1   What sensor should be used for this system?

2   What does the term 'logging rate' mean?

3   What logging rate should be chosen? Per second, per minute or per hour?

4   Define the term 'logging period'.

5   Which one of the following logging periods is most appropriate for this experiment? Two seconds, two minutes or two hours.

6   Why do you think this logging period is appropriate?

Case study

Catching car tax dodgers

The government is losing £188 million a year due to drivers who do not pay their road tax. When you pay car tax you get a circular piece of paper (called a tax disc) with the registration number of the car, the make and model of the car and the expiry date of the tax on it. This is displayed in the windscreen of your car.

A new system is being developed which will hopefully catch and fine the tax dodgers. This system is call the Stingray system.

The system must be capable of working without the need for human operators. It will need to recognise the registration numbers on the number plates of vehicles and to look them up in a database. If no tax has been paid or if it is not up-to-date, then it will need to find the details of the vehicle's owner. A letter will then be sent to the owner of the vehicle telling them that they must pay the tax or face a large fine.

The data that needs to be captured will be the vehicle registration number (from the number plate).

There are two input devices to the system:

■ Twin cameras (called Stingray cameras) which take digital pictures of the front of the vehicle and the number plate. These cameras are capable of reading the plates of more than 1500 vehicles per hour.
■ A global positioning satellite which records the location, time and date of each vehicle photographed.

Optical character recognition (OCR) software is used to recognise the number and then it is looked up in a database of all the plates that have paid tax. If it is not there then the road tax has not been paid. The number is then looked up in a large database containing the details of all the owners of vehicles on the road (called the DVLA computer). A letter is then sent out automatically to the offender.

continued over page

The system described above can be shown in a flowchart. The processes are described in the rectangles and there is a decision box that offers two different paths depending on whether the owner has paid tax or not.

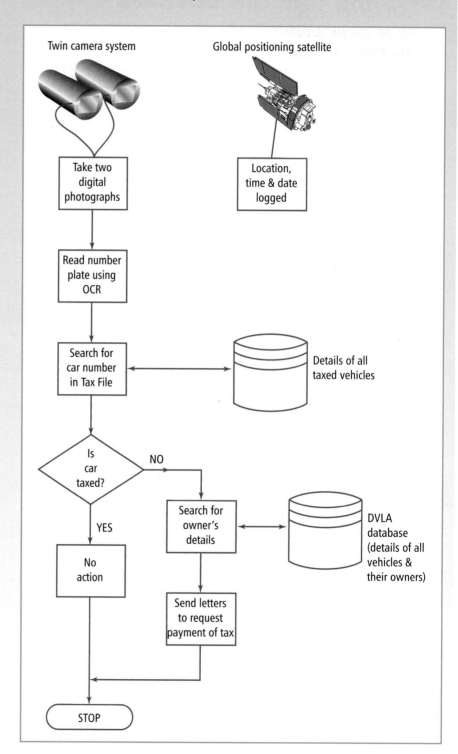

Figure 3.16

The 'Stingray' car tax dodger system

Because one of the cameras takes a photograph of the front of the vehicle, some people are worried that it could be used to take pictures of the occupants of vehicles. The system might be adapted for use by security services to look out for suspects. However, it is doubtful that the quality of the picture would be good enough for identification purposes.

The cost of developing and setting up the system is around £1 million. Each camera costs around £20,000. The recovery of the lost car tax, along with fines, will, however, bring in large amounts of money from tax dodgers. This will eventually more than cover the initial development costs.

1 The Stingray system makes use of two types of applications software: optical character recognition (OCR) software and database software.

   Explain why each of these types of software is needed.

2 Give the name of the main input device for this system.

3 It is important to test the system thoroughly before it is introduced. Explain what might be done to test this system.

4 a Explain what the term 'privacy' means.
   b People who have committed an offence or crime would not want to be photographed and recognised. Why might completely innocent people also object to having their photographs taken? Give one reason.

Activity 4

Your school probably uses computers to help with many of its administrative tasks. Here are some of them.

- recording details of students
- keeping records of attendance
- entering students for public examinations.

continued over page

Find out:

1 the different methods of data capture used in your school

2 what each method is used for

3 why each particular method of data capture has been chosen.

Build your notes

Here are some notes that summarise this chapter. The notes are incomplete because they have words missing.

Using the words in the list below, copy out and complete the sentences A to J, underlining the words that you have inserted. Each word may be used more than once.

scanner   OCR   OMR   voice recognition   MICR   data capture
sensors   logging rate   data logging   logging period

A _____ _____ is the way the computer obtains its data for processing.

B Barcode reading involves using a _____ to read a number or code contained in the barcode.

C Banks use _____ for data capture because it is extremely quick and very difficult to forge.

D _____ is used to mark registers, multiple-choice answer sheets and lottery tickets.

E To enter text from a printed page quickly into a wordprocessing or desktop publishing package a scanner and _____ software is used.

F Using your voice to enter commands and data into a computer is called _____ _____.

G Data may also be collected automatically in the form of electric signals from _____.

H In data logging, readings are taken at set intervals. This is called the _____ _____.

I In data logging, the total time over which the data is logged is called the _____ _____.

J Collecting data over a period of time using sensors is called _____ _____.

1 In data logging, the logging period is:

a the time that the computer is switched on for
b the time over which measurements are made
c how often the individual readings are taken
d a record kept by the operating system.

2 In data logging, the logging rate, or logging interval, is:

a the frequency at which the readings are taken
b the time the computer is switched on for
c the time a program takes to load
d the wait to log onto the Internet.

3 Which one of the following applications is least likely to use barcode reading as a method of data capture?

a recording loans and returns in a library
b reading the data on cheques
c recording the book numbers (called ISBNs) of books in a bookshop
d stock control in a supermarket

4 Collecting data at regular intervals over a set period of time is called:

a data logging
b data processing
c data communications
d data validation.

5 The main advantage of data logging is that:

a readings can be taken automatically
b the readings are more accurate
c computing equipment is needed
d no expensive equipment is needed.

6 All large stores make use of a barcode scanning system. Which one of the following is not an advantage of a barcode scanning system?

  a typing errors are eliminated
  b customers will spend less time at the checkout
  c the customers will obtain an itemised bill
  d the system is quite expensive

7 Voice recognition allows:

  a the computer to hold a conversation with you
  b you to enter data into the computer by using your voice
  c the computer to talk to other computers
  d the computer to use a loudspeaker as an input device.

Questions 8 to 11 refer to the following list of input devices:

  a barcode reader
  b optical mark reader
  c magnetic stripe reader
  d optical character reader

Which one of the above input devices is best used for each of the following?

8 Recording the fact that a book has been returned to a library after a loan.

9 Recording the answers given by students in a multiple-choice test.

10 Reading the account numbers when a customer pays a gas bill.

11 In a supermarket for reading and then obtaining the details (price, description) of a product.

very low, since simple

1 A lottery ticket is an example of a document that contains data (i.e. your lottery numbers). Marks are made on a card that is then read by a machine.

   a Give **one** reason why the staff in the shop selling the lottery ticket do not simply key in the numbers as the customer says them.

   b Give the name of the form of data capture that is used to capture the details on the lottery ticket.

   c Give **one** advantage of this form of data capture.

2 Here is a table containing applications and methods of data capture. They have become mixed up and you have to copy and complete the new table, matching the best method of data capture to each application.

Application	The best method of data capture
Luggage handling at an airport	Magnetic ink character recognition
Cheque clearing in a bank	Optical mark reading
Marking multiple-choice answer sheets	Barcode reading
Reading the details on a credit card	Magnetic stripe reading
Capturing the numbers on lottery tickets	Optical mark reading

New table to copy and complete:

Application	The best method of data capture
Luggage handling at an airport	
Cheque clearing in a bank	
Marking multiple-choice answer sheets	
Reading the details on a credit card	
Capturing the numbers on lottery tickets	

3 One method of data capture involves a person talking to a computer.

   a What is the name given to this method of data capture?

b Give the name of the input device that is needed for this method of data capture.

c Give one advantage of this type of system.

d Give one disadvantage of this type of system.

e Sometimes data is captured automatically using signals.

f Give the name of an application where data is captured automatically.

g Describe why the data is captured automatically in the application you have named.

F Questions

1 a Explain what is meant by the following terms:

data

information.

b For each item in the list below, say whether it is data or information.

the cat is black

barksdogthe

16th May 1970

16051970

(NEAB Tier F, June 2000, p2, q2)

2 In banking, magnetic ink character recognition (MICR) and magnetic stripes are both used for data input.

a MICR is used to enter data from cheques into the bank computer system.

Westshire Bank   31-22-05

Bury Branch
321 Park Place
BY2 8GL   20

Pay _____ only

                                              £ [   ]

_____

                                              Mr. M. Fletcher

_____

Cheque No.   Sort Code   Account No.

⑈408472⑈   31⑈2205   15277306⑈

(i) Give **one** item of data which is pre-printed on the cheque above and which is read by MICR when the cheque is processed.

(ii) After the cheque is used the amount is typed on by the bank in magnetic ink. Why is this necessary?

(iii) Give **one** reason why MICR is used in this situation rather than OCR.

b Credit card data is input from a magnetic strip on the back of a card. Give **two** reasons why this method of data input is used rather than MICR.

(AQA Tier F, specimen paper, q8)

---

3 The following are different methods of data capture that can be used.

questionnaires	data capture forms	data logging
feedback	OMR	OCR
MICR	barcodes	magnetic strip

From the list above, choose the most suitable method of data capture for each of the situations given below.

a To input cheque details including the cheque number and the value of the cheque.

b To input students' answers to multiple-choice examination questions.

c To collect information about pupils' views on their new cafeteria system.

d To capture and store temperatures every second during a chemical reaction.

e To input information such as the account number from credit cards.

f To input information about books being taken out of a library.

(NEAB Tier F, June 2000, p1, q14)

---

4 a Which of A, B, C and D is correct?

Data logging is:
A the collection and storage of data from sensors
B the use of sensors to enter data into a database
C the use of sensors to speed up processing
D the collection of data directly from barcodes using a sensor.

b Give **two** sensors that could be used in data logging.

c Explain what is meant by the terms:
  (i) logging interval
  (ii) period of logging.

(AQA Specification A Tier F, specimen paper, q6)

H Questions

1 **a** Explain the terms:
  (i) data logging
  (ii) logging interval
  (iii) period of logging.

b Give **two** sensors that could be used in data logging.

c Explain, with a clear example, why some data needs to be collected over a long period of time.

(AQA Specification A Tier H short course, specimen paper, q5)

2 **a** Briefly explain the difference between the terms data and information.

b Data can be quantitative or qualitative. Briefly describe the difference between these two terms.

c Here are some methods used for data capture. For each of the situations (i) to (vi), choose the method of data capture most suitable.

> OCR   MICR   voice recognition   barcoding
>   OMR   magnetic stripe reading

(i) Reading the account number on a cheque.

(ii) Allowing the answers to multiple-choice examinations to be input into a computer system.

(iii) Reading the account number when a customer returns part of the gas bill along with the payment.

(iv) Recording that a library book has been returned to the library after a loan.

(v) Inputting a large amount of text into a wordprocessor from a book without retyping it.

(vi) Inputting the account details on a credit card.

The consequences of wrong data

Wrong data can have several consequences, such as:

- it could cost a lot of money
- it could be very annoying
- it could even be dangerous or life threatening.

It could cost a lot of money ...

- A person could be wrongly arrested because they have been confused with someone else. They could then sue the police.
- A company could send someone a bill for the wrong amount of money. If the bill is for a much smaller amount than it should be, it could cost the company money.

It could be very annoying ...

- A travel agent could book your holiday for the wrong date, and it is not discovered until you arrive at the airport.
- You could be charged the wrong price at a shop.
- The wrong goods could be delivered.
- The wrong quantity of goods could be delivered.

It could be dangerous or life threatening ...

- A mistake in a patient's medical record could mean that the patient is given the wrong drugs or doses that could prove life threatening.
- An ambulance, police vehicle or fire engine could be sent to the wrong address.

The reason for data validation

Data validation is performed by a computer program. It checks to see whether the data being entered is allowable. A good program will be able to spot serious errors. It is impossible for a program to always spot every error.

Key Jargon

GIGO – Garbage In Garbage Out. It means that if you put rubbish into a computer then you get rubbish out.

What sorts of errors are made?

Think about the errors you can make when typing work into a computer. Here are some common errors:

- spelling mistakes
- grammatical errors
- typing the same information twice
- leaving an important field blank
- transposing words, letters and numbers (i.e. putting them in the wrong order). These are called transposition errors
- misreading a word or number from a document you are copying. This is called a transcription error.

Some of the errors that can occur are shown in Figure 4.2.

ORDER
Customer No.
187512

Customer No.
187521

Putting letters or numbers in the wrong place is a transposition error

Application Form

Entering the same details twice by mistake

Misreading/misspelling words (transcription errors)

Jack Jacobson

"Right … 'Jake Jackson' …"

"I'm sure I've already typed this in. Oh well, I'll type it in anyway and then go to lunch …"

Errors in the transfer of data

Figure 4.2

Types of error

Getting the right data into a computer
Data validation

When data is validated we ask: Is this data possible or reasonable? Data validation is performed by a computer program. When we build a database we need to think about the validation checks that we can set up to spot or 'trap' unreasonable data. We will look at this in a later chapter.

Activity 1

Here are some dates of birth written in different ways. You have to say whether they are possible.

1   19/12/78
2   12/19/90
3   3rd June 1999
4   30th Feb 2003

5   31st September 2001
6   29th Feb 2004
7   01/01/2003
8   1/3/78

Answers are given at the end of this chapter.

Two different ways of checking
Verification and validation

Two methods are used to check data: verification and validation.

Verification

Verification involves simply checking that the data being typed in matches exactly the data on the document used to supply the information. This document could be a bill, an order form, an application form and so on. This check makes sure that no errors are introduced during the typing.

verification – checking the accuracy of data entry.

In many cases, verification involves proofreading what has been typed in by comparing it against the source of the information. Sometimes verification can mean showing what's on the screen to the person who is placing the order or who is familiar with the data to check that it is right.

There is another way of verifying data. Two people can enter the same data. This is called the double entry of data. The data will only be accepted for processing if both sets of data are the same. Obviously this will involve a lot of work because the job of typing in the data is being done twice. Also, two people will need to be paid to do the work instead of only one.

Figure 4.3

The two methods of verification: (a) proofreading and (b) double entry of data

Validation

Validation is a check that is performed by a computer program. When creating the structure of a database, you can include **validation checks**. These checks restrict the data that can be entered.

The types of validation checks you can carry out

There are many different checks that the computer can perform. Here are the main ones.

Key Jargon

validation check – a check performed by a computer program to make sure that the data is allowable.

Range checks

Range checks are performed on numbers. They make sure that each number lies within a specified range. For example, a program that checks whether people are eligible for retirement pensions requires that all recipients are aged 60 or over. If a typist enters 16 instead of 61, a range check would detect this. However, not all errors would be detected – if the typist entered 69 instead of 96, both are valid so the range check would not spot the mistake.

Control total

A control total is used to check that data has been entered correctly. All the data is added together by the computer to create the control total. This is then compared with the actual total to check that it is correct.

Check digits

Bank account numbers and ISBNs (International Standard Book Numbers) are examples of long numbers that sometimes need to be entered into a computer. It is hard to enter long numbers without making mistakes.

A **check digit** is a number that is placed at the end of a long number and is used to check that the rest of the number has been entered correctly.

When a number like this is entered, the computer cuts off the last digit (i.e. the check digit). It then performs a calculation involving each of the digits and then compares the answer with the check digit. If the two are the same, then the number has been entered correctly.

How check digits are calculated

The ISBN number of the book whose barcode is shown in Figure 4.4 is 0-7487-6367-8.

1   Leaving off the check digit and getting rid of the dashes, we have:

    0 7 4 8 7 6 3 6 7

2   Starting with the 0 we multiply it by 10, the next number (7) by 9, the next number (4) by 8 and so on. You can set out the sum like this:

    $0 \times 10 = 0$
    $7 \times 9 = 63$

Key Jargon

check digit – a number placed at the end of a string of numbers to check that they have all been correctly input to the computer.

range check – a data validation technique which checks that the data input to a computer is within a certain range.

ISBN 0-7487-6367-8

9 780748 763672

Figure 4.4

A barcode

$$4 \times 8 \ = \ 32$$
$$8 \times 7 \ = \ 56$$
$$7 \times 6 \ = \ 42$$
$$6 \times 5 \ = \ 30$$
$$3 \times 4 \ = \ 12$$
$$6 \times 3 \ = \ 18$$
$$7 \times 2 \ = \ 14$$

3 Now add up all the totals of the multiplications:

$$0 + 63 + 32 + 56 + 42 + 30 + 12 + 18 + 14 \ = \ 267$$

4 Divide the total by 11 (267/11) and note down the remainder:

11 divides into 267 a total of 24 times with a remainder of 3.

5 Subtract the remainder from 11 to give the check digit:

$$11 - 3 \ = \ 8$$

So the check digit is 8.

6 If the check digit is 10, the letter X is used.

The calculated check digit is then compared with the check digit in the barcode. If both are the same, then the ISBN number has been entered correctly.

This calculation seems long, but computers can do thousands of these in a second.

Activity 2

The following number is an ISBN, which is a code found on all books. The last number, which we will call Z, is the check digit.

ISBN 0 09129931 Z

1 Using the method given above, calculate the value of the check digit Z. You need to show clearly how you have done the calculation.

2 A customer places an order for a book at a bookstore. The shop assistant keys in the ISBN incorrectly. They type in 0 7847 5774 3 instead of 0 7847 5747 3. Show how the check digit would show that the ISBN had been typed in incorrectly.

Parity checks

When data is transferred electronically from one place to another it can become corrupted. The computer receiving the data needs to know if this has happened so if necessary it can be re-sent. **Parity checks** are used to detect whether corruption has taken place.

Type checks

Type checks check that the right types of characters have been entered. For example, if a field (i.e. a space for data) has been set to 'numeric', then only numbers can be entered. If it has been set for characters, then numbers, letters and punctuation marks can be entered.

Table look-ups

Stock items are given a unique code to identify them. Whenever this code is used, it is checked against a table of codes stored in the computer to make sure that it is a valid stock code. If the code is not in the table then it is rejected. This prevents any incorrect codes being processed. Table look-ups are also called file look-ups.

Presence checks

When keying in data into a form on a computer, there are fields that are optional and fields that are compulsory. For example, your e-mail address would be optional whereas your name and address would be compulsory. Some fields, such as employee ID in a personnel system or National Insurance number in a payroll system, must always have data in them. A **presence check** checks to see if a field which should have data in it is left blank or not. If it is left blank, the user is informed.

Spelling and grammar checking

Any documents you produce on a computer should be accurate. This means that they should not contain any spelling mistakes and the grammar should be correct. To help you with both of these, most wordprocessing packages come with spelling and grammar checkers.

Spellcheckers
Spellcheckers are often provided as part of wordprocessing, desktop publishing and graphics packages. The spellchecker works by checking to see if each word in the document is in the

Key Jargon

parity check – a check to see if all the data has been transferred correctly from one place to another.

presence check – a check to make sure that data is present in a field.

spellchecker – a program, usually found with a wordprocessor, which checks the spelling in a document and suggests correctly spelt words.

type check – a check performed by a computer to see if data is of the right type to be put into a field. For example, it would check that only numbers are entered into numeric fields.

grammar checker – a program (usually part of a wordprocessing package) that checks a document for grammatical errors and suggests corrections.

spellchecker's dictionary. Spellcheckers aren't able to pick up every spelling error. For example, if you used the word 'care' instead of 'core' then as both are spelt correctly the spellchecker will not spot the error. If a word is not in the spellchecker's dictionary, it alerts the user who can then check the word and correct it. Spellcheckers are also able to spot if the same word has been typed in twice, one next to the other.

Grammar checkers

Grammar checkers can be used to check that:

- sentences end with only one full-stop
- there is a capital letter at the beginning of each sentence
- common errors like writing 'their' when 'there' should be used, and vice versa.

Here is some text that someone has typed in. Can you spot what is wrong?

> **I no their are mistakes in my spelling but I will use the spell cheque to cheque them.**

If you look at this sentence closely you will see that all the words are spelt correctly. You will also notice that some of the words are the wrong ones. The spellchecker will not pick up these errors because there are no spelling mistakes. Using the grammar checker may pick up some mistakes, such as the use of the word 'their'. This should read 'there'.

Type this sentence into a computer, then use the spellchecker and then the grammar checker. Which errors are picked up? Which are missed?

Spellchecking and grammar checking will not ensure that your document makes sense. It is therefore important also to proofread your document. It is a good idea to get someone else to read through your work as they might spot mistakes that you have missed.

Getting the customer to type in the data

When you buy goods or services over the Internet you have to enter certain details. Getting you to do this has two advantages:

- the company does not need to pay someone to do this for you
- you are less likely to make a mistake entering your own details than someone who is entering them for you.

Activity 3

There are lots of new terms to learn and understand in this chapter.

You have been asked to explain the following concepts to someone. Make sure that you explain them clearly. It is a good idea to use examples to help your explanation.

1 The difference between verification and validation.
2 The use of check digits.
3 The ways of checking wordprocessed work.

Case study

An examinations database

Each school has a person called the Examinations Officer, who is responsible for all the school's external examinations. It is a responsible job and it is essential that everyone is entered for the correct examinations.

At Grangeside School the Deputy Head is also the Examinations Officer. She has set up a database to help keep track of the examinations that each student is entered for. Here is part of the database:

Type of data	Example of data
Student number	10233
Surname	Jones
Forename	Zara
Sex (M or F)	F
Date of birth (dd/mm/yy)	02/03/87
Subject 1	Mathematics
Subject 2	English Language
Subject 3	Information Communication Technology
Subject 4	Double Science
Subject 5	Geography
Subject 6	Cookery

continued over page

This file uses the student number to access another file containing all the student's personal details such as address, phone number and name of parent or guardian.

1 As the school has 1700 students, why is it important that each student has their own unique student number?

2 For which type of data would a check digit be useful?

3 Each form teacher fills in a document with all the subjects each student is taking. This is given to the student to check. The Examinations Officer then uses the form to type the details into the database. After typing in the data, the Examinations Officer reads what she has typed and compares it with the data on the document.
   a Give the name of this form of checking.
   b Explain two things that could happen if the data in the database is incorrect.

4 Here are some validation checks that can be used:
   ■ range check   ■ presence check   ■ type check.

   The data in the table below contains errors. Copy and complete the table, placing a tick if the error can be detected using any of the above checks and stating which validation check should be used in each case. The first one has been done for you.

Type of data	Example of data	Tick if error could be detected	Validation check used
Student number	10333	✔	range check
Surname	Brwn		
Forename	Stephen		
Sex (M or F)	N		
Date of birth (dd/mm/yy)	31/02/87		
Subject 1	Mathematics		
Subject 2	English Language		
Subject 3	Information Communication Technology		
Subject 4	Double Science		
Subject 5	Geography		
Exam Fee	£45989		

5 Explain what a table look-up is and how it could be used with this database.

Build your notes

Here are some notes that summarise this chapter. The notes are incomplete because they have words missing.

Using the words in the list below, copy out and complete the sentences A to G, underlining the words that you have inserted. Each word may be used more than once.

> parity   verification   proofreading   range checks
> presence check   processing   validation   type checks
> transposition   check digit

A One method of _____ is to let two people type in the same data. Only if they make identical keystrokes will the data be accepted for _____.

B Another, more feasible method involves getting the user to check carefully what has been typed in. This is called _____.

C _____ is performed by a computer program. Validation checks include the following: _____ _____ to make sure that the right type of characters have been entered and _____ _____ to make sure that the data lies within a certain range.

D When a large number is entered, mistakes often occur, so an extra number is added at the end which is calculated from the other numbers. This extra number is called a _____ _____.

E The commonest type of error is the _____ error which is caused by letters or numbers being typed in the wrong order.

F _____ checks are checks to make sure that data has not been corrupted as it is transferred from one place to another.

G Some fields must always have data entered in them. A _____ _____ checks to make sure that such a field has data entered into it.

1 **Which one of the following statements is false?**

a Validation is performed by a computer program.

b Errors caused by mistyping are called transcription errors

c Letters or numbers that are swapped around by mistake are called transposition errors

d Validation checks are able to detect all errors.

2 **Instead of entering the student number 009089, the user enters in the incorrect number 009098. This is an example of:**

a a parity error

b a transposition error

c a transcription error

d a range error.

3 **Which of these is not classed as a method of verification?**

a range check

b presence check

c character type check

d double entry of data

4 **A total is found by adding all the product numbers together.**

Product number	Product
129	Rulers
107	Pencils
<u>004</u>	Sellotape
240	

This total can be used for checking the data. It is called a:

a range check

b hash total

c control total

d check digit.

5 An extra digit added to the end of a long number such as a bank account number or International Standard Book Number (ISBN) is called a:

a   check digit
b   parity digit
c   binary digit
d   length check.

6 Making sure that data being entered is present in a table or file is called:

a   look-up
b   look-out
c   a check digit
d   an ISBN.

7 Checking that a number is not too big or too small is best carried out using a:

a   presence check
b   range check
c   data type check
d   ISBN.

8 Checking that a wordprocessed document contains no spelling mistakes is best performed using a:

a   grammar checker
b   spellchecker
c   virus checker
d   validation check.

9 **Which one of the following would not be part of a validation check?**

a a range check

b proofreading information on the screen before it is accepted for processing

c a data type check

d an existence check

10 **Which one of the following would not use a check digit?**

a a product code on an item of clothing

b the International Standard Book Number (ISBN)

c a bank account number

d a student's surname

1 A call centre is a place where customers can ring up and place orders or make enquiries about orders. When a customer places an order, they give their personal details along with the details of their order. Before the data is accepted for processing, it is first verified by the operator and then validated by the computer.

  a Explain the meaning of each of the following terms:
    (i) verification
    (ii) validation

  b Explain how an order could be verified by the operator.

  c Here is an order line in the customer's order:

Product number	Product description	Price	Quantity	Total cost
1019210121	Jaz Drive	£75.00	3	£225.00

    (i)   Say which data is most likely to use a check digit.

    (ii) When the product number is typed in, a look-up table is used to obtain the product description and price. Give **one** reason why it is better to use a look-up table rather than get the operator to type in the details.

    (iii) Give the name of the field that the operator types in that would be best validated using a range check.

2 An application form for a passport arrives at the passport office where the details are typed into a computer. The details are then verified after typing. Explain briefly how the details may be verified.

3 Here are some of the checks that can be performed on data in order to validate it.
- character type check
- range check
- check digit.

Here is some data in a record as part of a database:
Customer Name: Mr Sean Hughes
Product Number: 19102100102
Order Quantity: 12

Explain how each of the following checks could be used to validate the entry of data into the record shown above.

a   data type check
b   range check
c   check digit

4   Here is a table containing the names of validation checks and what they are designed to check. The only problem is that they have been mixed up. Copy and complete the new table, writing the correct checks in the spaces.

Name of validation check	Description of what it is designed to check
Range check	A number placed at the end of a string of numbers to check that they have been correctly input into the computer
Data/character type check	Makes sure that the entered data is in a table or file
Presence check	Makes sure that a number lies within a certain range
Check digit	Makes sure that the right type of data is entered. For example, numbers can only be entered into a numeric field
Look-up	Ensures that data has been entered into a field

New table to copy and complete:

Name of validation check	Description of what it is designed to check
Range check	
Data/character type check	
Presence check	
Check digit	
Look-up	

5 a What is meant by a check digit?

b Give two situations in which check digits are used.

6 Explain the meaning of the following errors and give an example of each.

a transcription error

b transposition error

7 The human resources department of the APEXAN manufacturing company keeps a file of employee records on a computer. This is part of the file:

Employee number	Family name	First name	Sex	Number of years employed
0127	Ryan	Jean	F	15
2971	Hussain	Sabina	F	200
5234	Ryan	Pauline	F	5
1253	Mercadal	Jean	F	7
1074	Razaq	Fazal	M	11

The contents of a field in one record cannot be correct.

a Say what the error is.

b Explain why the contents cannot be correct.

c Say which **one** of the validation checks below could detect the error.

(i) check digit

(ii) range check

(iii) type check

(iv) table look-up

(v) double entry verification

F Questions

1 Supermarkets use point-of-sale (POS) terminals to process goods at the checkouts by scanning the barcodes on product labels.

a Barcodes contain a check digit, which is used for data validation.

Explain what is meant by **data validation**.

b Say which is the check digit on the barcode shown below.

9 770039 519675 >

c Explain how check digits are used to validate barcodes when they are scanned.

d Give **two** other methods of data validation.

(AQA Tier F, June 2001, p2, q7)

---

2 Fill in the gaps in the paragraph below using the words from the following list:

correct	presence	range
digit	processing	sensible
input	output	software

a Data validation is the checking of data when _____, using _____ to make sure it is _____.
Two common methods of data validation are a _____ check and a _____ check.

b Why is the use of data validation so important?

(AQA Tier F, June 2001, p1, q15)

H Questions

1 **a** What is meant by the term 'data validation'?

b Explain the following methods of data validation, giving a clear example of each.
(i) presence check
(ii) range check

(AQA Specification A Tier H full course, specimen paper, q5)

Answers to Activity 1

■ 1, 3, 7 and 8 are all possible.

■ 2 could be possible or impossible. In the USA it is usual to put the month first, then the day and finally the year. This date could therefore be possible.

■ 4 is not possible because February has 28 days (unless it is a leap year when it has 29).

■ 5 is not possible because September has 30 days.

■ 6 is possible because 2004 is a leap year.

5 Doing Things with Data

Once data has been gathered and input into the computer, it is stored and processed to produce the output (i.e. the results). This chapter looks at how data can be organised, stored and processed.

Organising and storing data

Manual filing systems

Companies need a lot of files to run their business. Figure 5.1 shows three files used by a business for different purposes. These files are kept by different departments in different places.

Personnel File

Employee Number:	1765
Surname:	Jones
Forename:	Jenny
Date of Birth:	19/09/72
Job Title:	Sales Manager

Payroll File

Employee Number:	1765
Surname:	Jones
Forename:	Jenny
Date of Birth:	19/09/72
Salary:	£24000

Department File

Employee Number:	1765
Surname:	Jones
Forename:	Jenny
Experience:	10 years

Figure 5.1

The three files containing employee details

The simplest type of filing system uses a card box. A more complicated system uses a filing cabinet, with different files in different drawers.

Some of the data is the same in each file (i.e. it is duplicated). Data duplication wastes time because someone has to enter the data more than once. Also, keeping these three files up to date becomes harder. If Jenny got married her surname would change and this would need to be changed in three files. There is a danger that it would only be changed in one or two of them. This could be a problem for the people who use the database.

Data duplication also causes problems because:

● a lot more data is stored than is really necessary

● somewhere has to be found to store the data

● more people are needed to look up the data and keep it up to date.

These are some of the main problems with data duplication:

● We sometimes need to obtain data held in more than one file. Suppose we wanted to find out the names of sales managers who had less than 10 years experience and earned over £22,000 per year. This would be difficult because all three files would need to be used, and each is probably held by a different department.

● Changing some information in one file could mean changes need to be made in other files.

All organisations need to hold a store of data. In a school the data could be about students or staff. In a company, it could be

about customers, orders, suppliers or stock. These stores of data need to be organised in some way so that information can be found quickly. When these organised stores of data are computerised, the result is called a **database**.

How is data broken down in a database?

Look at Figure 5.2. It shows how you would store data using a card box filing system. Notice the structure with the items of data in **fields** written on the cards. Each card is about one person and is called a **record**. Lots of records go to make up a **file**.

Key Jargon

database - a series of files/tables stored in a computer that can be accessed in a variety of different ways.

field – an item of data or a space for data in a database.

file – a collection of related records.

record – a set of related information about a thing or an individual.

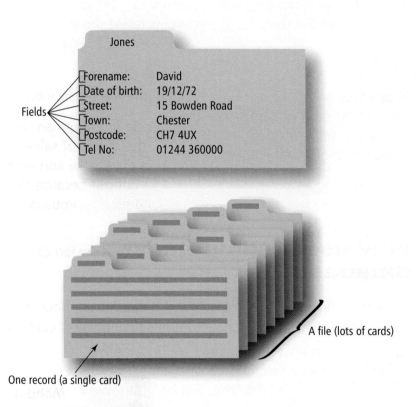

Jones

Forename:	David
Date of birth:	19/12/72
Street:	15 Bowden Road
Town:	Chester
Postcode:	CH7 4UX
Tel No:	01244 360000

Fields

A file (lots of cards)

One record (a single card)

Figure 5.2

How data is organised into fields, records and files

Here are some database terms you will need to know about:

Data

This is the details about a specific person, place or thing.

Information

Information is data that has been rearranged into a form that people can use.

Fields

A field is an item of data on a form. In other words, it is a fact about a person, place or thing. A surname would be an example of a field.

Records

Information about a particular person, place or thing is called a record. A record consists of a number of fields. All the information about a particular student (e.g. student number, surname and forename) is contained in a record.

Files

A collection of related records is called a file. The group of records for all the students in a school is called the student file.

Tables

In one type of database, called a relational database, we do not store all the data in a single file or table. Instead, the data is stored in several tables. The data in the separate tables can be combined together if needed.

Why use a computerised database?

Using a computerised database to hold data has many advantages:

- It is easy to alter the structure of the database, for example if you miss out a field and need to add it later. Suppose you left out a pupil's telephone number from your database design. As soon as you realise it is missing, you can add it to the database.
- Keeping the database up to date is much easier. You can modify, delete or add details.
- You can process the data in many different ways. You can summarise, calculate, select or sort the data.
- Reports (another name for printouts) of the results can be produced, such as a list of all the students who are in a certain form.

What are the disadvantages of using a computerised database?

- If the computer breaks down, you are not able to access the records.
- It is easy to copy computer files, so sensitive personal data needs to be protected by passwords.
- People need to be trained to use the system and this costs time and money.

Creating a database
Preparing the database structure

A school keeps details of all its students on a database. As well as personal details (name, address, etc.), the school also holds details of each student's form and form teacher.

The person who is developing the database asks the headteacher for a sample of the data.

This sample of the data is shown below:

Description of data stored	Sample data
Pupil number	1029
Surname	Jones
Forename	Luke
Date of birth	15/03/87
Street	1 Queens Road
Town	Wavertree
Postcode	L15 3PQ
Contact phone number	0151-202-1414
Home phone number	0151-305-1010
Form	5A
Teacher number	112
Form teacher title	Dr
Form teacher surname	Hughes
Form teacher initial	J

Pupils table

Pupil number
Surname
Forename
Date of birth
Street
Town
Postcode
Contact phone number
Home phone number
Form

Forms table

Form
Teacher number

Teachers table

Teacher number
Teacher title
Teacher surname
Teacher initial

Figure 5.3

By linking tables, you can combine data in any of the fields

The database developer looks at this sample and decides to use three tables to hold the data rather than one.

The three tables are called Pupils, Forms and Teachers. The fields in each table are shown on the left.

The data is put into three tables rather than one because it saves time; you don't need to type in the details about the same teacher over and over again for each student. If there were 25 students in each form, the teacher's details (e.g. Teacher number, Teacher title and Teacher surname) would need to be entered 25 times. If instead we put these details in their own table, we can access them from the Form field and only need to type them in once.

Linking files or tables

To link two tables together there needs to be the same field in each table. For example, to link the Pupils table to the Forms table we can use the Form field, as it is in both tables. Similarly, the Forms table and the Teachers table can be linked through the Teacher number field.

Figure 5.3 shows the links (shown as lines) between the tables.

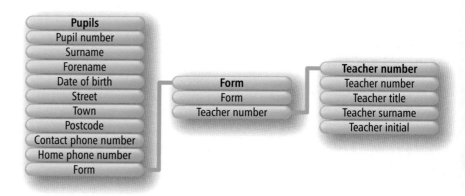

Data types

Once you have given a field a name you have to specify the type of data that is allowed in the field. This means you can only enter a certain type of data in the field.

The possible data types available in Access (and most other databases) are shown in the table on page 107.

Data type	Description
Text	Used for storing names, words and numbers that are not used in calculations (e.g. telephone numbers, code numbers, bank account numbers)
Number	Used for storing numbers that can be used in calculations
Date/Time	Used for storing dates and times
Currency	Used for storing money values to two decimal places
AutoNumber	These are numbers given in sequence by the computer. Each record is given a different number. If you use AutoNumber the number given will always be unique
Yes/No	Used for storing data such as Yes/No, True/False, etc.
OLE Object	Used for storing data from other programs. It can include pictures
Memo	Used for storing long notes which are not suitable for putting in a field

Picking a key field

When a table is created a key field needs to be chosen. The **key field** is a field that uniquely defines a particular record (i.e. a row) in a table or file.

In the case of the Pupils table, we could use surname but it is quite common to have students with the same surname. How many Smiths or Jones are there in your school? Date of birth might be chosen, but what if you had twins in the same class? It is hard to think of a field that would be unique in the Pupils table. Instead, we can create a field called Pupil number that would give each student a unique number that is used to identify them. If you look at the table above, there is a data type called AutoNumber which is a number that is automatically allocated to each student. The computer remembers the last number it has given so when a new student joins, they are given the next number in sequence.

In the Forms table there is already a unique field. There are no two forms the same, so Form can be used as the key field.

The Teacher number is the unique field in the Teachers table so this is chosen as the key field.

Key Jargon

key field – a field that has a different value in every record.

Storing data in files

Data storage

The space for an item of data in a database is called a field. Storage space needs to be allocated by the computer for each field. The trouble is that the computer cannot always know how much space is needed for a particular field. Some fields always contain data of a certain length. For example, a person's date of birth can be written in the form dd/mm/yy. If the user is told that they have to enter dates of birth in this format then the field length is always eight characters (including the slashes). With a person's surname, on the other hand, it is not always possible to know the longest surname that could be entered, so we usually allocate far more than we would ever be likely to need, just in case. But any spaces that do not have characters in them are wasted. Wasted spaces make the file size bigger and make data processing much slower. More storage is needed on the computer, which is expensive.

Fields in databases can be of two types:

- fixed length fields – where the length of a field is fixed, e.g. Date of birth can be fixed at eight characters
- variable length fields – where the length of a field is determined by the characters put into it by the user, e.g. Surname can be any length.

File size and data storage

The more information that you store, the greater the disk space it takes up.

- Large files take longer to save and back up.
- It takes longer to look for specific information in a large file than in a small one.
- Large files cost more to maintain.

You should therefore try to reduce the size of files whenever possible. One way to do this is by using file compression. Another way is to code some of the data in the file so that there are fewer characters. These two ways of making files smaller are described below.

File compression

If you put a lot of photographs or other artwork into a wordprocessed document and try to save it on a floppy disk, you may not be able to. This is because the file is too big for the storage capacity of the disk (1.44 MB).

It is possible to save artwork files in certain formats which take up less space. The other option is to reduce the size of the entire document file by compressing it using special software. Usually the file can be reduced to a quarter of its original size. One program used to do this is called WinZip. Once the document file is compressed using WinZip it can be saved on a floppy. Before it can be used again it needs to be decompressed, or expanded.

Compressing files has the following advantages:

- Compressed files can be stored on media (e.g. floppy disks) which would normally not have enough storage capacity for them.
- They are much faster to send over the Internet.
- They take less time to download.
- They allow hard disk drives to store more data.

One of the disadvantages is that if a file is given or sent to someone else, then the other person needs to have the correct software to decompress the file.

Here is an icon for a file that has been compressed using

WinZip: .

Design.zip

Coding data

Data is often coded before being entered using a keyboard. For example, we can have M or F for Male or Female. Here are some commonly used codes:

- S, M, L, XL, XXL for small, medium, large, etc.
- U, PG, 12, 15, 18 for film classifications
- MAN, ATH, CFU are the airport codes for Manchester, Athens, Corfu
- GBP, USD, GDM are the currency codes (for Great Britain Pound, United States Dollar, German Deutsch Mark).

Why code?

Coding data can make data harder to understand, so why code?

Coding data has the following advantages:

- There is less to type in (this makes it quicker and more accurate).
- Coding reduces the file size (and hence the amount of storage needed).
- It makes it quicker to do searches and sorts.

Making up your own codes

Bear in mind the following when making up your own codes:

- It is best if all codes are the same length. This helps to validate the data.
- Codes must be easy to use.
- Codes need to have room for expansion. If too few characters are used, you may run out of codes in the future.

Activity 1

Here is a list of the subjects taken at GCSE in Grangeside School.

Mathematics	Biology
English Language	Physics
English Literature	Information Communication Technology
History	PE
Geography	Cookery
Chemistry	Design Technology

The Examinations Officer at the school has asked you to come up with a coding system for these subjects.

Using the advice above, produce a set of codes for the subjects in the list. Make sure that you explain fully how your coding system was developed. You should mention any other coding systems that you developed along the way and the reasons for arriving at your final choice.

Getting information from data

Processing data

When raw data is processed, we get information. For example, we might want to produce a list of the students in a certain form in a school in order of date of birth. The data in the database would need to be processed to produce this list. The information can be output from the database using **queries** and **reports** (see below).

The results of a query can be shown on the computer screen or printed out. With reports, though, you have more control over what the output looks like. Reports are used to present the output from a database in a more attractive or interesting way. They are ideal when the data is to be published, for example in a school prospectus or a company report.

Putting data into a structure, calculating, sorting and searching are all examples of processing.

Key Jargon

query – extracting specific information from a database.

report – the production of output from software such as a database for a specific purpose.

Searching and matching

Searching involves finding records in a database that match specified criteria. Searches for specific information contained in a database are called queries. Queries are used to ask questions of databases.

Here are some questions you might want to ask a database in a school:

- How many students qualify for free school meals?
- What are the names and details of all teachers who are within two years of retirement age?
- Which rooms are free from 1 until 2 on a Friday?
- What percentage of students got grade A or A* in their GCSE ICT exam?

In order to ask these questions, a query is used. Once you have created a query it can be saved and re-used in the future. It will give you different answers each time because the data in a database is constantly changing as students and teachers leave and join the school.

Using logical operators in queries

To search for information we use the **logical operators** AND, OR and NOT.

AND

Two expressions are combined with AND when both must be true for a record to qualify. Suppose we need to know how many students have the surname Jones and live in Liverpool. We could use: surname = "Jones" AND town = "Liverpool". (NB: When matching text, you always enclose the text in inverted commas.)

OR

Two expressions are combined with OR when either one or the other needs to be true for the record to qualify. For example, we might want the surname Doyle OR Prescott.

NOT

NOT can be used to display all the records that do not meet a criterion. For example, we may want details of all people who live in a city which is NOT Liverpool.

Suppose we want to extract the name and address of a video library member whose membership number, stored as text, is 0001. We could use: Membership number = "0001". This will match the record having the membership number 0001 and the contents of this record will be displayed.

The following examples show how logical operators can be used to narrow down a search.

Example 1

It is necessary to extract the names of all employees earning over £30,000 per year in the production department of a company. We could use:

> Department = "Production" AND Salary > 30000

Example 2

Suppose we wanted a list of the names and addresses of employees who work in the production or marketing departments. We could use:

> Department = "Production" OR "Marketing"

Sorting files

Data in a table or file is normally arranged in the order it appears in the key field. The data may need to be sorted into a different order.

To do this a **sort** is performed. To perform a sort you need to specify the name of the field in which you want the data sorted.

You then have to decide whether you want to sort in ascending order (A to Z or increasing numbers) or descending order (Z to A or decreasing numbers).

Merging files

Merging files means combining two files into one. This means that a file with 100 records could be merged with a file with 50 records to give a new file consisting of 150 records. For example, if two people are inputting data into a database, they may need to combine both files at the end of the day.

If the files being merged are on magnetic tape then a new tape is produced containing all the data from the two files.

If files on magnetic disk are merged, then merging is much easier. This is because the data from one of the files is simply added onto the end of the other file. Once this has been done the resulting file can be put into any order the user wants. Merging files in this way by adding them onto the end of another file, is called **appending**.

Updating files

Updating a file means altering a file to reflect recent changes in the data. Updating is a type of merging. Updating includes:

- inserting – this means adding new data, for example adding new customer details to a customer file would involve inserting new records
- deleting – involves removing records from a file
- amending – involves altering some of the existing data in a record, for example a student in a school could change their address.

In some systems the changes are not made immediately. Instead, they are saved up and the updating is performed in one go. This is an example of batch processing (see Figure 5.4 on page 114).

In batch processing a **transaction file** is produced containing all the changes that need to be made to the **master file** (i.e. the main file). To change the master file, the transaction file and the master file are merged to produce a new updated master file.

Key Jargon

append – add new data to a table or file.

master file – the most important version of a file, since it is the most complete and up-to-date version.

merge – put two sets of data together to form one larger set of data.

sort – put into a new order.

transaction file – used to hold temporary data which is used to update the master file. It contains the details of changes (transactions) that have occurred since the master file was last updated.

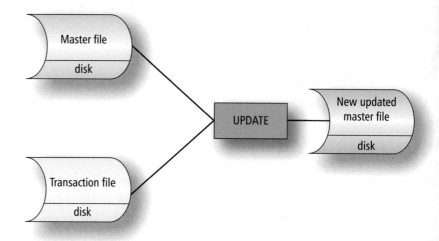

Figure 5.4

Updating using a batch
processing system

If the files are stored on magnetic tapes, the data in both files
needs to be in the same order (usually the same order as in the
key field). If the files were in different orders, one of the tapes
would have to be constantly wound forwards and backwards to
find the next record. To make sure both files are in the same
order, the transaction file needs to be sorted before it is used to
update the master file. Figure 5.5 shows the sorting and
updating process.

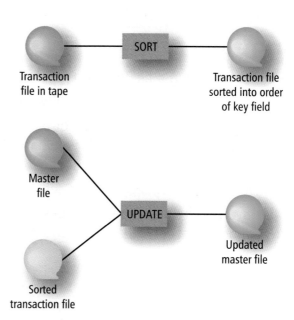

Figure 5.5

Updating a master file on tape

The grandfather-father-son principle is a method of keeping
copies of master and transaction files for security reasons. It
involves updating a master file using a transaction file. This
principle will be looked at in the next chapter.

Moving data around

The transfer of data

In ICT you often have to transfer data between different software packages and between different types of computer. Luckily the people who develop software have made it fairly easy for us to do this.

For example, a piece of clip art is stored as a certain type of file. When you place the clip art into a wordprocessed document, the wordprocessing software is able to recognise the file automatically, without you having to do anything to it.

When you use a digital camera or a scanner to produce an image, you will use a piece of software to alter the image in some way. For example, you might only want to use part of the image or you might want to enlarge or reduce it. Images are usually saved in a standard file format so that different types of applications software can be used to alter (or manipulate) them.

When you download files from the Internet you will come across many different file formats. The way you can identify the file format is by looking at the file extension. The file extension appears after the filename and is represented by a dot followed by 2 to 4 letters.

When you wish to do something with a file, it is important to know whether your software will work with the file. Sometimes you will need to decompress the file before it can be used.

For example, you might want to save a file in Word using the filename: chapter one.

When you look at the contents of the disk you've saved it on you will notice that a file extension has been added, so the file appears as: chapter one.doc.

The .doc is the file extension for a formatted text file. This means that if you downloaded a file from the Internet that had a .doc on the end of the filename, then it needs a wordprocessor or similar program to open the file.

Case study

A database for the job centre

A job centre uses a database to store information about the available jobs. Some of this data is shown here:

Job-ID	Employer	Min. age	Min. qualifications	Pay (£/year)	Type of job	Area
10021	Wiggins Ltd	25	3 GCSEs	10,870	Sales	Walton
10024	Thornes Ltd	18	5 GCSEs	13,450	Secretarial	Widnes
10025	ESP Skills	30	2 A levels	20,098	Clerical	Liverpool
10027	A1 Utilities	16	4 GCSEs	9,800	Clerical	Bootle
10045	Kardan Ltd	18	5 GCSEs	15,400	Sales	Liverpool
10050	Hewitts & Co	450	none	20,340	Management	Liverpool
10065	Kitchen Studio	25	3 years exp.	21,900	Sales	Southport

In the past, the jobs available were typed onto cards and these cards pinned to the walls of the Job Centre. Now, the people working at the job centre use a database to search for suitable jobs for people coming into the job centre.

When creating the database, one of the requirements was that each job should be allocated a unique number. The database designer specified the data type for this field as an AutoNumber.

The computerised system allows users of the database to construct queries to match each job hunter's requirements. These queries make use of logical operators and apply to the field names listed in the above table. Here are some examples of the queries that they use:

- Minimum age >= 25 (this picks only those jobs with a minimum age of 25 or older)
- Minimum age >= 25 AND Pay >= 15000 (this picks only those jobs with a minimum age of 25 or older and where the pay is £15,000 or greater)
- Area = "Bootle" OR "Liverpool" (this picks those jobs in the areas Bootle or Liverpool)

Most of the job hunters want a printout of the jobs that match their requirements. Although the results of a query can be printed out, it is better to print out a report. The report will have a title and a date, along with the job details arranged in neat columns.

1 One of the fields in this database has the data type AutoNumber.
 a Give the name of the field which uses AutoNumber.
 b What does AutoNumber do when data is added to the database?

2 The person typing the information into the job centre database has made a mistake.
 a Give the Job-ID of the job where the mistake has occurred.
 b Give the name of the validation check that would trap this error.

3 Give **three** advantages of using the computerised database rather than cards pinned to the walls.

4 Queries are constructed to search for a job hunter's requirements. Write down the Job-IDs of the jobs picked out by running the following queries:
 a Minimum age > 18 AND Area = "Liverpool"
 b Employer = "Wiggins Ltd"
 c Type of job = "Sales" OR "Clerical"
 d Type of job = "Clerical" AND Pay > 20000.

5 Write down the query you would use to search for all jobs which pay more than £10,000 per year.

6 Write down the query you would use to search for all the jobs for people aged 18 or over in sales which pay more than £15,000.

7 Give one reason why it is better to produce a report rather than simply print out the results of a query.

Activity 2

For this activity you will need to use the Internet. Using the Internet, access the following website:

www.learnthenet.com/english/html/34filext.htm

continued over page

This website tells you about the different file extensions. Although you will not be asked specifically about file extensions in the GCSE exam, you will often come across them in your work.

Here are some file extensions. Use the site above to say whether the file is a text, graphic, audio or video file. You should also describe briefly what the file is used for. Here is an example:

File extension	Type of file	Purpose of file
.doc	text	used for documents in Word

1 .html
2 .pdf
3 .jpg
4 .gif
5 .mpeg
6 .mp3

Activity 3

You have been asked to produce a sheet showing the different types of hardware for a PC, such as mice, printers, scanners, etc. You need to include a photograph of the hardware and a couple of sentences explaining what the hardware is used for.

To do this you need a supply of photos to put in your document. One place to look for these is on the Internet. A supplier of equipment can be found at **www.dabs.com** but feel free to use other sites.

When you see a picture of hardware that you like, place your cursor over the photograph and right-click on the mouse. A menu appears and you need to click on the Save As option. Change the file format to bitmap (Word is able to use files of this type) and save your picture with a suitable filename.

Now start a new wordprocessed document. Click on Insert, then on Picture, and finally on From File…. A screen appears like the one on the next page.

To select your picture, click on it in the list and then click on the Insert button situated at the bottom right of the screen.

The picture will now be inserted into your document.

Build your notes

Here are some notes that summarise this chapter. The notes are incomplete because they have words missing.

Using the words in the list below, copy out and complete the sentences A to I, underlining the words that you have inserted. Each word may be used more than once.

> report   records   key field   database   master   files
> compress   transaction   fields

A An organised collection of data is called a _____.

B A database consists of a series of _____.

C Files consist of a series of _____, each one about a certain company, person or thing.

D Within each record we have _____ such as name, address and date of birth.

E A _____ _____ is a field that uniquely defines a particular record (i.e. a row) in a table.

F WinZip is an example of software used to _____ files.

G The printout of information from a database is called a _____.

H A _____ file is the complete, up-to-date version of a file.

I Master files are kept up to date using a _____ file.

1 **Before data is entered into a computer, it is often coded. Why is this done?**

a Codes prevent unauthorised access.
b It makes it harder for people to understand what the data means.
c Codes are quicker to type in.
d Codes can be kept secret.

2 **Which of the following parts to a database are in the right order, with the largest first?**

a file, field, record
b file, record, field
c field, record, file
d record, field, file

3 **What is the main reason for not using the surname of a person as the key field in a large database?**

a Surnames can be long so there will be too much typing.
b More than one person could have the same surname.
c Surnames can be hard to spell.
d For security reasons.

4 **The data in a database can be brought up to date. Which one of these processes would not be classed as updating?**

a deleting
b amending
c inserting
d sorting

5 **Which one of the following is not a reason for coding data?**

a It is faster because there is less to type in.
b It takes up less storage space.
c It makes the data harder to understand.
d Searches and sorts are performed faster.

6 Which one of the following pieces of software is used to make a file smaller?

a file compression
b database
c wordprocessor
d presentation

7 To find specific information from a database you would need to perform a:

a query
b print
c sort
d validation

Questions 8 to 10 refer to the following table:

Here is a table from a relational database. The table is called MEMBER and it is used to store the details about the members of a video library.

MEMBER table

M. no.	Surname	Forename	Title	Street	Town	Postcode	DOB	Tel_no
0001	Bell	John	Mr	12 Queens Rd	Crosby	L23 6BB	12/12/56	924-8882
0002	Smith	Jenny	Ms	1 Firs Close	Crosby	L23 5TT	01/08/79	924-9090
0003	Cannon	Paul	Mr	12 Bells Rake	Crosby	L23 5FD	09/03/65	924-0098
0004	Charles	Steve	Mr	8 Moor Grove	Crosby	L23 7YY	02/07/69	924-1121
0005	James	Karen	Miss	3 Meols Rd	Crosby	L23 4RR	01/09/45	924-8111
0006	Brady	June	Mrs	9 Fox Close	Crosby	L23 5EE	20/01/59	924-0232

8 How many records are shown?

a 6
b 36
c 9
d 1

9 **Which field should be chosen as the key field?**

a Membership_number (M. no.)
b Postcode
c Date_of_birth (DOB)
d Tel_no

10 **The shaded information in the table refers to a:**

a file
b field
c character
d record.

1 There are a lot of specific terms that are used with databases.

In the table below, the terms and their definitions have been mixed up. You have to match each term with the correct definition.

Term		Definition	
1	Record	**A**	A set of records
2	Key field	**B**	A set of related information about a thing or person
3	Field	**C**	A field that uniquely defines a particular record (or row) in a table
4	Database	**D**	An organised collection of data
5	File	**E**	Facts about a specific person, place or thing
6	Data	**F**	Data that has been rearranged into a form that is useful
7	Information	**G**	An item of data

2 A sports club has recently installed a computer system. The aim of the system is to help with the administration of the club. At the moment the club stores the details about each club member in a database.

a By giving a suitable example in each case, explain what is meant by each of the following terms:
(i) File
(ii) Record
(iii) Field

b Give **three** advantages of the sports club using a database rather than a manual system to hold all its members' details.

c Give **two** disadvantages of the sports club holding members' details using a database rather than manually.

d Give the names of **four** fields other than Surname, Forename, Address and Telephone number that the sports club might use in its Members database.

e The sports centre will design a form which members will fill in to provide the club with their details. Using the fields given in part d, along with your four new fields, design a form that could be used for this purpose.

F Questions

1 A large theatre has started to run a drama group for young people aged between 12 and 18. A database is used to store information on the young people who have become members of the drama group. Part of the database file is shown below.

ID number	Surname	Forename	Sex	Date of birth
1001	Ali	Ahmed	M	05-09-86
1002	Bell	Claire	F	12-10-85
1004	Brown	Susan	F	23-12-84
1005	Collins	Sarah	F	30-04-84
1006	Ellis	John	M	01-01-83
1008	Graham	Amy	F	18-07-85

a How many **records** are shown in this database file?

b How many **fields** are shown in each record of this database file?

c (i) Name **one** field in which the data has been coded.

(ii) Give **two** advantages of coding data.

(iii) Give **one** possible disadvantage of coding data.

d Which field would you choose to be the **key field** in this database file?

e Explain why the field you have chosen is suitable to be used as the key field.

f Give **four** fields, which are **not** given above, that the theatre may reasonably wish to hold on the members' database.

g The theatre will collect information from new members by asking them to fill in a form. This is used to update the database.

Using your answers to part f, add your four fields to complete the design of the form below. Follow the examples given on the form.

Drama Group membership details

ID number ☐☐☐☐

Forename ☐☐☐☐☐☐☐☐☐☐☐☐☐☐☐☐☐☐☐☐☐☐

Surname ☐☐☐☐☐☐☐☐☐☐☐☐☐☐☐☐☐☐☐☐☐

Sex ☐

Date of birth ☐☐☐☐☐☐

(AQA Tier F, June 2001, p1, q9)

2 A primary school holds personal details about its pupils. At present the data is kept manually in filing cabinets. The headteacher of the school would like to keep the details on a computer system. He is currently looking into putting the pupils' details on a database.

  a Give **three** advantages of holding the pupils' details on a database.

  b Give **two** disadvantages of holding the pupils' details on a database.

  c Each pupil is given a unique number when they join the school. Give **one** reason why this unique number is used.

  d Other than name, address and telephone number, give the names of **five** different fields that could be held in the pupils database.

H Questions

1 An employment agency keeps a database of the jobs available.

This is part of the database.

Reference_Number	Area	Job_Type	Employer	Pay £ per year
923	Carnforth	Driver	Zenco	11200
145	Ireby	Sales Assistant	Wilson Clothing	9000
14W	Fairbourne	Waiter	George Hotel	8250
877	Sleaford	Waiter	Sleaford Hotel	7500
402	Carnforth	Sales Assistant	Jean's Army Surplus	6750
549	Ireby	Waiter	Three Crowns Hotel	8500
267	Ireby	Driver	Xport	13000

a **(i)** The Reference_Number 14W is incorrect. Say which validation check from the list below would detect this error.

Reference_Number is not 549.
Reference_Number is alphabetic.
Reference_Number is alphanumeric.
Reference_Number is less than zero and bigger than 999.
Reference_Number is numeric.

(ii) Using a word from the list, complete the sentence below.

bank   digit   range   type   field

The type of validation check that would detect this mistake is called a _____ check.

b The Job_Type field is to be coded.
(i) Design a suitable code for the jobs shown above.
(ii) Give **three** advantages in coding information.

c **(i)** Write down the Reference_Number(s) of the record(s) selected using the following search conditions.

Search condition 1: Pay is less than 8000
Search condition 2: Area is Sleaford OR Employer is Zenco
Search condition 3: Area is Ireby AND Job_Type is NOT Waiter

(ii) Write down the Reference_Numbers in the order the records will be after they have been sorted into **descending** order on the **Pay** field.

d The database extract is shown again below.

Reference_Number	Area	Job_Type	Employer	Pay £ per year
923	Carnforth	Driver	Zenco	11200
145	Ireby	Sales Assistant	Wilson Clothing	9000
14W	Fairbourne	Waiter	George Hotel	8250
877	Sleaford	Waiter	Sleaford Hotel	7500
402	Carnforth	Sales Assistant	Jean's Army Surplus	6750
549	Ireby	Waiter	Three Crowns Hotel	8500
267	Ireby	Driver	Xport	13000

(i) Name the key field.

(ii) Write down the value of a valid key field for a record which is not shown above.

(iii) Explain why a key field is used.

(AQA Specification B Tier H full course, specimen paper, q3)

2 A company accepts telephone orders for a large range of products. They have a number of staff to answer the calls and each member of staff works at a terminal connected to a local area network.

The system flowchart shows how an order is processed.

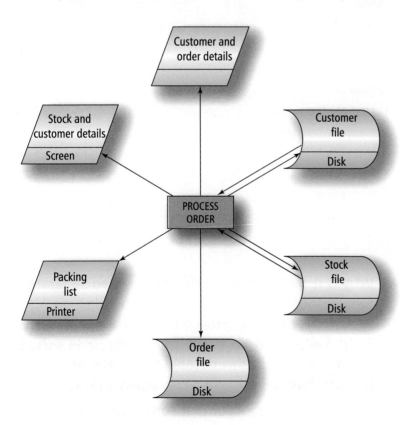

a The packing list is printed on the warehouse printer. Why does this output need to be on paper rather than on a screen?

b The stock file contains a field called 'current stock level'. This field is updated as each order is placed.
(i) What do we call this type of processing?
(ii) Why is it essential in this application that the stock level is updated straightaway?

c Describe **one** way in which the company could make use of the data in the customer details file other than for processing orders and accounts.

d Give **three** reasons why details of all orders processed have to be stored.

(AQA Specification A Tier H full course, specimen paper, q8)

3 A pupil database contains two data files. The structure of the two files is shown below.

Pupils
Pupil number
Surname
Forename
Date of birth
Address 1
Address 2
Address 3
Contact phone number
Home phone number
Subject code 1
Subject code 2
Subject code 3
Subject code 4
Form

Subjects
Subject code
Subject name

a Why is it better to store the data in two separate files, rather than keeping it all in one file?

b Why is date of birth stored rather than age?

c To find all the pupils in the same form, a search can be carried out. In this database package searches take the form:

<fieldname><comparison><value>

A search for **surname = "Robinson"** would find all pupils with the surname Robinson.

Write down the search you would carry out to find all the pupils in the Form called 7B.

d The Head Teacher wants to be able to send personalised letters to the pupils' parents or guardians.
What extra field would be needed to allow the letters to be produced?

e The pupil record contains four subject code fields. Each of these contains the code of an optional subject studied for GCSE. Subjects can appear in any option group. The system can produce this report.

Pupil Options Report
Pupil name: Paul Freeman
Form: 10S
Optional subjects studied:
1. History
2. Geography
3. Information Technology
4. Spanish

(i) Explain how subject names were included in this report.

(ii) The system also produces subject lists like the one shown below:

Subject: Spanish
Form: 10S
Name:
Rachel Brown
Graham Ellis
Paul Freeman
Sunita Patel
May Williams

The subject code for Spanish is 12. Simple searches can be linked together using logical operators AND, OR and NOT. Brackets are used to make sure the separate parts are handled in the correct order.

Write down the search needed to select the correct records from the pupil file for this report.

(NEAB full course, June 98, p2, q8)

4 A book club uses batch processing to send out monthly statements to its customers. The system uses a master file and a transaction file to carry out this task. These files are held on magnetic tape. Members only receive a statement if they have ordered a book or paid for a book which they have received. Some of the fields in the files are shown below:

Master file
Member number
Member name
Member address
Amount owing
Date of last payment

Transaction file
Member number
Amount of transaction
Payment or order

a The transaction file has to be sorted before processing can take place.
   (i) What order must the records in the transaction file be in?
   (ii) Why must the records be in this order?
b How would the **Payment or order** field be used during processing?
c During processing, records have to be read from the files and matched. To produce each statement the following steps take place:

   ■ read the next file from file A
   ■ read records from file B until a matching record is found
   ■ produce a statement for the member.

   (i) What fields will be compared to find matching records?
   (ii) Which of the two files is file A?
   (iii) Why might it be necessary to read more than one record from file B?
   (iv) What name is given to this type of file access?
d Describe the method of back-up which would be used to make sure that if the master file was damaged it could be restored.

(NEAB full course, June 98, p2, q9)

Security

The importance of security

Hardware and software can be replaced if they are lost. Data is a lot more difficult to replace. Patient data on a computer in a GP practice would have been built up over many years. If the data were lost and there was no copy, then it would be very serious.

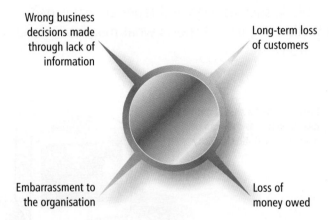

Figure 6.1

What the loss of a computer system can mean

Even if a home computer or laptop were stolen it could contain irreplaceable family photographs or video clips. It is therefore important to protect your computer system and also to keep a spare copy of the data held on it. In this chapter we will be looking at security to prevent the loss of data and also at how to restore data using back-up copies.

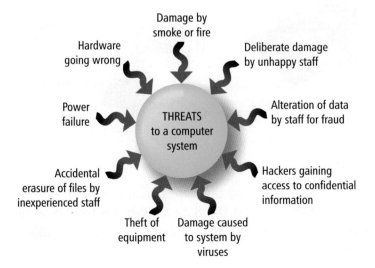

Figure 6.2

The many threats to a computer system

Keeping computers safe

Physical security

Physical security is about things that restrict entry to a building, room or computer. Physical security will usually prevent outsiders from gaining access to a computer system but will not prevent employees from accessing the system. It will also protect against natural hazards such as fire, lightning and water damage, and also deliberate damage or theft.

Magnetic media such as disks and tapes are easily damaged and need protection. Figure 6.3 shows what magnetic media need protection from.

Computers should never be left outside – sunlight, rain, etc. can damage magnetic media

Magnetic media should not be left near monitors as they can be damaged by static electricity

Liquids, heat and magnetic fields can all cause damage to magnetic media

Figure 6.3

Protecting magnetic media

Theft of hardware is a big problem because it usually involves the theft of the software and the data as well. Laptop computers are particularly prone to theft as they are often used in public places or left in cars.

Physical security on its own will not protect against someone accessing or stealing confidential data. If a network is connected to the Internet, it is possible for **hackers** to access the data from anywhere in the world. They do this by simply adding their own computer to the network.

Key Jargon

hacker – a computer enthusiast who tries to break into a secure computer system.

physical security – measures to protect computers against physical harm (usually theft or damage).

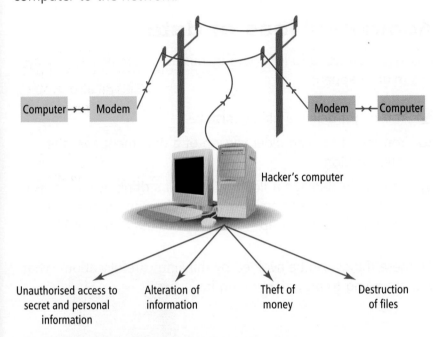

Figure 6.4

Some consequences of hacking

Preventing computer theft

- All computer rooms should be locked (keypads, swipe cards, etc. offer easier access than keys).
- Fire exits should be alarmed.
- Computers should be bolted onto the desks.
- All equipment should be security tagged (this makes it hard for a thief to sell it on).
- All staff should wear ID badges.
- Rooms containing computers should be located away from the general public and not on the ground floor if possible.

Preventing damage to computers

- Smoke detectors should be installed throughout the buildings.
- Sprinkler systems should be installed so that a fire is put out as soon as it starts. In computer rooms, gas flooding systems are used to put out fires because water can cause large amounts of damage to computer systems.

Preventing data from being lost

Keeping data safe

Accidental loss of data

It is very frustrating to lose data by mistake. Here are some ways this might happen:

- You might delete a file by mistake.
- You might save an older version of a document over the latest version.
- You might damage a floppy disk, spill a drink over it or, as I once did, drop a floppy disk on the floor and move your chair back to pick it up – straight onto the floppy disk!

All these things can be avoided by thinking carefully about what you are going to do before doing it.

Machine malfunction

Computers, like all machines, can break down. They normally do so at the worst possible moment. The moving parts are the least reliable, so the disk drives sometimes fail. This can cause damage to the disks and hence to the data on them.

The only thing to do to protect against this kind of accident is to make sure you have recent back-up copies of all your data.

Viruses

Computer **viruses** are programs designed to get into other people's systems and cause damage. As their name suggests, viruses are designed to spread from one computer to another. If a virus manages to get into a computer networked to other computers, then it can spread rapidly.

Some viruses come with e-mails so it is important that you *think* before opening an e-mail that has a file attached to it. You should only open e-mails with file attachments that have been sent by people that you know and trust.

Virus scanners

A **virus scanner** (sometimes called antivirus software) is an essential piece of software. It looks for any viruses in, or trying to enter, your system. Once a virus has been detected, the same piece of software is used to remove it.

Because viruses are being produced all the time, a virus scanner, or virus checker as it is sometimes called, needs to be updated regularly. Once you have bought the software you can receive regular updates from the software developer's site on the Internet.

How to avoid viruses entering a computer system

Here are some tips to prevent viruses infecting your system:

- Do not buy secondhand or illegally copied software.
- Scan all e-mails with file attachments.
- Regularly check your computer for viruses.
- Do not download free copies of music or games off the Internet.
- Do not use lots of different computers as this will increase the risk of getting a virus.

Key Jargon

virus – a program that has been created to do damage to a computer system.

virus scanner – a program that detects and removes viruses and prevents them entering a system.

Figure 6.5

One of the most popular virus checkers is called Norton AntiVirus

Protecting your work

You will have to do some coursework as part of your GCSE exam. You will have to be very careful not to lose this work. Here is some advice about looking after your work:

- Save your work regularly (wordprocessors such as Word are set to do this automatically).

- **Back up** your work at the end of each session. Never rely on just one version of your work.

- Print your work out regularly. If the work is then lost, at least you can type it in again.

- If you are working on a network and do not have a disk to save your work onto, you can attach it to an e-mail and send it to yourself at home.

Preventing unauthorised access to computers

System security

System security is making sure that only authorised people can access a computer system. This is normally done using user identifications (**user-IDs**) and **passwords**. System security is provided by computer software. Most computer operating systems provide systems of user-IDs and passwords.

Identifying the user (user-IDs)

A user-ID is a name or number that is used to identify a certain user of the network. Once the network has identified a particular user, the network manager can:

- allocate space on the network for the user

- give the user access to certain files

- keep track of what files the user is using

- make sure the user is not accessing inappropriate Internet sites.

Using passwords

A password is a string of characters (letters, numbers and punctuation marks). It is chosen by the user and only the user knows what it is. When you enter a password it does not appear on the screen. (Usually an asterisk appears each time you enter a character.) You are only allowed access to the network if the correct password has been entered.

Advice about passwords

Passwords should:

- be changed regularly
- not be obvious, such as your name, your dog's name, your favourite singer, etc.
- not be written down (e.g. on a bit of paper in your drawer, in your diary or on a sticky note stuck on the screen).

Activity 1

Stephen Jackson's favourite football team is Manchester United and he has a pet dog called Roger. Stephen is taking GCSE ICT at school. All the computers in the school are networked and before Stephen can use any of them, he needs to **log on**. He was given his user-ID by the network manager at the start of term. He also has his own password which he thinks up himself. Every month, the system tells Stephen to change his password. He has to choose a different password every time.

1 Explain the purpose of a user-ID.
2 Explain the purpose of a password.
3 Here are some of the passwords that Stephen has considered using:
 Stephen
 MUFC
 Roger
 Jackson
 R3521J
 One of these is a much better password than the others. Say which one it is and why the others should not be used.
4 Explain why a password is never shown on the screen.
5 Passwords should be changed regularly. Give one reason for this.

Key Jargon

log on – to supply your user-ID and password successfully and be allowed to use a network.

Levels of access

When computers are networked the person in charge of the network (usually the network manager) can give different levels of access to the data. For example, one user may only be allowed to view the data but not alter it. This is called read-only access. Another user may be allowed to view and alter the data. This is called read-write access.

By giving people different levels of access, you can prevent someone who does not know what they are doing altering data by mistake.

Access rights

Access rights restrict a user to only those files they need in order to do their job. So, for example, someone in accounts would not be able to access the personnel records. However, some senior managers would need access to all the files held by the company.

Like levels of access, access rights are set by the person in charge of the network. They are set when you log on to the computer, according to your user-ID.

Transaction logs

Think of a simple database. Once you have typed over an item of data and saved the change, it is simply replaced and no record is kept of the original data. This would be unacceptable in most organisations, as they would not be able to protect against staff making alterations for their own benefit. For example, if you had a friend who worked for a credit card company, you could get them to alter the amount you owed.

Transaction logs are able to record alterations that are made and also record the user-IDs of the people making them. This way, any alteration can be traced back to the person who made it.

File dumps

File dumps are copies of files that are transferred quickly to another media (e.g. CD or DVD) and then stored in case they are ever needed. They are done in case the normal back-up routine fails.

Encryption

If you have bought goods over the Internet then you will have used **encryption**. Encryption scrambles data as it is passed along communication channels. Even if the data is intercepted by someone, it will make no sense to them. Once it has arrived at its destination the data is de-scrambled back to its original form.

If you have sensitive documents stored on your computer, you can encrypt them to prevent other people from seeing them. This means that even if the data is stolen it cannot be used.

Figure 6.6 shows the screen that appears when personal data such as name, address and credit card number are transferred over the Internet.

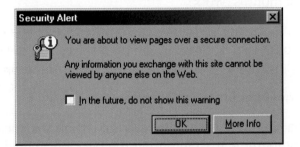

Key Jargon

encryption – the processes of coding sensitive files before they are sent over a network. To be read they have to be decoded (also called decrypted).

Figure 6.6

The screen that appears when your details are encrypted and sent over the Internet

Firewalls

A firewall is a piece of software, hardware or both that is able to protect a network from hackers. Firewalls are also used to prevent users from accessing undesirable parts of the Internet.

Activity 2

Here are a number of important facts about protecting your work. These facts are very important, especially as students often lose their work.

- Label your disks with your name and your teacher's name.
- Save your work regularly.
- Never rely on just one file. Always back up your work.
- Do not keep the back-up copy with the original copy.
- Always close applications properly.
- Disks should always be scanned for viruses.

continued over page

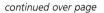

The way these facts are presented is boring and needs livening up. Your task is to use this text to produce a wordprocessed document. Make it look lively and interesting by using:

- different fonts
- colour
- clip art or other artwork.

Back-up

Have you ever lost work on the computer? It is frustrating to have to do even a small amount of work again. How would you feel if you lost six months' work?

Back-ups of software and data are kept to protect against loss. Using the back-ups, your work can be restored to how it was before the loss. Back-ups are therefore copies of the original data.

Here are some important points about back-ups:

- The back-up media should never be left on the computer. If the computer was stolen, then the back-ups would be lost as well.

- Back-ups should be kept in a different place from the computer. (If the computer was damaged by flood, fire or explosion, then if the back-ups were in the same place they'd be damaged too.) Some companies keep the back-ups in a fireproof safe.

- Back-ups should be taken regularly.

What happens if you can't access your files?

For your coursework you will have to do work at school/college and at home. To transfer work between the two computers you will probably store your work on a floppy disk. Sooner or later you will find that you cannot access the files on your disk because they have become damaged or corrupted.

You have two alternatives:

- You can use special software that may be able to recover or repair the file. Programs such as Norton Utilities or Disk Doctor could be used for this.
- You can restore the data from the back-up copies you have taken.

The grandfather-father-son principle

There is always the chance that data contained on a master file could be accidentally or deliberately destroyed, for example by an inexperienced user, a power failure, a machine malfunction, theft, etc. For any company the loss of vital data could be disastrous, so a back-up method is needed to re-create the master file. This method is called the grandfather-father-son principle.

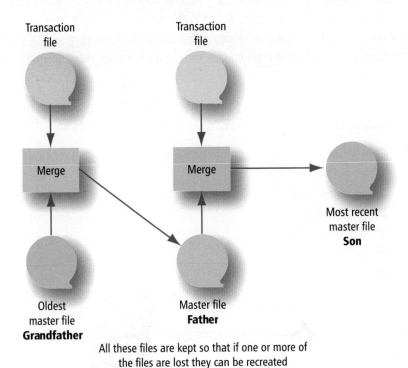

All these files are kept so that if one or more of the files are lost they can be recreated

Figure 6.7

The grandfather-father-son principle, used for file security for batch processing systems

The principle works like this. Basically, three generations of file are kept. The oldest master file is called the **grandfather** file and it is kept with its transaction file. These two files are used to produce a new master file called the **father** file which, with its transaction file, is used to create the most up-to-date file called the **son** file. This process is repeated, so the son becomes the father and the father the grandfather and so on. Only three generations are needed, and the files can be re-used over and over again. Although the diagram shows tapes being used, the system can also be used with a disk-based system.

Activity 3

A credit card company keep records of all its customers on magnetic disk in the form of <u>customer files</u>. On each <u>master file</u>, details are kept such as name, address, amount owed, minimum payment and date due. Each customer pays a certain amount of money each month and every month the computer department receives a disk called the <u>transaction file</u> which contains details of all the payments that have been received from all the customers.

The transaction file is <u>processed</u> with the master file to produce a new <u>up-to-date</u> master file which now has all the new amounts on it.

1   Explain what is meant by the following words, which are underlined in the above passage:
■   customer file
■   master file
■   transaction file
■   processed
■   up-to-date.

2   Often, computers make use of the grandfather-father-son system. What does this mean?

3   Why is the grandfather-father-son system used?

Activity 4

We all know that one way to back up small files is to use a magnetic floppy disk. Floppy disks only hold 1.4 MB of data which is a very small amount. If you had a database taking up 1.4 GB then you would need 1000 floppies to store it on. Clearly you could not insert this number of disks in the computer, one after the other.

Any form of back-up needs to:

- avoid having to use more than one disk
- transfer the data quickly
- be easy to use.

Your task is to use the Internet and suitable searches to find out about different devices used to back up data.

For each of the devices you find out about:

1 give the name of the device
2 say whether it is an optical, magnetic or other type of device
3 state what the cost of the device is and also the cost of any removable media
4 work out the cost, per megabyte, of storage using the device.

Produce a wordprocessed document outlining what you have found out.

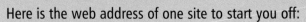

Find it out yourself

1 By using computer equipment suppliers' catalogues and websites, find out about the devices that are available to provide physical security for a computer system.

Here is the web address of one site to start you off:

www.dabs.com

2 Here is a good site for you to look at:

www.howstuffworks.com/virus

Use this site to learn about computer viruses and what they do. You can also learn about Worms and Trojan Horses, and viruses with names such as Melissa and I Love You.

continued over page

Produce a short wordprocessed document outlining what viruses are, how they can get onto your system and what damage they can do. You can also mention what precautions can be taken to avoid viruses getting onto your system.

3 A software company called Symantec produces a virus scanner called Norton AntiVirus.

It has a site at:

www.symantec.com

Check out this site. You can actually check your computer for viruses while you are on-line using this site.

Build your notes

Here are some notes that summarise this chapter. The notes are incomplete because they have words missing.

Using the words in the list below, copy out and complete the sentences A to K, underlining the words that you have inserted. Each word may be used more than once.

> user-ID   encrypted   back-ups   hacking   physical   virus   data
> father   viruses   firewall   son   password

A Computer security is concerned with protecting the hardware, software and _____.

B _____ security is used to protect against fire, theft, etc.

C Copies of data or programs kept for security purposes are called _____.

D Programs that are written to disrupt serious computer use are called _____.

E _____ scanner software is used to detect and remove viruses.

F Another name for unauthorised access to a computer system is _____.

G To prevent hackers from gaining access to confidential data, a _____ is used.

H Personal data and credit card details should be _____ before they are sent over the Internet.

I Three generations of files are kept along with their transaction files. They are called the grandfather, _____ and _____ files.

J In order to identify a user to a network a _____ is typed in by the user.

K The user then types in a secret combination of characters called a _____ to make sure that they are the person using the user-ID.

1 **Back-up copies are:**

a copies kept for management
b copies kept for security purposes
c copies of lists of passwords
d copies of documentation.

2 **Why should back-up copies be kept off-site?**

a It is harder to access them.
b If the building is destroyed, then the back-up copies will be safe.
c It is cheaper to keep them off-site.
d It saves the effort of keeping them close by.

3 **A mischievous program whose purpose is to do damage to other people's data is called a:**

a bug
b virus
c bacteria
d antivirus.

4 **Which one of the following best describes a firewall?**

a A system for putting out a fire in a computer room.
b A fireproof door to prevent a fire from spreading.
c Hardware/software to prevent hackers entering a network connected to the Internet.
d A type of operating system.

5 **Which one of these is not classed as physical security?**

a locks on doors
b computers bolted to desks
c a sprinkler system in case of fire
d a password, user-ID system

6 **A file kept to show any changes made to another file is called a:**

a transaction log
b floppy disk
c back-up file
d secret file.

7 **An example of software security is:**

a bolting computers to the desks to prevent theft
b the use of passwords and user-IDs to restrict access
c the use of keypads on doors to restrict access to computer rooms
d the use of fire extinguishers.

8 **A piece of software designed to detect and remove viruses is called a**

a wordprocessor
b database
c virus scanner
d spreadsheet.

9 **Personal details and credit card details are encrypted before being sent over the Internet. This is to ensure that:**

a they are turned into code to prevent hackers from reading them
b the card details are correct
c the details can be sent along a telephone line
d they are backed up.

10 **Which one of these is not a natural hazard that could cause damage to computer systems?**

a earthquakes
b floods
c lightning
d theft

1 There are two main types of security: physical security and software security. Copy and complete the following table with either 'physical' or 'software' to indicate the type of security described.

Description	Physical security or software security?
Keypad on the computer room door	
Password to gain access to a network	
Virus checker installed on all computers	
ID badges worn by all staff	
Bolts or clamps to attach the computer to a desk	
Smoke detectors installed in computer rooms	
All disks brought from outside scanned with a virus checker before being used	

2 Computer security takes care of hardware, software and data.

a Describe **one** consequence to a business of losing its data.

b Describe **two** things that can be done to minimise the chance of the theft of hardware from a computer room.

c Data is often more valuable than the hardware or the software. Explain briefly why this is.

3 Computer viruses pose a serious threat to all computer systems.

a Explain what is meant by the term 'computer virus'.

b Give the name of the piece of software that can be used to check for viruses and also to remove them.

c Describe **two** actions that may be taken, other than using software, to prevent viruses from entering a computer system.

4 If a computer is stolen, then the data on it is also stolen. To prevent the complete loss of data a regular back-up should be taken.

  a Explain what is meant by the term 'back-up'.

  b It is important to keep the back-up copy away from the computer system. Give one reason why this is so.

  c To prevent unauthorised personnel from reading certain data, the file containing the data is encrypted. Explain what the term 'encrypted' means.

5 Normally, a password has to be entered in order to gain access to a network.

  a Give **one** reason why a password is needed.

  b Give **one** reason why this password should be changed regularly.

6 a Explain what is meant by the word 'transaction'.

  b When the contents of a file are changed, a transaction log is often kept. Explain briefly the reason for the transaction log.

7 Many medical practices and health centres now store patient information in computer files.

  a Name **three** items of personal information (other than name and address) that could be stored in these files.

  b Patients may be worried about their records being read by people who have no need to see them. Give **three** ways of preventing this unauthorised access.

F Questions

1 In a medical centre, data about the patients is stored on the hard disk of the network file server.

  a Give **two** physical precautions that could be taken to keep the data secure.

b Doctors need to see all the information about patients. Receptionists only need to see some of the information about patients.
Describe **one** way in which software could be used to restrict access to patient information.

(AQA Specification A Tier F full course, specimen paper, q10)

2 A student is trying to access a file saved on a floppy disk. The file cannot be opened because it is damaged or corrupted.

a Describe **three** possible ways that the file could have been damaged or corrupted.

b Give **one** method that the student could use to continue with the work saved in the damaged file.

(AQA Tier F, June 2001, p2, q9)

H Questions

1 Computer systems can be protected using physical security and software security.

a (i) Explain what is meant by 'physical security'.
(ii) Give **two** examples of threats that physical security will protect against.

b Software security is provided by programs.
(i) Give **two** examples of software security.
(ii) Explain **two** threats to computer systems that software security protects against.

2 Most organisations make use of computer networks so that they have shared access to programs and data. It is important to make sure that there is no unauthorised access to such networks.

a Give the name given to the unauthorised access of computer systems.

b System security is provided by a network operating system using a system of passwords and user-IDs.
(i) Give **two** purposes of a user-ID.
(ii) Briefly explain the difference between a user-ID and a password.

(iii) For passwords to be effective, they should be changed regularly. Give **two** other things you should consider when using passwords for them to be effective.

c Network operating systems provide levels of access to data. One level of access is called read-only and another is read-write.
Explain the difference between read-only and read-write access to data.

d The manager of a network issues each user of the network with access rights. Explain what access rights are and why they are needed.

e When members of staff make alterations to databases, a transaction log is kept. Explain the purpose of a transaction log.

3 a Give **three** methods of preventing computers from being stolen.

b Describe **three** ways that data may be lost accidentally.

c Data and programs may be damaged by viruses infecting a computer system.
(i) Explain what is meant by a computer virus.
(ii) Describe **one** way in which a computer virus can enter a computer system.
(iii) Describe **two** ways in which viruses can be prevented from entering a computer system.

7 Networks

Networks are about sharing

If you link two or more computers together you have a **network**. Networks allow each of the computers to share things (called resources). Resources include hardware, such as a printer or a scanner, and software (i.e. programs). Resources can also include shared data such as student details in a school. You can even share a connection to the **Internet**.

Key Jargon

Internet – worldwide network of computer networks. The Internet forms the largest connected set of computers in the world.

network – a group of computers which are able to communicate with each other.

The two types of network

LANs and WANs

Key Jargon

LAN (local area network) – a network of computers on one site.

WAN (wide area network) – a network in which the terminals/computers are remote from each other and communicate using telecommunications.

There are two types of network: a local area network (**LAN**) or a wide area network (**WAN**).

Basically, a WAN is much bigger than a LAN and covers a much wider area. This table gives you the main features of each type of network.

LAN (local area network)	WAN (wide area network)
Confined to a small area	Covers a wide geographical area (e.g. connects cities, countries and even continents)
Usually located in a single building	In many different buildings, cities, countries, etc.
Most often just uses cables or infra-red links	Uses satellite, microwave and telecommunication links
Cheap to build	Expensive to build
Cheap to run	Expensive to run

Large networks

It is common to find a LAN connected to a WAN. A company could have a LAN in its head office, connected by WAN to computers in small, local offices in different parts of the world. In order to connect a LAN to a WAN, a **gateway** is needed. The gateway allows a computer in the LAN to communicate with a computer in the WAN and vice versa.

gateway – the device/software that translates between two different kinds of computer networks (e.g. between a WAN and a LAN).

Connecting computers together
Networking

Connecting computers is more complicated than just joining them with wires. First, a network interface card needs to be fitted to each computer acting as a terminal. Then you need to install software that tells the whole system how to operate as a network. This software is called a network operating system.

Network interface cards (NIC)

Network interface cards (NIC), sometimes called network cards, are cards that are inserted inside each computer on the network. The purpose of these cards is to provide a connection between the workstation and the **transmission medium**. Like most hardware devices, such as printers and scanners, network interface cards need drivers to get them to work.

transmission medium – the material through which data travels from one terminal to another.

Basically, a NIC does the following:

- it prepares data ready for sending
- it sends data
- it controls the flow of data from a terminal to the transmission media.

Network operating systems

A network operating system is systems software that allows PCs connected together to function as a network. Most operating systems, such as Windows 2000 and Windows XP, have a network operating system built in. These are quite popular operating systems, and many networks, both small and large, make use of them.

Linking computers together

Figure 7.1 shows some of the ways that computers can be linked.

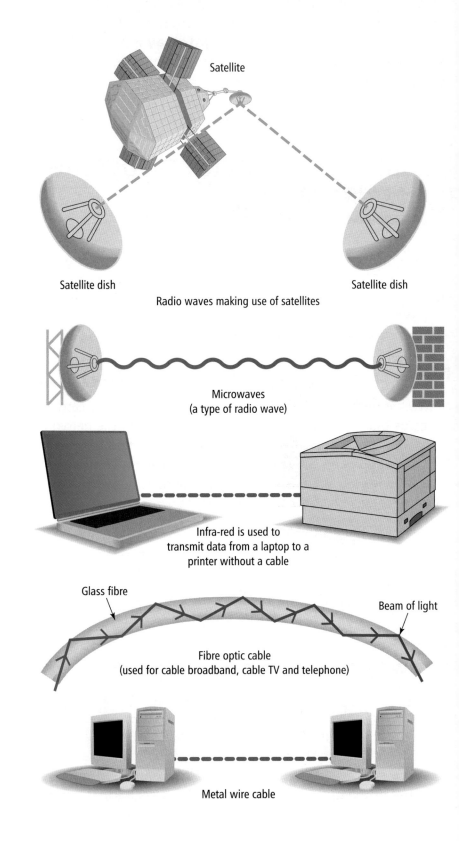

Satellite

Satellite dish

Satellite dish

Radio waves making use of satellites

Microwaves
(a type of radio wave)

Infra-red is used to
transmit data from a laptop to a
printer without a cable

Glass fibre

Beam of light

Fibre optic cable
(used for cable broadband, cable TV and telephone)

Metal wire cable

Figure 7.1

Computers can be linked in
many ways

154

Operating a network

Peer-to-peer and client-server

There are two main ways to operate a network, called peer-to-peer and client-server. Which one is used is determined mainly by the size of the network.

Peer-to-peer networks

Here are the main features of peer-to-peer networks:

- All the computers/terminals on the network are considered equal (i.e. they are peers).
- All the computers/terminals are able to share each other's resources (storage devices, printers, scanners, etc.).
- They are only suitable for small networks with less than ten users.
- All the users need to have some basic knowledge of networks in order to use them.
- As more users are added to the network, the whole network slows down considerably.

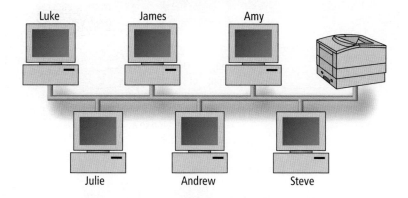

Luke   James   Amy

Julie   Andrew   Steve

Figure 7.2

Peer-to-peer networks are ideal for small networks (2–10 users)

Client-server networks

These are the main features of client-server networks:

- There is one computer, called the server, which is usually (but not always) more powerful than the rest and is used to store all the data and programs needed by the network. The server controls the network.
- They are the more popular choice of large organisations.

- They are simple to run because software installation, file back-up, etc. is all done on the server.
- The network is totally dependent on the server. If the server breaks down, then the network cannot function.

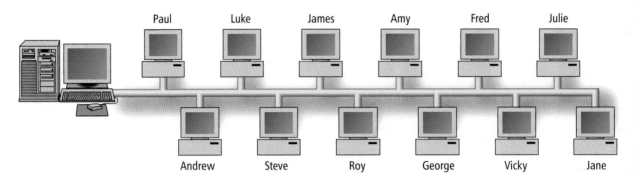

Figure 7.3

A client-server network. All the data and the programs to be shared are stored on the server

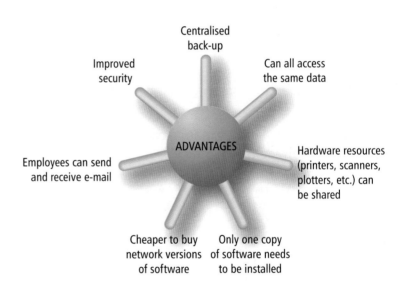

Centralised back-up

Improved security

Can all access the same data

ADVANTAGES

Employees can send and receive e-mail

Hardware resources (printers, scanners, plotters, etc.) can be shared

Cheaper to buy network versions of software

Only one copy of software needs to be installed

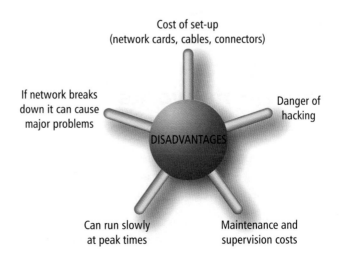

Cost of set-up (network cards, cables, connectors)

If network breaks down it can cause major problems

Danger of hacking

DISADVANTAGES

Can run slowly at peak times

Maintenance and supervision costs

Figure 7.4

Advantages and disadvantages of networking

Networks where one or more computers are more powerful than the rest are sometimes called hierarchical networks.

Servers

To run a client-server network a powerful computer is needed to act as the server. A server is responsible for storing data and moving it around a network.

Many PCs are now capable of acting as servers, but it is better to use one specifically designed for the task.

There are servers which each have a specific function in a network:

File server

A file server is a high-speed computer in a network that stores programs and data files shared by users. It deals with the requests made by the users on each terminal for programs and data.

Print server

A print server is a computer in a network that controls one or more printers. It feeds the users' print jobs, one at a time, to the printer. Each print job goes into a printer queue where it waits until the printer is ready to deal with it. On very small networks, the printer server and the file server may be the same computer.

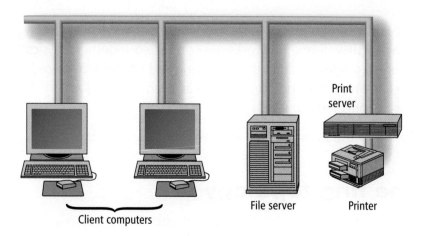

Client computers

File server

Print server

Printer

Figure 7.5

A network with both a file server and a print server

Web server

A web server is a computer on a network whose purpose is to supply access to the Internet to all the users on the network.

Activity 1

A small firm with eight computers uses each of them as stand-alone machines.

1 What is meant by the term 'stand-alone machine'?

2 They decide to network the computers together. There are two types of network: peer-to-peer and client-server.

Describe **one** main difference between these two types of network.

3 The firm decides to use a client-server network. Give **one** possible reason why they made this choice.

Connecting a network

Topologies

topologies – maps of networks showing how the various devices are connected together.

Networks can be arranged in many different ways, called **topologies**. Some networks are connected together physically, whereas others, such as those making use of radio, infra-red or satellite links, have no connections as such but behave as if they were connected by wires.

The main topologies in use are the ring, bus and star.

The ring topology

With a ring topology all the terminals are connected in a circle (see Figure 7.6). Data passes around the network in one direction. As each terminal receives data, it checks to see if the data is for that terminal and if not it sends the data on to the next terminal. Since the data signal is being generated repeatedly, the signal strength is maintained.

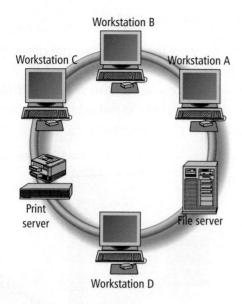

The bus topology

With the bus topology, sometimes called a line topology, all the terminals are connected to a single cable, which is often called the backbone (see Figure 7.7). Signals are normally passed in either direction along the backbone. At each end of the cable there are terminators. These prevent signals that have reached the end of the cable from reversing direction and interfering with the other signals.

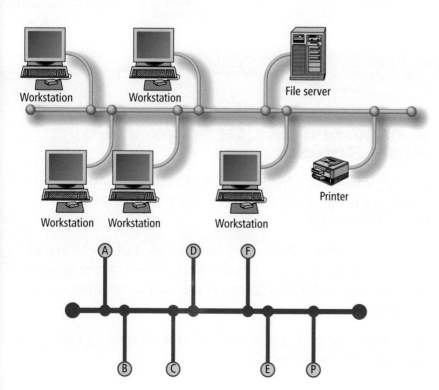

Figure 7.7

The arrangement of terminals in a network with a bus topology

The star topology

With the star topology, all the devices on the network are connected to a central computer (see Figure 7.8). This computer controls the network. It receives all the signals and then transmits them to the correct device on the network. Star networks use more cable and are therefore more expensive than other topologies.

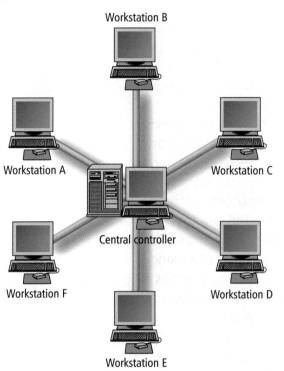

Workstation B

Workstation A

Workstation C

Central controller

Workstation F

Workstation D

Workstation E

A schematic diagram of the star network on the right (notice the central controller node, S)

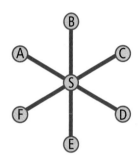

Figure 7.8

The arrangement of terminals in a network with a star topology

Case study

A network for Grange Valley High School

Grange Valley High School has just received a large grant which is going to be used to set up a computer network within the school.

The school already has many computers, but these are all stand-alone computers, which means users can only access the resources attached to or on the computer they are working on.

On the next page are some of the advantages of installing a network in the school.

- **Resource sharing:** You can have just one printer and one scanner in each classroom, which any of the computers in the classroom can use.
- **Improved security:** Students can save their work on the network. The person who looks after the network will make sure that the students' work is backed up. Passwords are used to make sure that people cannot interfere with other students' work or copy it.
- **Speed:** It is very quick to copy and transfer files.
- **Cost:** The school can buy network versions of software. This is much cheaper than buying individual copies for each computer.
- **Software installed on file server only:** Software need only be installed on the central computer used to run the network (called the file server). This makes it much easier to upgrade the software. With stand-alone computers, each computer has to have the software installed on it.
- **Electronic mail:** Students and teachers are able to communicate using electronic mail. The headteacher could send e-mails to her staff rather than paper-based documents which have to be photocopied and delivered.
- **Access to a central pool of data:** Staff in the school can use the network to access timetables, meeting dates, syllabuses, exam results, student details, etc. from any terminal provided they have the password. Students do not have to return to the same computer to access work they've done previously.

There are some disadvantages:

- **A network manager needs to be employed:** A special person will need to be employed to manage the network, or else an existing member of staff will need to be trained to do the job.
- **Security problems:** A virus could get onto the system and spread to all the computers on the network, causing problems.
- **Breakdown problems:** If the network breaks down, the users will not have access to the information held on the server.
- **Cost:** The installation of a network can be expensive.

continued over page

1 A school network is to be linked using metal wires. The school already owns all the computers it needs. At the moment, the computers are being used as stand-alone machines.
   a Give **two** other ways computers can be linked without the need for metal wires.
   b Explain what is meant by a 'stand-alone machine'.
   c Give **two** items of hardware or software that the school will need in order to turn their system into a network.

2 The school has a choice of two types of network: client-server or peer-to-peer. If the network has a total of 80 terminals, which type of network should be chosen? Give a reason for your answer.

3 A network expert recommends that the school has a network based on the star topology.
   a Explain what is meant by the term 'topology'.
   b Draw a diagram with six terminals and a server connected in a star topology.
   c Give the names of **two** types of server that you might find connected to a network.

The largest network in the world

The Internet

The Internet is the biggest network of computers in the world, and every time you log on with your computer you are adding to the size of the network.

Websites

All organisations, including schools and colleges, are reaping the benefits of having their own websites. Basically, a website allows communication between the organisation and the outside world. For commercial organisations, it allows potential customers to learn about the organisation, its products or services. Some websites allow the user to place electronic orders. The cost of conducting business on the Internet is often low compared with other more traditional methods.

Activity 2

Consider the following:

- In what ways is it cheaper to conduct business over the Internet?
- Why would it be useful for a school to have its prospectus on a website?
- What other information might a school put on a website?

Websites can be written using Hypertext Markup Language (**HTML**), which is easy to use, and you can get instructions on how to create a website on-line using your Internet Service Provider (**ISP**). Some websites include a counter to count the number of visitors to the site.

When you create your own website, it is stored on space allocated to you by your ISP (e.g. AOL or BT).

HTML (Hypertext Markup Language) – a language used for the development of websites.

ISP (Internet Service Provider) – a company that provides users with a connection to the Internet.

Accessing the Internet

There are a number of ways you can get onto the Internet using your computer. The method you choose depends on the speed of access you require and your budget. Like buying a car, the faster you want to go the more you have to pay.

Transmission speeds

How fast data is transmitted is measured in bits per second (bps). A bit (binary digit) is either a 0 or a 1. Data is coded as groups of binary digits. Because it is possible to send several thousand or even million bits per second through a transmission medium, transmission rates are abbreviated as follows:

kbs (kilobits per second i.e. 1000 bps)
Mbs (megabits per second i.e. 1,000,000 bps or 1 million bps)
Gbs (gigabits per second i.e. 1,000,000,000 bps or 1 billion bps)

Modems

If you hear screeching noises when you connect your computer to the Internet, then this is the modem working. The modem converts the digital data from your computer into a form that can be sent along an ordinary telephone line. When the data arrives at the other end of the line, the signal needs to be converted back to digital data before it can be understood by the receiving computer. Modems are usually inside the casing of the computer so you cannot see them.

External modem | Internal modem

Figure 7.9

Modems can be inside or outside the computer

The speed of a modem is how fast it can send data along a telephone line. The speed is measured in bits per second. The fastest modems transfer data at 57,600 bits per second. You will be lucky to send and receive data to and from your modem at this speed, as other network traffic can slow it down.

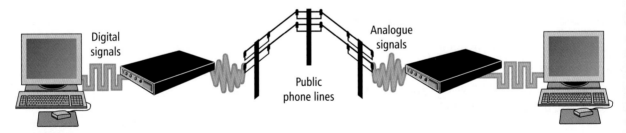

Figure 7.10

Using modems to transmit signals down telephone lines

Bandwidth

The speed with which you can send and receive data depends on the **bandwidth**. If you want to surf the Internet faster, then you need greater bandwidth. With a digital system, the bandwidth is expressed as the data transmission speed in bps, so a modem with a speed of 28,800 bps has half the bandwidth of a modem operating at 57,600 bps.

A page of text (ordinary letters, numbers and punctuation marks) requires less bandwidth than a digital photograph if it is to be transmitted during the same time period. The bandwidth requirements for digital video are very high, because the signal consists of data, images and sound.

Broadband

Broadband can be thought of as a high bandwidth, and is a method used to transmit more data along a single cable during a given time period. It does this by using different channels, with each channel being used for different types of data. For example, these channels could be used for voice communication (telephone conversations or voice mail), still images (diagrams, charts, photographs, etc.) video pictures and other types of data. Basically, instead of a single cable carrying a single signal, broadband divides the capacity of the cable in a way that allows multiple signals to be passed. You can think of broadband as a multi-lane motorway, and the data as the traffic; the more lanes there are, the faster the traffic can flow.

Key Jargon

bandwidth – determines how fast data can be passed through a transmission medium.

broadband – a very high-speed Internet connection (usually cable).

MP3 – a format for music files that makes use of compression. It is often used when music files are downloaded from the Internet.

Transferring data using a modem is like transferring water along a narrow pipe with a tap on it. The narrowness of the pipe means that it is hard to get a lot of water through it. The tap means that to make the water flow you have to turn the tap on

With broadband the pipe is much fatter so lots of water can flow. The water flows all the time so you do not have to wait for the tap to be turned on

Figure 7.11

Transferring data using a modem compared with broadband

Advantages of broadband

- It is extremely fast (ideal for watching videos, downloading music as **MP3** files, surfing the web, etc.).
- It is always on. You do not need to wait for the system to dial up, as you do with an ordinary modem.
- You only need one line. You can use the phone while you are surfing the net.
- It is unmetered.

Disadvantages of broadband
- The monthly charge is higher.
- You usually need a card called a **network interface card** installed inside your computer.
- A cable may need to be laid to your computer from outside your house.
- It is not available in all areas.

Look at the following websites for more information on broadband:

BlueYonder site:
http://www.blueyonder.co.uk/

A campaign site to encourage greater broadband facilities:
http://www.broadband4britain.co.uk/

ISDN

ISDN is a method of sending voice (i.e. telephone conversations), video and other types of data over either digital telephone lines or normal telephone lines. It is much faster to send and receive data using ISDN compared with a modem, but it is not as fast as broadband.

A typical data rate (speed of transmission) for ISDN is 128 kbs (kilobits per second).

For ISDN you need an adaptor rather than a modem. Like modems, two adaptors are used, one at each end of the transmission line.

Advantages of ISDN compared with a modem
- It is faster to send and receive data (up to 128 kbs compared with 57.6 kbs) for a modem.
- Very fast connection time.
- It can be used for videoconferencing.

Disadvantages of ISDN compared with a modem
- It is a more expensive service.
- It uses two telephone lines.

Look at the following graph (Figure 7.12). You can see how much faster broadband is compared with a modem or ISDN. BlueYonder is a broadband service that makes use of fibre optic cable and is provided by the telecommunications company Telewest.

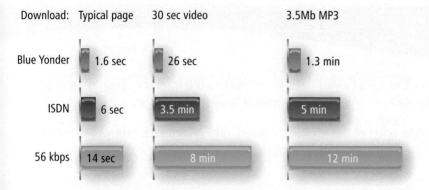

Download:	Typical page	30 sec video	3.5Mb MP3
Blue Yonder	1.6 sec	26 sec	1.3 min
ISDN	6 sec	3.5 min	5 min
56 kbps	14 sec	8 min	12 min

ADSL (Asymmetrical Digital Subscriber Line)

ADSL allows broadband speed using an ordinary telephone cable between the computer and the telephone exchange. The system is 'always on' so there is no need to wait for connection. ADSL is able to send data and voice at the same time, so only one telephone line is needed. ADSL is faster than ISDN.

The role of an Internet Service Provider

To connect to the Internet directly is very expensive and only suitable for large companies and organisations. Most people connect to the Internet via an Internet Service Provider (ISP). This is a company that supplies connections to the Internet as well as other services. These can include:

- storage space on their server where you can store a website
- e-mail facilities
- instant messaging, in which you can send short messages to your friends when they are on-line
- access to on-line shopping
- access to news, sport, weather, financial pages, etc.

When you log on to the Internet using a modem, your modem will dial the number of your Internet Service Provider. You will then be asked for your user-ID (or screen name) and a password. Once this has been validated, you are allowed access.

America On Line (AOL) is an example of an Internet Service Provider.

Uploading and downloading

When you send an e-mail or other file to someone else, you are uploading.

When you receive data, files or e-mails you are downloading. When you are visiting websites (i.e. surfing), data is sent to your computer so you are downloading. With one type of broadband service, called ADSL, uploading is slower than downloading.

Activity 3

For this activity you need to connect to the Internet using an Internet Service Provider. Once connected, look at the facilities offered by the ISP.

Write a list of the facilities offered, and under each one write one or two lines explaining why it is useful.

Electronic mail (e-mail)

An e-mail is an electronic message that is sent from one computer to another. It involves using a telecommunications link (telephone line, cable, satellite, radio waves, etc.). Sending and receiving e-mails is not just restricted to computers. Many mobile phones, landline telephones and personal digital assistants (**PDAs**) can also be used to send and receive e-mails.

Using e-mail you can:

- keep in touch with friends and family
- communicate between businesses
- attach files (photos, long wordprocessed documents, spreadsheets, music files, etc.)
- send one message to many different people.

How do e-mails work?

1   You type in the e-mail message and send it to the recipient's e-mail address.

2   The message is sent to the mail server or Internet Service Provider's server. A server is simply a powerful computer with lots of storage space.

3   The message is sent on to the Internet where it arrives at the recipient's mail server or Internet Service Provider's server. Here it is stored.

4   When the recipient logs on, they are told that there is e-mail waiting for them. The mail is then sent from their mail server or Internet Service Provider to their computer.

Replying to an e-mail

When you receive e-mail you will notice that there is a button to click for your reply. All you have to do then is type in your reply, as the e-mail address of the person you are sending it to is included automatically. You can also include a copy of the message that was sent to you. This means the recipient knows which message you are replying to.

Figure 7.13 shows the e-mail preparation screen from AOL. Notice that you can format the text (bold, italics, etc.). Notice also that there is an Address Book and you can attach files using **Attachments**.

attachment – a file that is attached to an e-mail.

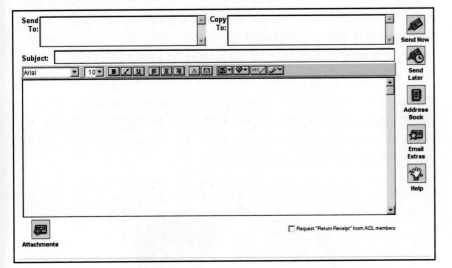

Figure 7.13

The e-mail preparation screen from AOL

Address Book

Internet Service Providers have a feature called an Address Book for managing your e-mail addresses. In the Address Book are the names and e-mail addresses of all the people to whom you are likely to send e-mail. Instead of having to type in an address each time you write an e-mail, you can simply click on the e-mail address of the recipient in the Address Book.

Mailing lists

Mailing lists are lists of people and their e-mail addresses. They are used when a copy of an e-mail needs to be distributed to all the people in a particular group. For example if you were working as part of a team and needed to send each member of the team the same e-mail then you would set up a mailing list. Every time you needed to send the members of the team e-mail, you could use the list to save time.

File attachments

You can attach files to e-mails. For example, you could attach a file containing a photograph of yourself obtained from a digital camera, a piece of clip art, a picture that you have scanned in or a long document. Basically, any kind of electronic file can be attached to an e-mail.

You can attach more than one file to an e-mail, so if you had six photographs to send, you could attach each of them to one e-mail and send them all together.

Before you attach a file, you must first prepare an e-mail message to send with the file explaining the purpose of your e-mail and giving some information about the file that you are sending with it (what its purpose is, what format it is in, etc.). Once the e-mail message has been completed, you click on the File Attachment button. A box will appear to allow you to select the drive, folder and eventually the file that you want to send.

If you want to send more than one file, repeat the file attachment process until all the files have been attached. Usually, if there is more than one file to send, the files are compressed to reduce the time taken to send them.

Although Jim knew about file attachments, address books and mailing lists he still couldn't work out where his e-mail messages came from

The main advantages of e-mail

● E-mail is fast. It takes just a few seconds to send and receive e-mail. If the recipient checks their e-mail regularly, then a reply can be sent very quickly.

● It is ideal for communicating with people over long distances. An e-mail can be sent to someone anywhere in the world in a matter of seconds and for very little cost. You don't need to worry about the time difference when sending an e-mail abroad, as the recipient will simply read the e-mail when they next log on.

- E-mails are quick to write and less formal than letters and the odd spelling mistake is acceptable.

- It is inexpensive and easy to send the same e-mail message to many different people.

- It is easy to attach a copy of the sender's e-mail with your reply, and this saves them having to search for their original message if they need it to refer to.

- E-mail is cheaper than a letter. No stamp, envelope and paper are needed. E-mails sent across the world cost no more than a local e-mail. Large electronic documents and other files can be attached to an e-mail at no extra cost.

- You do not have to go out to the post office or a post box, and you do not need to spend time shopping for stamps, envelopes and paper.

The main disadvantages of e-mail

- Not everyone has the equipment to send and receive e-mail. However, with Internet access available from televisions, landline phones and mobile phones it could soon take over from traditional paper-based mail.

- Junk mail is a problem. You can waste time looking through e-mails that are just adverts.

- E-mails are not as secure as traditional letters because they can be accessed by 'hackers'.

- The efficiency and speed of the system relies on people checking their e-mail regularly.

● People who do not have access to the Internet, or who are unfamiliar with the technology, may feel alienated.

● The equipment needed to send and receive e-mail is expensive compared with traditional methods of communication.

fax machine – a machine capable of sending and receiving text and pictures along telephone lines.

E-mail versus fax

A **fax machine** is like a long-distance photocopier. You put a document in the fax machine at one end and then enter the telephone number of the fax machine it is to be sent to. The page is scanned, passed along the telephone line and finally printed out on the recipient's fax machine. Documents containing text as well as pictures can be sent by fax. It is possible to use a computer with a scanner and a printer as a fax machine.

More people now have e-mail than fax, particularly at home. Faxing documents is less convenient than e-mailing; with a dedicated fax machine (i.e. not a computer) you have to scan the document before you can send it, and it has to be printed out at the other end. This can take time, and the quality of the output from the recipient's fax machine is often poor. There is also the problem of having to store the faxes, and a lot of paper is wasted.

E-mail versus the telephone

Nowadays, businesses are using e-mail for communicating with each other far more than the telephone. The advantages of e-mail compared with the telephone are huge.

● You may need to phone someone a number of times before you get through to them (the phone might be engaged, they might be out, etc.). With e-mail, you send the message once, and then simply wait for them to reply.

● You can waste time making conversation on the phone rather than sticking to the main points of your message. E-mail is more concise.

● If there is a large time difference between the country you are in and that of the person you are phoning, you need to time your call carefully to avoid disturbing them at unsociable times of the day (or night).

● Phone calls can be expensive compared with e-mail, especially to other countries.

Activity 4

A company has offices all around the world. They use e-mail to communicate with their staff.

1 Give **three** advantages of contacting staff by e-mail rather than by post.

2 Describe **two** features of e-mail that would allow the company to send the same e-mail to many different people easily.

Protecting a network
System security

Because so many people use a network it is important to ensure that the system is secure. If there is access via the network to the Internet then there needs to be protection against **hackers**. These people could intercept and read e-mail, alter data or even collect credit card numbers and use them to commit fraud. **Encryption** is used to protect data as it travels over the Internet.

Key Jargon

encryption – the process of encoding sensitive data before it is sent over a network.

hackers – people who try to break into a computer network.

Encryption and digital signatures

Encryption works in the following way. Suppose Jayne in London wants to send a secure e-mail to Jack in Paris. When Jayne has typed in her e-mail she presses the 'encrypt' option. The software verifies who she wants to send the e-mail to. It does this by presenting a list of all the people to whom Jayne can send encrypted messages. She chooses Jack's name from the list. The encryption software then automatically mixes and re-mixes every binary digit (bit) of the message with every bit in Jack's **public key**. The result is a mix of data which can only be unscrambled by the same software using Jack's **private key**.

When Jack receives the e-mail in Paris he selects the 'decrypt' option and the software then asks him for a password which he types in. This decrypts his private key, and a large number of calculations are then performed which unscrambles the encrypted message sent by Jayne.

If the message had been intercepted, it could not have been read as you need the private key of the recipient to perform the calculations needed to unscramble the message.

For added security, Jayne could have added a 'digital signature' to the message. This would then have been checked by Jack's software to ensure that the message really came from Jayne, and not from another user pretending to be Jayne.

Encryption is used to make sure that your personal details, credit card details and other sensitive information are secure when you send them over the Internet, for example when ordering goods or carrying out bank transactions.

User-IDs

A user-ID is a name or number that is used to identify a certain user of the network. The person who looks after the network uses this name or number to allocate space on the network to the user. It also allows the network manager to give the user access to certain files, and to keep track of what files they are using.

Passwords

A password is a string of characters (letters, numbers and punctuation marks) that the user can select. Only the user knows what their password is. When the user enters the password it will not be shown on the screen. Only when they enter the correct password will the user be allowed access to the network.

Transaction logs

When transactions ('bits of business') are performed on a computer, there may not be a paper-based record of them. Instead, the software used may have a function built in which provides an audit trail. The audit trail is a record of what has happened in the system. For example, if a file has been altered it will provide evidence of the file before it was altered, along with the date, time and name of the member of staff who performed the alteration, and even the reason why the file was altered.

Firewalls

Firewalls are used to filter out unauthorised requests from outside users to gain access to the network. This prevents hackers from accessing the system. Firewalls also filter data so that only allowable data is able to enter the system.

All networks that have access to the Internet should have a firewall.

Activity 5

Explain briefly how each one of the following helps improve the security of a network.

1   user-ID
2   password
3   encryption
4   transaction log
5   firewall

Backing up programs and data

Back-ups are copies of data and program files kept for security reasons. If the originals were destroyed then the back-ups could be used instead. Using a file server and storing both programs and data on it means that back-ups can be made in one place rather than on individual computers. The person in charge of the network will make the back-ups when needed, rather than each user having to make their own.

Squashing files

Big files such as e-mails with photos attached can take a long time to upload (send) or download (receive). To cut down on this time, files can be squashed or compressed. This is done using a special compression program. The file is compressed and sent, and then decompressed by the recipient when they have downloaded it.

WinZip is a popular program for compressing and decompressing files.

The icon for WinZip is a press squashing a filing cabinet .

 If you download a file from the Internet and it has an icon like this, then you will need to decompress it before you can open the file and look at its contents.

If an e-mail attachment needs compressing before it can be sent, some ISPs will do this automatically. Similarly, when you log on to download the file it will be decompressed automatically.

Find it out yourself

The Internet is full of unfamiliar terms, many of which you will not find in an ordinary dictionary.

Here is a list of terms in alphabetical order. Copy it down, and put the meaning next to each term. If you don't know what the meaning is, use one of the glossaries available on the Internet to look it up.

Term	Meaning	Term	Meaning
Browser		Hacker	
Chat room		ISP	
Cookie		Hyperlink	
Download		Modem	
E-mail		Surfing	
FAQ		User-ID	
HTML		Web page	

Build your notes

Here are some notes that summarise this chapter. The notes are incomplete because they have words missing.

Using the words in the list below, copy out and complete the sentences A to S, underlining the words that you have inserted. Each word may be used more than once.

> website   network interface card   bandwidth   ring   LAN
> topology   peer-to-peer   network   bus   print server   electronic
> WAN   star   modems   Internet   Internet Service Provider
> cable   client-server   broadband

A A group of computers linked together in order to share facilities is called a _____.

B Small networks confined to a single site are called _____.

C Networks that use communication lines and are separated by a long distance are called _____.

D The card which is inserted into a computer so that the computer can be connected to a network is called a _____ _____ _____.

E A network where all the computers are of equal status is called a _____-_____-_____ network.

F A network where there is one powerful computer that controls the network is called a _____-_____ network.

G In some networks there is a computer used to control the printing services for the network. This computer is called a _____ _____.

H The way the computers in a network are connected is called the _____.

I A network where the computers are connected in a circle is called a _____ network.

J A network where the computers are connected in a line is called a _____ or line topology.

K A _____ topology is one where there is a computer at the centre and all the other computers are connected to it.

L Computers connected together using a communications line need two _____, one at each end of the line.

continued over page

177

M _____ mail allows messages to be sent from one terminal to another which may be in the same building, another part of the country or even in a different country.

N The _____ is the biggest network of computers in the world.

O A company whose file server is permanently connected to the Internet and who you can use to gain access to the Internet is called an _____ _____ _____.

P If you want to access the Internet faster, then you need to have greater _____.

Q Wide bandwidth is often referred to as _____.

R _____ is classed as a broadband service.

S Most companies and organisations have a _____ which outsiders can use to access information about it.

1 **A group of computers connected together that are able to communicate with each other is called a:**

a   stand-alone computer
b   network
c   terminal
d   file server.

2 **Which one of the following is not an advantage of a network?**

a   It is possible to share resources such as a printer.
b   All users can access the same data.
c   You can use e-mail internally.
d   Expensive equipment is often required.

3 **A network confined to a single building is called a:**

a   WAN
b   PAN
c   WAP
d   LAN.

4 **Which one of the following is not a network topology?**

a   star
b   ring
c   bus
d   tram.

5 **Which of the following is not an advantage of e-mail?**

a   It is less formal than a letter and so takes less time to write.
b   You do not need a stamp and an envelope.
c   It is easy to send the same e-mail to several people.
d   Everyone can be contacted using e-mail.

Multiple-choice questions

6 The main advantage of using an ISDN adaptor compared with using a modem is:

a it is cheaper to buy
b it allows faster transfer of data
c you can use e-mail
d you can download files.

7 Which one of the following is a disadvantage of e-mail compared with ordinary post?

a You cannot contact everyone as not everyone has e-mail facilities.
b You can send e-mail from your own home. There is no need to go to the post box.
c E-mail is cheaper than a letter (no paper, no envelope and no stamp to buy).
d E-mail can be sent and received using many mobile phones.

8 To log on to a network, a user must supply:

a a user-ID and a password
b their name and address
c their mother's maiden name
d a credit card.

9 Small networks where all the terminals have equal status is called a:

a client-server network
b stand-alone system
c print server network
d peer-to-peer network.

10 To transfer video along a cable you need a cable with a high:

a bandlength
b bandwidth
c baseband
d diameter.

1 A network is set up in the computer room of a junior school. Each computer is attached to a local area network (LAN).

   a Draw a labelled diagram of a LAN consisting of eight computers. You should include any other hardware devices that you would expect to be connected to this network.

   b Most large networks are client-server networks.
     (i) Explain the main feature of a client-server network.
     (ii) In a client-server network, where would the programs be stored?
     (iii) Describe **one** advantage of a client-server network.

2 A network topology is an arrangement of terminals/computers in a network to show the way that they are connected. Draw diagrams to show the following topologies:

   a star topology
   b ring topology
   c bus topology

3 A school has a room of networked computers and also a room of stand-alone computers.

   a Explain clearly the difference between a networked computer and a stand-alone computer.

   b The ICT teachers in this school prefer to teach in the room with the networked computers.
     (i) Give **two** advantages to the teachers of using the networked computers.
     (ii) Give **one** advantage to the students of using the networked computers.

   c One teacher says that the networked computers also have some disadvantages. Give **one** disadvantage that the networked computers might have.

4 Here are some terms and their definitions that have been jumbled up. Copy the table, writing the names of the terms next to their correct definitions.

Term	Definition
modem	A way of sending messages electronically from one computer to another
WAN	A small network that is usually confined to a single site
e-mail	A network covering a wide geographical area
LAN	A device needed to convert the signals from a computer so that they can be sent along a telephone line

5 A password normally has to be entered in order to gain access to a network.

  a   Give **one** reason why a password is needed.
  b   Give **one** reason why a password should be changed regularly.

F Questions

1 LAN and WAN are both types of computer network.

  a   (i)   What do the letters LAN stand for?
      (ii) What do the letters WAN stand for?
  b   Give **two** differences between a LAN and a WAN.
  c   Give **three** advantages to computer users of a LAN, rather than working on stand-alone machines.
  d   Give **one** method which can be used to prevent data from being misused when it is being transferred between computers.

  (AQA Tier F, June 2001, p2, q3)

2 A teacher uses the Internet to communicate with some students, who cannot come to school, by sending them e-mails.

  a   Give **three** advantages, other than cost and speed, of using e-mail to communicate, rather than by telephone.
  b   Give **two** reasons why it may not be possible to send e-mail to every student who cannot attend school.
  c   Give **two** other ways that a student could use the Internet to help with schoolwork at home.

  (AQA Tier F, June 2001, p2, q8)

H Questions

1 A building firm buys a computer system and some software to help run the business. As the business expands it gets two more computer systems for the office. The owner of the business wants to use the same wordprocessing package on all three machines.

   a Explain why he should buy extra copies of the software.
   b He wants to keep records of his customers on the three computers and thinks it would a good idea to install a network.
      (i) Give **three** advantages to the staff of having the computers connected to a local area network (LAN).
      (ii) Give **one** possible disadvantage (other than cost) of having the network installed.

(NEAB Tier H, June 1998, q5)

2 A doctors' practice uses a local area network (LAN). The practice has four doctors and each doctor has a terminal in their room which they use to access patient records. Each terminal has a printer attached and this printer is used to print out prescriptions, letters to hospitals, etc.

   The network is a client-server network and the server is located in the office.

   a Give **two** advantages of using this network instead of stand-alone machines in each doctor's surgery.
   b The local hospital uses a network and the practice would like to link their network to it so that information can be passed between the hospital and the practice and vice versa.
      (i) What extra device is needed so that data can be passed from one network to the other?
      (ii) Explain the function of this device.
   c Explain **one** difference between a LAN and a WAN.
   d The LAN is a client-server network. Explain what this means.

8 Communications

Years ago people usually lived where they worked. If you look at the mining towns of Wales or the cotton towns of Lancashire you will see that the houses were all built within walking distance of the mine or factory. The people couldn't afford cars so they either cycled or walked to work. The surrounding shops relied on the people from the mines or factories for their custom. People did not go abroad for their holidays and most people never even met anyone from another country. Communication was limited to where they worked or lived.

Times have changed. Many people travel large distances to get to work. Some people are able to work from home. People are able to work on the move on trains, planes, etc. You can go on holiday virtually anywhere in the world and make friends with people from other countries and cultures. The Internet allows people all over the globe to communicate with each other.

There is no doubt about it; the world is now a much smaller place.

Global communication

What does it mean?

Key Jargon

e-commerce – conducting business by making use of the Internet.

teleworking/ telecommuting – working from home by making use of ICT equipment.

If you have a connection to the Internet, then you can make contact and communicate easily with people all over the world. You are no longer restricted by where you live. You may be lucky and have the type of job where you can work from home. Working from home using ICT equipment is called **teleworking** or **telecommuting**.

Modern businesses operate in many different countries. To do so successfully they need to have effective communication links. Most large businesses have websites and some are able to take orders directly from customers using the Internet. Doing business using the Internet is called **e-commerce**.

Large international businesses such as Coca-Cola and Macdonalds rely on global communications to operate successfully.

Advantages of global communication

- You can communicate with anyone anywhere in the world. This helps people understand about other cultures and nationalities.
- You can communicate easily with relatives and friends in other countries.
- You are able to buy and sell goods anywhere in the world.
- It makes it much cheaper and easier for businesses to deal with customers and suppliers in other countries.
- It makes it easier to shop around for goods. You can buy the cheapest goods, no matter where they are being sold.

Disadvantages of global communication

Global communication is usually a good thing, but there are a number of disadvantages:

- Large international companies can dominate the marketplace and put smaller local businesses out of business.
- There is the danger that sensitive information could be intercepted by hackers.
- Computer viruses can spread rapidly to computers all over the world.
- It can cause legal problems; what is legal in one country may be illegal in another.
- It can widen the gap between the rich and poor countries because poorer countries cannot afford to invest in the latest technologies, such as satellite links, broadband, etc., and therefore cannot compete with the countries that can.

Freedom of information

'Freedom of information' means that there are no secrets. If all information were freely available, governments, schools, hospitals, etc. would not be able to keep information from us.

Some people argue that all information, no matter how undesirable, should be freely available. They say that it is up to the individual to decide what information they see, and not the state.

Most people, however, take the opposite view. They say that there is a lot of information people should not be able to see, for example:

- where to buy illegal drugs
- how to join terrorist organisations
- the private addresses of members of parliament
- how to make bombs
- how to create and distribute viruses.

Arguments for freedom of information

- Freedom of information is vital for democracy, since leaders should not impose their wishes on people without consultation.
- There are always two sides to any argument so it is essential to be able to make up your own mind about something. In order to make an informed judgement, people need to see all the available information.
- If all information is made available, individuals can decide for themselves if they want to see or use it. For example, pornographic material is available, but people are free to decide whether to look at it or not. (There are some serious flaws in this argument, can you say what they are?)
- The views of minorities should be heard, even if their views differ from those of the government and society as a whole (e.g. animal rights activists, extreme political groups, terrorist groups, etc.).
- If information is freely available, then people can copy any material they need and include it in work they've produced themselves.

Arguments against freedom of information

- Some types of material (such as pornography) are not suitable for everyone, e.g. children.
- Not all information is accurate, so if there was no policing of information it could lead to people being misinformed.
- People could give information about others that is not true, and that could cause them upset and distress.
- Some information could be dangerous if it were freely available. If you were a witness to a serious crime, for example, then you would not want everyone to know your name and address.

- Students could copy coursework off the Internet, or look up exam questions. This would undermine the examination system.

- If all types of material were freely available, such as photographs, music, diagrams, maps, text, web page designs, etc., then it would be very difficult to protect the rights of the people who had created or developed the material in the first place.

- People may choose not to make certain information available, so what information was available would depend on individuals rather than the state.

- Freedom of information would allow criminal records, school reports and medical details to be seen by anyone who wanted to see them. Would you be happy for people to have access to this kind of information about you, or a member of your family?

Websites

Websites allow communication between an organisation and the outside world. For commercial organisations, it allows potential customers to learn about the organisation, its products or services. Some websites allow the user to place electronic orders. The cost of conducting business on the web is low compared with other more traditional methods.

Figure 8.1

The Amazon on-line order form

Individuals can also produce their own websites so that people who have similar interests can contact them. When you make your own website, it is stored on space that has been allocated to you by your Internet Service Provider (the company that provides you with your Internet connection).

Web browsers

A web browser is a program that allows you access to the World Wide Web (WWW).

The World Wide Web is part of the Internet where graphics, sound, video and animation are used as well as text. Web browsers allow you to move quickly from one page to another, and from one site to another. They also allow you to navigate around a site and to perform certain actions.

Using global communication
Finding information on the Internet

There are three ways to find information on the Internet:

1 **By typing in a web address.**
   If you know the web address of a website, then you simply type it in. Web addresses are everywhere; you can find them in magazines, advertisements and even on the sides of planes. Web addresses look like this:

   www.nelsonthornes.com

Figure 8.2

The Internet is so important to easyJet's business that it has the website address on the sides of its planes

2 **By 'surfing' the Internet.**
   Surfing the Internet means moving rapidly from one web page or website to another until you find something of

interest. To do this you make use of the **hypertext links**. These appear as either underlined text or text in a different colour. When you move your mouse pointer over a hypertext link it changes shape (usually to a hand). On double-clicking the left mouse button, you are taken to the new site.

3   By using a search engine.
One of the main problems with the Internet is finding what you want easily. This is why **search engines** are used. Search engines are special programs that allow keywords to be entered so that sites can be located that contain those words.

Search engines

To find what you want on the Internet you need to perform a search. To do this you need a program called a search engine. A search engine is a **web portal**, which is a website where you go to get redirected to another website. Your Internet Service Provider (the company you use to connect you to the Internet) will provide one, but there are others to choose from. These include:

- Yahoo
  www.yahoo.com
- Lycos
  www.lycos.com
- WebCrawler
  www.webcrawler.com
- Excite
  www.excite.com

If you perform a search and get a huge amount of information, or no information at all, you are probably searching the wrong way.

Searching using a single keyword

The simplest search uses a single keyword. Here is some useful advice when searching for a single word:

- Start by entering something very specific.
- If you don't find anything, then broaden your search.
- If you still don't find anything, then broaden your search further.

Key Jargon

hypertext link – a link that allows you to go from one web page to another.

search engine – a program that can be used to search for information on the Internet.

web portal – a website where you get redirected to another website.

Searching using a phrase

Searching using a phrase means searching using several words. If you type in 'computer laws' you will get a huge number of references because as well as those to computer laws, you will also get references to 'computer' and all references to 'laws'.

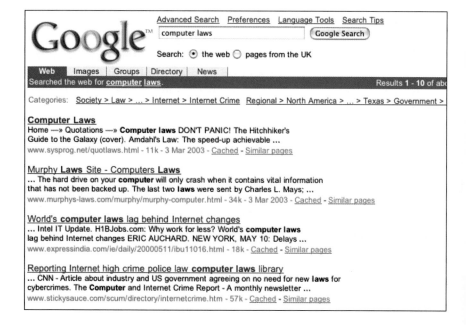

You need to tell the computer to group the words 'computer' and 'laws' together, and this is done by placing them in inverted commas like this:

"computer laws"

This tells the search engine to find the words only when they appear next to each other on the page.

Suppose you want to search the Internet for information on a football club such as Liverpool Football Club. If you type in **Liverpool Football Club** then the search will also find references to **Liverpool** (all about the city of Liverpool, businesses in Liverpool, etc.); **Football** (all about the game in general, football clubs both amateur and professional, etc.) and **Club** (clubs in general such as night clubs, chess clubs, tennis clubs, health clubs, etc.). You need to type in **"Liverpool Football Club"**.

Multiple search criteria

Multiple searches make use of simple logic when performing searches. They are called Boolean searches. Multiple search criteria use keywords (AND, OR and NOT) in the following way:

AND   Search on Term 1 AND Term 2

OR   Search on Term 1 OR Term 2

NOT   Search on Term 1 but NOT Term 2

Examples

- Retail AND Computers will search for web pages containing both the words 'Retail' and 'Computers'.

- Retail OR Computers will search for web pages that contain the word 'Retail' or the word 'Computers' or both words.

- Radiation NOT Nuclear will search for web pages that contain the word 'Radiation' but not 'Nuclear Radiation'.

Activity 1

By making use of search conditions, search the Internet for information on:

- the latest mobile phones
- personal digital assistants (PDAs).

Is the information accurate?

You should always ask the question 'is it right?' after you have found information using the Internet. There are sites that are specifically designed to misinform.

Here are some things to look for:

- What organisation or individual made the site, and have you heard of them?

- Does the site look as if it was produced professionally, or by someone with a limited knowledge of website design?

- Has the website got the expected address? For example, you would expect Microsoft to have a website with the address **www.microsoft.com**, which it does. Bogus sites often incorporate deliberate spelling mistakes in the domain name.

- Is the page with the information on dated? Information can go out of date very quickly.

- Are there spelling or grammatical mistakes?

Global networks

How they affect our lives

Key Jargon

e-commerce – buying and selling goods or services over the Internet, as opposed to using traditional methods such as shops or offices.

E-commerce

Most companies have their own websites. In some cases the websites are simply to make people more aware of their business and for advertising. Other companies use their websites to conduct **e-commerce**. Customers can use these websites to place orders on-line.

Here are some advantages of e-commerce to a company:

- It is cheaper than renting shops and offices.
- Fewer staff are needed. Much of the administrative work is done by the customers themselves (e.g. checking the price, checking availability, typing in the order, etc.).
- The company can operate 24 hours a day, 365 days a year.
- It can reach many different countries.
- The warehouses can be located anywhere in the world.

There are also advantages to the customers:

- Goods and services can often be bought more cheaply than from high street shops and offices.
- You can visit other Internet shops without leaving your home to make sure you are getting the best deal.
- The goods are delivered straight to your house. There is no need to go and pick them up.
- You can order goods from anywhere in the world.

There are, however, some disadvantages too:

- Poorer people may not be able to afford the equipment and ISP costs to connect to the Internet.
- You need some ICT skills to use the Internet. Some people, such as older people, may not have these skills.
- You often need a credit card to make on-line purchases. If you do not have a credit card you cannot buy on-line.
- Many people are wary of typing in their personal details and credit card number because of the risk of hackers getting hold of the information.

Activity 2

Find out about e-commerce on the Internet. You need to look at the following sites:

www.amazon.co.uk
www.cd-wow.com
www.ebay.co.uk

You need to look closely at these sites and investigate some of their features.

After doing this, answer the following questions:

1 What does the site offer?
2 Write a few short paragraphs to explain what advantages the site offers compared with making a purchase from a shop or catalogue.
3 What are the main advantages to the consumer in using the site?
4 How does a user pay for the goods they have bought?

Now find some e-commerce sites of your own.

Write down the web addresses of the sites you have visited.

Find it out yourself

Where is the best place to find information about the Internet? The Internet of course! Here are some very good websites:

www.internet-guide.co.uk/
This is a basic guide to the Internet – what it is, how to get started, what an ISP is, etc.

www.webteacher.org.uk/
This site has a good explanation of the difference between the World Wide Web and the Internet. There is also information on browsers and other aspects of the Internet, some tutorials and a glossary of Internet terms.

Using the glossary at:
www.webteacher.org.uk/

continued over page

find and write down a definition for each of the following terms:

- ADSL
- attachment
- bandwidth
- browser
- cookie
- encryption
- firewall
- hyperlink
- ISP
- ISDN
- search engine
- uploading
- web browser.

Case Study

Buying goods and services globally

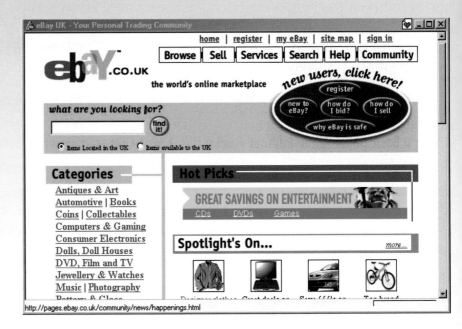

Figure 8.4

The home page of ebay.co.uk

194

E-bay is an auction site, set up to put sellers of goods in contact with buyers throughout the world. The seller puts a description and a picture of the goods they want to sell on the site. They have a minimum price below which they do not wish to sell the item. Users of the site are not told this price. People are able to bid for the goods and if they make the highest bid and it is above the minimum price, the buyer accepts the bid and the goods are sold.

E-bay has some advantages over an ordinary auction:

- You do not need to attend the auction.
- There is a huge variety of goods for auction; you have a much wider choice than with an ordinary auction.
- Because the auction is conducted over several days or weeks, you have time to think about your bids.

There are, however, some disadvantages:

- You cannot see the goods before you buy unless you live locally.
- There may be customs duties to pay when you buy from abroad.
- Postage from abroad could be high if the item is heavy.

A company like e-bay could not have existed before the Internet. The Internet has made it possible for buyers and sellers to do business even if they are in different countries. Multinational parcel companies such as FedEx allow you to send and receive parcels quickly and easily. You can even track your parcel as it leaves the depot to find out where it is and when it is likely to be delivered.

To use e-bay you have to register. It is important that only people who have the money to pay for the goods are able to make bids. You therefore need a credit card. When you register you have to supply your personal details (name, address, telephone number, e-mail address, etc.). You also have to supply your credit card details. To prevent hackers gaining access to this data, it is encrypted before it is sent.

1 e-bay makes use of the Internet. Briefly explain what is meant by the Internet.

2 To gain access to the e-bay site, the web address is typed in. What is meant by the term 'web address'?

continued over page

3 The e-bay auctions operate in 'real time'. Explain why the system must operate in real time.

4 This auction site is a very popular site, and many people who have never bought anything in an auction take part.

Give **two** advantages of using an on-line auction rather than a conventional auction where you have to be present to bid.

5 To participate in an e-bay auction you need a credit card. Give one reason why this may be a problem.

6 When a person's personal details and credit card details are entered, the data is encrypted.
  a Explain what 'encrypted' means.
  b Give **one** reason why it is necessary for these details to be encrypted.

Teletext

Teletext is an information service provided on most televisions. It has been around for a lot longer than the Internet, but in some respects they are similar. It consists of pages of information about television programmes, news, weather, share prices, sports results, airport arrivals, traffic problems and so on. The pages are accessed using the television remote control and you can either select the pages from a menu or type in their page number.

There are some differences between the Teletext service and the Internet. They are shown in the table below.

Teletext	The Internet
Free	Costs money to connect via an Internet Service Provider (ISP)
Transmitted at the same time as TV pictures	Sent via telephone, fibre optic cable or radio signals
Limited number of topics and pages	Unlimited information
Non-interactive. You cannot order goods using Teletext	Interactive. You can play on-line games and order goods and services
Provided by TV companies	Provided by everyone who is connected to the Internet

There is a version of Teletext available over the Internet. It can be found at:

www.teletext.co.uk

This is very different from the television version of Teletext because it is interactive. Incidentally, this is an excellent site, and you can use it for searching for cheap, last-minute holidays.

Banking from home

You may have noticed that many bank branches have closed recently and are now restaurants or wine bars. Many banks have closed up to a quarter of their branches.

They are not closing because they have too few customers – they are closing because their customers are banking in a different way. Rather than use branches, they can do their banking from home by making use of either the Internet or their telephone.

Home banking, or virtual banking, has many advantages:

- You can bank 24 hours a day, 365 days a year.
- You do not have to visit the bank to make use of its services.
- You do not have to wait in a queue.

There are a few disadvantages.

- People are concerned about the security risks of banking on-line.
- You can move money from one account to another and check your balance, but you still need to go out of the house to get cash.
- Some people, particularly older people, prefer the personal service offered by a conventional bank.

Figure 8.5

You can keep control of your bank account from home, using the Internet

(© Copyright. [HSBC Bank plc] [2003] ALL RIGHTS RESERVED No part of this publication may be reproduced, stored in a retrieval system, or transmitted, on any form or by any means electronic, mechanical, photocopying, recording, or otherwise without the prior written permission of HSBC Bank plc.)

On-line booking services

The use of ICT in the travel industry has led to a lot of changes. Here are some of them:

Travel information

The Internet provides a huge source of information about public transport. In the past, if you wanted information about bus or train times, then you would have had to get it from the library or train/bus station. Now you have access to all the timetables on the Internet.

Travel agents

Travel agents use computers all the time. They are used to check whether a particular flight or holiday is available. Once a holiday is found they can tell the customer the cost and book it for them. As well as booking holidays and flights, travel agents can also book rail tickets, accommodation, hire cars, etc.

Figure 8.6

Travel agents use computers for checking holiday availability, flights, etc.

Using the Internet to book holidays

If you want to book a flight or a holiday, then the first place to look is the Internet. There are many sites where you can pick the dates you wish to travel and the approximate price you want to pay, and it will search for suitable holidays.

Such on-line systems have to be real-time systems because as each holiday or flight is sold the system needs to be updated immediately to prevent double booking.

Using the Internet you can:

- book from the comfort of your home
- check the availability and prices of flights and holidays
- make savings when you book direct
- read reports from people who have been on the same holiday
- arrange your own travel and accommodation
- find out about the resort before you go.

In the future, more people will book their holidays direct using the Internet as it will be cheaper than booking them through a travel agent. Travel agents may therefore become a thing of the past. Some people even think that the package holiday's days are numbered as more people are able to create their own holidays by booking their own travel and accommodation arrangements.

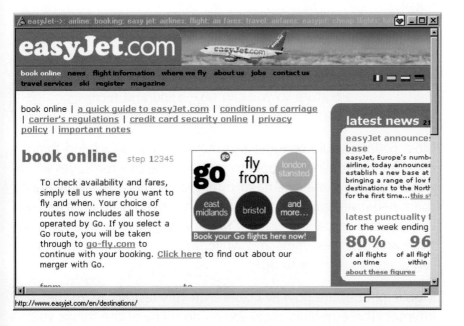

Figure 8.7

Booking flights on easyJet.com means the cost savings can be passed to the customers

Mobile telephones

The current trend is for manufacturers to combine the functions of digital TVs, web browsers, mobile phones and digital cameras. People want to have access to all these methods of communication all the time, even when they are on the move, so they want just one device that does everything. That device is the mobile phone.

Figure 8.8

Do you know anyone who doesn't have a mobile phone?

At one time a mobile phone was exactly that – a device that you could carry around with you to make phone calls. Now you can use a mobile phone to send and receive text messages, send and receive e-mail, surf the web and access a database of contact details.

There are times when you would like to take a photograph but haven't got your camera with you. Most people, however, carry their mobile phone all the time. Some mobile phones now have a digital camera feature so you can take, send and receive photos whenever you want.

Most people would consider text messaging to be a good thing. For example, it allows people to send and receive messages when watching a film in a cinema or during a meeting. But there are some negative issues. Text messaging has been used in cases of bullying and sexual harassment, and people have been known to write and send text messages while they are driving – clearly a very dangerous thing to do!

Mobile phones are now available with very fast access to the Internet. These phones allow you to do many of the things you could only have done before using a computer, such as:

- obtain football scores for your team and then see a video clip
- download a street map of a city
- send photographs to friends
- play Internet games.

Digital television

Digital broadcasting is a new transmission system which uses binary signals to transmit information. Representing a signal digitally (i.e. as 0s and 1s) makes it less prone to errors.

Here are some reasons why **digital** TV is better than **analogue**:

- The pictures are much clearer.
- The sound is crystal clear.
- You have greater choice of TV channels.
- You can get interactive TV (e.g. home shopping, banking and Internet access).

Key Jargon

analogue – data represented by a continuously changing quantity.

digital – data represented by groups of the binary digits 0 and 1.

Build your notes

Here are some notes that summarise this chapter. The notes are incomplete because they have words missing.

Using the words in the list below, copy out and complete the sentences A to F, underlining the words that you have inserted. Each word may be used more than once.

> portal   web browser   e-commerce   Teletext
> search engine   surfing

A A program that allows access to the world wide web is called a

_____ _____.

B A _____ _____ is a program that is used to search the Internet for information.

C Using the links in websites to move from one website to another is called _____.

D Conducting business over the Internet is called _____.

E _____ is an information service that is sent at the same time as television signals.

F A web _____ is a site where you go to get redirected to another site.

1 The main purpose of an Internet Service Provider (ISP) is to:

a provide a permanent connection to the Internet
b sell computer equipment
c spy on computer users
d provide a banking service.

2 Conducting business over the Internet is called:

a e-commerce
b WAP
c www
d http.

3 Which of the following is not an advantage of shopping on-line?

a The goods are usually cheaper.
b Some traditional shops may have to close.
c Orders can be placed at any time of the day.
d There is a much bigger choice of products.

4 Which one of the following is not a negative aspect of Internet use?

a pornography
b Internet addiction
c hacking
d opportunity to find out about and join voluntary groups

5 Which of the following is not an advantage to a company in using e-commerce?

a fewer staff needed
b premises can be located anywhere
c the equipment is expensive to buy
d can operate 24 hours per day, every day

6 What is the name of the service that uses a television signal sent at the same time as TV programmes?

  a the Internet
  b ISDN
  c ISP
  d Teletext

7 A program that allows access to the World Wide Web is called a:

  a web browser
  b spreadsheet
  c e-commerce
  d database.

8 The software used to search for information on the Internet is called:

  a a web browser
  b a search engine
  c a query
  d a report.

9 Which one of these is not an advantage of banking over the Internet?

  a You can move money between accounts without leaving your home.
  b Your balance can be checked 24 hours per day.
  c You can check statements on-line.
  d You can get cash out of your account.

10 Unlike Teletext, the Internet is:

  a interactive
  b up to date
  c used only for business
  d used only to send e-mail.

Multiple-choice questions

1 Many banks have home banking available to customers who have access to the Internet.

   a Here are **two** of the services available using home banking:

- balance enquiry
- order a new cheque book.

     Give **two** other services that might be available.

   b Give **two** advantages of home banking to a customer.

   c Give **two** disadvantages of home banking to a customer.

2 The development and use of global networks has affected the way people work.

   a Give **one** example of a global network.

   b Give **two** examples of how global networks have affected the way people book holidays.

   c People often need to find out information such as the costs of flights or train departure times. Give **two** examples of information services, other than the ones mentioned, that are useful.

F Questions

1 a The increasing use of IT at work and the development of global networks, such as the Internet and the World Wide Web, have affected employment.

     (i) From the list below, write down **three** ways some workers may be affected.

       More workers will be able to afford televisions.
Teleworking will be more widespread and more workers will work from home.
Workers will be paid in cash.
Workers will need IT skills.
Workers will need less education.
Some workers in the UK will compete for jobs with workers throughout the world.

     (ii) From the list below, write down **three** ways some employers may be affected.

Businesses will be virtual reality organisations.
Employers will use the World Wide Web for
advertising.
Employers will train their workers using
computer-based learning materials.
Employers will use e-mail to communicate with
their workers.
Employers will need to make sure that all their
workers live locally.
Employers will need more reference books.

b State **three** ways in which documentation or help
can be obtained using IT or global networks.

c Using global networks, people can access a wide
range of information.
Some people say that anyone should be able to put
information on global networks, and that it should
be available to everyone.
  (i) Give **three** reasons for freedom of information
  on global networks.
  (ii) Give **three** reasons against freedom of
  information on global networks.

(AQA Specification B Tier F full course, specimen paper, q8)

H Questions

1 a The increasing use of IT at work and the development
of global networks, such as the Internet and the
World Wide Web, have affected employment.
  (i) Describe **two** ways some workers may be
  affected.
  (ii) Describe **two** ways some employers may be
  affected.

b Using global networks, people can access a wide
range of information.

Some people say that anyone should be able to put
information on global networks, and that it should
be available to everyone.

Give a reasoned argument for and against freedom
of information on global networks.

(AQA Specification B short course, specimen paper, q8)

2 A school library has recently been extended to include an IT resource centre. This has six multi-media PCs which are all connected to the Internet.

  a Give **two** possible advantages to pupils of using CD-ROMs to find information rather than the traditional method of looking up information in books.

  b Give **two** possible advantages to pupils of using the Internet to find information rather than using a CD-ROM.

  c Give **two** possible reasons why some school library users will look up information in books.

(AQA Specification A short course, specimen paper, q9)

3 The development of the Internet has changed our lives in many ways.

  a Describe **two** ways in which it has changed the way people work.

  b Describe **two** ways in which it has changed the way people spend their leisure time.

  c The Internet is the main way people can find out information without leaving their home. Describe **two** different ways of finding out information on the Internet.

  d Information obtained from the Internet is not always accurate. Describe **one** precaution you can take to ensure the accuracy of information.

4 Many companies sell goods and services direct to the public over the Internet via their own e-commerce sites.

  a Give **three** advantages to a company of using e-commerce.

  b Give **three** advantages to a customer of buying goods from an e-commerce site.

  c Some customers are worried about keying in their credit card details when paying for goods on an e-commerce site.

    (i) Give **one** reason why they might be worried.

    (ii) Describe **one** step the company could take in order to prevent the customers' credit card details from being misused.

9 ICT and Society

Most people will agree that far more good things come out of ICT than bad things. However, ICT can be misused. Laws need to be developed to cover the misuse of ICT.

Keeping data about you private

Data protection

It is hard to keep information about yourself private. Everyone seems to want to find out about you. Think of the number of times you supply personal information. When you fill in forms it seems you are asked so many questions that you wonder what all the information will be used for.

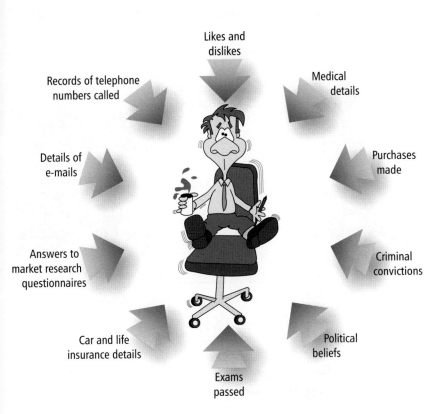

Likes and dislikes

Records of telephone numbers called

Medical details

Details of e-mails

Purchases made

Answers to market research questionnaires

Criminal convictions

Car and life insurance details

Political beliefs

Exams passed

Figure 9.1

Some of the personal data held about you

To many companies, personal information means money. By getting this personal information they can market goods and services better. Some even sell your personal data to other companies.

It is not just commercial organisations that collect information about you. Hospitals, schools, tax offices and so on all need to hold some personal information about you.

What is personal data?

Personal data is:

Your exam results have been incorrectly entered by your school

- about an identifiable person (i.e. about someone who can be identified by name, address, etc.)
- about someone who is living
- specific to an individual (e.g. their medical records, criminal record, credit history, religious or political beliefs, etc.).

What if personal data is wrong?

"But the teacher told me I had an A* for my coursework"

Details in your medical records have been mixed up with someone else's

Inaccuracies in your personal data held on computer can cause all sorts of complications (see Figure 9.2). You may find your life is becoming more difficult, but you don't really know why. Unless you see the information held about you yourself, it is hard to know if it is wrong. This is why part of the Data Protection Act allows you to see, and have corrected, your own personal data.

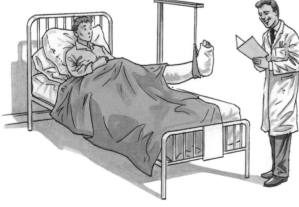

A database says you have a criminal record when you haven't

"I don't know why I didn't get the job!"

"According to these records, you're pregnant Mr Jones!"

Figure 9.2

Some of the effects of inaccurate data in files of personal information

A database says you are a bad credit risk

Why is computer data easier to misuse than paper-based data?

When data is stored and processed by a computer it makes it much easier to misuse. This is why the Data Protection Act 1998 was created.

Here are some of the reasons why computer data is much easier to misuse:

- It is easier to take a copy without being noticed – there is no need to stand by the photocopier making copies.
- It is quicker to make a copy – you can copy a data file to a disk or attach it to an e-mail and send it to yourself within a few seconds.
- It is harder to spot if data has been altered deliberately.
- It is much easier to search through a computer file to find specific information.
- Networks that are connected to the Internet make it possible for hackers to gain access to personal data stored on the network.
- It is easier to combine personal data from one database with that from another using computers.

Privacy

Privacy is about keeping some of the personal aspects of your life private.

We all make mistakes in our lives, and hopefully learn by them. Many people do things that they become ashamed of in later life.

Imagine that you become famous or successful. You are chatting to a friend on the Internet and discuss with them something you did in the past. You trust them but, unknown to you, someone has intercepted your message. This person sells your secret to a newspaper and a few days later you are on the front page.

This will have been a violation of your right to privacy.

The Data Protection Act 1998

Computers make it easy for organisations and businesses to store and process information about individuals. In this way they can build up a complete profile about someone. Much of this is done without the person being aware of it.

Key Jargon

privacy – being able to decide what information about yourself can be known by others.

To protect individuals against the misuse of personal data, the government brought out a law called the Data Protection Act in 1998. This act covers all personal data, whether it is processed by a computer or not.

The responsibilities placed on data users

The **Data Protection Act 1998** ('act' is another name for a law) protects individuals by placing responsibilities on the data users in the following ways:

Registration (notification)

Anyone who uses personal data is required to register with the Information Commissioner (formerly called the Data Protection Commissioner) who is the person in charge of the act. They must say what data they intend to hold and what they intend to do with it.

Individuals can see their own personal data

Anyone can apply to see the personal data held about them. Organisations have to show it and if there is any wrong information, then it must be corrected.

Data must be kept secure

Data must be kept secure and up to date. **Data subjects** (the people who the data is about) can sue an organisation who does not keep their personal data secure. The person in charge of the data in an organisation is the **data controller**.

The rights of data subjects

Data subjects have the right to see the personal information kept about them. If the information is incorrect they have the right to have it corrected.

The Data Protection Principles

Here is a brief summary of the eight Data Protection Principles covered in the act. If you want detailed information then there is a complete copy of the Data Protection Act at the following website:

www.dataprotection.gov.uk/

The Data Protection Principles state that personal data should be:

1 processed fairly and lawfully

2 obtained for only specified purposes

Key Jargon

data controller – the person in charge of the data in an organisation. They make sure that all the terms of the Data Protection Act are complied with.

Data Protection Act 1998 – a law that restricts the way personal information is stored and processed on a computer.

data subjects – the individuals to whom the personal data refers.

- adequate, relevant and not excessive
- accurate and kept up to date
- not kept any longer than is necessary
- processed in accordance with the rights of the data subject
- kept secure
- not transferred to another country unless it has a comparable data protection law.

Exemptions from the Data Protection Act

There are a number of partial exemptions from parts of the act:

Exemptions from registration/disclosure

- where the data is used for personal, family, household affairs or recreation
- where the data is being used for preparing the text of documents (e.g. compiling references using a wordprocessor)
- where the data is used for producing accounts, wages and pensions
- where the data is used for advertising and marketing
- where the data is used by a sports or recreational club which is not a limited company

Exemptions from disclosure

You can see most of the personal data held about you, but there are exceptions. You may not be able to see data used for:

- the prevention or detection of crimes
- catching or prosecuting offenders
- collecting taxes or duty
- medical or social worker reports.

Activity 1

Use the Internet to access the following website:

www.dataprotection.gov.uk/

The Data Protection Act 1998 is quite complicated. Luckily, you only need to know some brief details.

continued over page

Use this site to answer the following questions:

1 What is the name of the current Information Commissioner?

2 What are the names of the two acts that the Information Commissioner is in control of?

3 How do you find out whether an organisation holds personal information about you?

4 Most organisations store some personal data. Explain what they nee to do in order to make sure they comply with the act.

Key Jargon

Freedom of Information Act 2000 – a law which gives the public access to recorded information held by public bodies that could affect them in some way.

The Freedom of Information Act 2000

The **Freedom of Information Act 2000** gives a right of access to all types of recorded information held by public authorities such as local councils, hospitals, the police, schools, etc. Like the Data Protection Act, there are some exemptions.

Under the Data Protection Act, you are able to see most of the personal data held about you. However, it only covers access to personal data. There is a lot of data kept by public authorities that affects you but which is not about you, and until now you would not have been allowed to see. The Freedom of Informatio Act 2000 requires the public authorities to release the information they hold if it is not covered by one of the exemptions.

The exemptions from the act are:

● where the information would jeopardise the prevention or detection of a crime

● where it is more in the public interest not to show the information than it is to show it.

The person who enforces the Freedom of Information Act 2000, as well as the Data Protection Act 1998, is called the Informatior Commissioner.

Making sure ICT is used properly
Computer misuse

The Computer Misuse Act 1990

The **Computer Misuse Act 1990** covers the following:

- deliberately planting **viruses** on computer systems
- copying computer programs illegally (i.e. software piracy)
- **hacking** into someone's system with a view to seeing or altering the information held on it
- using a computer to commit a fraud (e.g. to steal money)
- using a firm's computer and time to carry out unauthorised work

To prosecute someone under the act it must be proved that they intended to do one of the things in the above list. If they did it by accident, then they would not be found guilty.

All these misuses are made an offence punishable by fines or imprisonment.

Key Jargon

Computer Misuse Act 1990 – a law that covers the misuse of computer equipment.

hacking – the process of trying to break into a secure computer system.

virus – a program created specifically to do damage to a computer system.

The Copyright, Designs and Patents Act 1989

Most people would never dream of going into a supermarket to steal a tin of soup costing 50p. Yet the same people would think nothing of copying software or music that cost much more.

Activity 2

John is under pressure because he has a lot of coursework to do for his GCSE. He hears from a friend that there is a website where people submit essays and coursework that they have done in order to help others. It is free to use the site.

Take a look at the site at:

www.essaybank.co.uk

Discuss with your friends and your teacher the moral implications of such a site. Is it a good or a bad thing?

Think about the following issues:

- ◼ What are the implications of John simply copying one of the examples on the site and passing it off as his own work?
- ◼ What are the likely consequences if John submitted the work as coursework and it was recognised by the assessment board?

Copyright, Designs and Patents Act 1989 – a law making it a criminal offence to copy or steal software.

The **Copyright, Designs and Patents Act 1989** makes it a criminal offence to copy or steal software. Under this act it makes it an offence to:

- ● copy or distribute software or manuals without the permission or licence from the copyright owner
- ● run purchased sofware covered by copyright on two or more machines at the same time unless there is a software licence which allows it
- ● compel (i.e. force) employees to make or distribute illegal sofware for use by the company.

Activity 3

The following two acts cover some IT issues:

A   The Computer Misuse Act 1990

B   The Copyright, Designs and Patents Act 1989.

Which act (either A or B) covers the following situation?

1 Distributing the music on a CD to a friend using the Internet.

2 Copying a CD containing software using a CD-rewriter and then selling the copy through the local paper.

3 Hacking into your school's computer system using your home computer.

4 Distributing a virus with the deliberate intention of damaging the data and programs on another person's computer.

5 Putting a copy of a piece of software on a server and then allowing it to be used by many terminals when a licence for more than one user has not been obtained.

Misuse of the Internet

There is no doubt that the Internet is one of the greatest developments in recent times. But, not everyone uses it properly. Figure 9.3 shows some of the ways that the Internet can be misused.

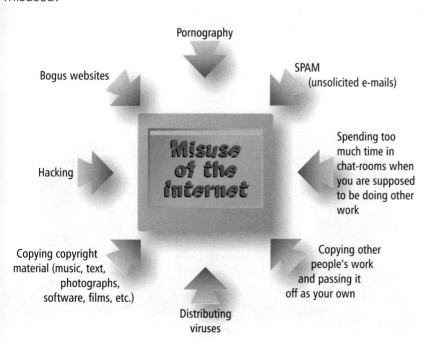

Figure 9.3

There are many ways that the Internet can be misused. This diagram shows some of them

Hacking

Hacking means gaining access to a secure computer system from outside. Usually it involves a person trying to access a network protected by user-IDs and passwords. Once a hacker has gained access they may leave a message. The main danger is that they could accidentally or deliberately alter or erase data.

Misuse of chat-rooms, text messaging or e-mail

Too much of anything can be a bad thing. Some people spend hours chatting in chat-rooms or communicating by e-mail. With some people this behaviour can become addictive. More seriously, paedophiles have been known to use chat-rooms to make contact with children.

You know you are addicted to e-mail when your best friend has an @ in their name

spam – unwanted e-mail.

Spam

Spam is unwanted e-mail. It is e-mail that has been sent to many people in the hope that it will interest someone. You may think that this is acceptable – after all, you only have to delete it. However, some people receive hundreds of these e-mails a day and it takes a long time to sift through them and delete the ones you don't want.

It's the worst case of spam I've ever seen.

Flaming

Flaming means communicating emotionally using e-mail. Often it means sending messages that are rude or impolite. Flaming can offend people and should be avoided.

Introducing viruses

Viruses are software that are designed to do damage or cause problems. Introducing a virus onto a computer is illegal.

Deliberate misinformation

It is easy to spread rumours on the Internet. You only have to tell something to a few people in a chat-room or put it on a website and it will soon spread. Rumours that are not true can cause distress to the people they concern. It can be difficult to trace the person who started a rumour, but it is not impossible as the Internet is not completely anonymous.

People can also be deliberately misinformed by organisations or politicians, and this is made much easier using the Internet.

Dealing with misuse of the Internet

Here are some ways of preventing misuse of the Internet.

Firewalls

The main purpose of a firewall is to prevent hackers from accessing a computer system. Firewalls can also be used to filter out unwanted material from the Internet. They can be set up to prevent users from downloading games and looking at inappropriate websites. Spam can be filtered out so that people do not waste time deleting unwanted e-mail.

Virus scanners/checkers

Virus scanners/checkers can scan downloaded files and e-mails with file attachments for viruses. If a virus is found, the software then removes the virus.

Monitoring employees

Most companies monitor their employees' use of the Internet. By using the user-IDs, the person in charge of the network can monitor what each person logged onto the system is looking at. They can also keep records of the time each person spends on-line. Such records can be used to discipline staff if necessary. Some companies even read their employees' e-mail.

Key Jargon

flaming – emotional, often rude, e-mail messaging.

Parental control

If you had young children, you would not want them to have full access to the Internet. They could, for example, see pornographic images and talk to adults (who could be paedophiles) in chat-rooms. All Internet Service Providers have parental controls which restrict access to parts of the Internet (see Figure 9.4).

All Internet Service Providers have a way for parents to control what their children see and do on the Internet. This is the AOL Parental Control screen

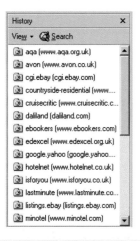

Figure 9.5

History allows you to view the sites that have been visited recently

Some parents may choose to sit with their children while they use the Internet, or monitor what they have looked at by looking at the history (which gives the addresses of all the recent websites visited, see Figure 9.5).

Figure 9.6 shows how parents can control what their children see and do on the Internet.

On-line timer

E-mail control
Parents can set whether their children can send or receive all e-mail, or just selected people

PARENTAL CONTROL

Web Control
Parents can set the age range suitable for their child (e.g. 12 & under, 13 to 15, 16 to 17 & full access to all web sites)

Instant Message (IM) Control
parents can control whether their child can send and receive IMs

Figure 9.6

How parents can control what their children see and do on the Internet

How does ICT affect our lives?

The wider issues

Globalisation

If you have been abroad you may have noticed that despite the obvious differences, many things are similar. People drink the same drinks, drive similar cars, eat the same fast-food and wear the same designer clothes. In Europe many countries now share the same currency, the euro. Globalisation means that many of the barriers between countries are disappearing and the world is operating more as one.

Figure 9.7

Coca-Cola can be found all over the world – this is an example of globalisation

You may think this is a good idea. Some people disagree because they want to keep the individual identity of their own country.

ICT has helped globalisation in a number of ways. It makes it easier for the large multinational businesses like Macdonalds and Coca-Cola to operate in hundreds of different countries. It has also enabled ideas, views and information to be spread quickly around the world. International travel has been made easier, bringing people together from all different cultures.

Widening the gap between the rich and poor countries

Rich countries have money to invest in the latest ICT developments. This makes the organisations in those countries more profitable and gives them the opportunity to expand into other markets. Some of these large organisations have more money than entire countries in less developed parts of the world.

Poorer countries do not have the money or the skills to invest in ICT. They have to do things using out-of-date systems. It is difficult for these countries to improve their standard of living.

This means that the rich countries are getting richer while the poorer countries remain poor, thus widening the gap between them.

Environmental issues

Protecting the environment is important. Here are some ways that ICT can be used to help save resources.

Computer-controlled heating systems

Heating systems can be designed so that they only come on when they need to. This means valuable sources of fuel, such as coal and gas, are used more efficiently. For example, if you want the temperature of your house to be 70°F when you wake up at 7:30 a.m. then the system will work out when the heating should come on based on the temperature outside. If it is really cold outside, then the heater may need to come on at 6:00 a.m. If it is fairly warm outside then the heating may not need to come on until 7:00 a.m.

Refilling toner/ink cartridges

There are companies that specialise in refilling ink-jet and toner cartridges; this avoids them having to be thrown away each time they run out of ink.

The impact of the paperless office

ICT allows organisations to deal with each other and with members of the public electronically. This reduces the amount of paper they use, which helps save trees.

Telecommuting

Telecommuting means working from home by making use of ICT equipment. Telecommuting helps the environment because fewer people have to drive to work. Travelling by car wastes resources and generates greenhouse gases that pollute the atmosphere.

Ethical issues

Ethics is about behaving properly towards other. Here are some uses of ICT which raise important ethical issues.

Figure 9.8

Telecommuting could help prevent rush-hour traffic jams like this

Monitoring employees

Many employers monitor their staff's use of the Internet. They usually do this to make sure their staff do not waste time on non-work related use. This can, however, be seen as an infringement of the employees' privacy.

Spyware

Spyware is software that is put on someone's computer without their knowledge to monitor their use of the computer. It could be put on to look at the person's e-mails or to follow their conversations in chat-rooms. People could use it to see what their partner is up to when they are on-line.

Cookies

Internet 'cookies' record details of the websites you have visited, without you knowing.

Loyalty cards

Loyalty cards, such as Nectar, allow companies to monitor what purchases you are making. When you use these cards, stores know what papers you read, what drinks you like, what pets you have, whether you smoke, and so on.

Social issues

ICT can improve, or have some impact on, the lives of many different members of the community.

People with special needs

There are many ways that ICT can improve the lives of people with special needs.

Figure 9.9

Older people can find the Internet invaluable

- The Internet is interactive, which means you can send as well as receive information. This helps to cut down the isolation that many housebound people feel.

- You can shop from home using the Internet – e-commerce helps housebound people to shop around for goods and services.

- Teleworking (working from home using ICT equipment) becomes possible for disabled people who might otherwise be unable to go out to work.

- ICT equipment can be used anywhere – as ICT equipment becomes smaller and lighter it becomes more mobile, and people can use it wherever they are, not just at home.

- Disabled people are able to access information on benefits, health, finances, entertainment, etc. directly from the Internet. This gives them more independence, and allows them to have more control over their affairs.

Finding information

Finding information is a lot easier using the Internet. Here are some types of information that you might need and which is available on the Internet:

- the names, addresses and opening times of museums, art galleries, etc. in a city that you are intending to visit
- the routes and times of buses in your area
- what is on at your local cinema or theatre
- a map to give to your friends who are coming to a party at your house
- the nearest venue of your favourite band/singer during their current tour
- what other people think about a particular holiday you are thinking of booking.

The impact of ICT on work

In the future, people will need to be more flexible in their work. They will no longer spend their whole working lives doing the same job. Constant retraining will be needed so that they can take advantage of the new technologies being developed. Here are some of the effects ICT will have on the way people work.

Telecommuting

Telecommuting allows people to work from home. To some people it sounds ideal, but it will not suit everyone. You need to be self-motivated, and there must be a quiet place in your house to work.

ICT skills

Being able to use a computer is such an important skill that the government makes all schoolchildren do ICT as part of the National Curriculum. For older people, there are plenty of courses available at colleges. Because ICT changes so rapidly, people will continually need to update their skills.

Mary thought Jim's computer classes weren't going too well when she saw him sending his first e-mail

Working with computers
Health and safety

Life can be a dangerous business. Most people would consider working in an office or at home with computers a fairly safe occupation. It is, but you do have to be careful that you use the equipment properly so you do not have an accident or health problem in the future.

There is a difference between using a computer now and again and using one all the time. Using a computer regularly over a long period of time can affect your health.

Health and Safety at Work Act 1974

Under the Health and Safety at Work Act 1974, employers have to make sure that their employees have a safe place to work and, as far as possible, have a safe system of work.

Wherever people work there are always some hazards around. When you are at work you need to know about these hazards and this will help you to prevent accidents and make a safe place for others to work in.

Hazards in the workplace may include:

Wires trailing across the floor, creating a tripping hazard

Not lifting properly (back should be kept straight with legs bent)

Overloaded power sockets can cause fires

Wedging a fire door open which should be kept shut at all times

Large quantities of paper lying around, particularly if people are allowed to smoke in the office

Figure 9.10

Hazards in the workplace

Figure 9.11 shows how you should be seated when using a computer.

Figure 9.11

Get into the habit of sitting like this when you are using your computer

- The chair should have five castors, otherwise it might tip up.
- The height of the base of the chair should be adjustable.
- The back of the chair should be adjustable too.
- Your feet should be firmly on the floor if a foot-rest is not available.
- The upper arm should be at right angles to the forearm.
- Your wrists should be kept straight.

What are the health problems?

People who work with computers a lot may experience some health problems. These include:

- eyestrain
- stress
- backache or joint aches.

Eyestrain

Eyestrain causes blurred vision and headaches. Refocusing your eyes as you shift between paperwork and the computer screen can cause eyestrain. Another cause of eyestrain is reflections on the screen preventing you from seeing the screen properly. Eyestrain is common in older computer users. If you work with computers a lot then your employer (i.e. the person or organisation you work for) is required to pay for regular eye tests and for any special glasses you might need.

Stress

Using computers can be stressful. Losing an important file or discovering that there is a virus on your machine is a very stressful situation. If you are using new software and can't work out how to do a simple task, this is also stressful. All these things seem to happen when you have an important deadline coming up. To reduce the amount of stress you are under, try to get into the habit of not leaving things to the last minute.

Backache or joint ache

Backache can occur if you slouch in your chair while you are using your computer. Try to sit upright with both feet flat on the floor. If you do not adopt this posture then it may lead to backache in the future.

Key Jargon

RSI – repetitive strain injury. A muscular condition caused by repeatedly using certain muscles in the same way. It builds up slowly until every muscle movement can be agony.

People who spend long periods typing at a keyboard at high speed may develop a medical problem called repetitive strain injury (**RSI**). Basically, this is caused by shock waves travelling into the joints of the hands, arms and neck during typing.

The Health and Safety Regulations 1992

The person or organisation who you work for (i.e your employer) is required by law to:

- look carefully at the terminal/workstation where you work to see if there are any health and safety risks. If there are any, they must be fixed immediately
- plan your work so that there are changes in activity or breaks
- arrange eye tests and provide special glasses if they are needed
- provide health and safety training (e.g. show you how to sit properly, how to lift properly, etc.).

You will now look at how employers can abide by these regulations.

Inspections

Employers should periodically inspect the workplace environment and equipment being used to check that they comply with the regulations. Any shortcomings should be reported and corrected. Desks, chairs, computers, etc. should be assessed for risks to workers' eyesight and physical and mental well-being.

Training

All employees should be trained in the health and safety aspects of their job. They need to be told about the correct posture to adopt for using keyboards, etc.

Job design

Each employee's job should be designed so that the worker has periodic breaks or changes of activity when using computers.

Eye tests

For computer users there should be regular free eye tests, with special glasses provided if necessary at the employer's expense.

The law also lays down certain minimum requirements for computer systems and furniture. All new and existing equipment should now meet the following requirements:

Display screens

These must be easy to read, stable and have no flicker. Brightness, contrast, tilt and swivel must all be adjustable and there must be no reflection off the screen.

Keyboards

These must be separate from the screen and tiltable. Their layout should be easy to use and the surface should be matt in order to avoid glare. There must be sufficient desk space to provide arm and hand support.

Desks

Desks must be large enough to accommodate the computer and any paperwork and must not reflect too much light. If you are keying in information from a document, an adjustable document holder should be provided so as to avoid uncomfortable head movements between the screen and the document.

Chairs

Chairs must be adjustable and comfortable, and allow freedom of movement. A foot-rest must be available if needed.

Lights

There should be suitable contrast between the computer screen and the background. There must be no glare or reflections off the computer screen, so point sources of light should be avoided and the windows should have adjustable coverings such as blinds to eliminate reflections caused by sunlight.

Noise

This should not be loud enough to distract attention and disturb speech.

Software

This must be easy to use and should be appropriate to the user's needs and experience.

Other matters

Heat, humidity and radiation emissions must be kept to suitable levels for a safe and comfortable working environment.

Reducing the risks to your health

- Make sure that there are no reflections off the screen. If sunlight is pouring into the room, take time to adjust the blinds. Doing this will reduce eyestrain and prevent headaches.

- Use a copyholder to hold documents rather than laying them on the surface of the desk. This means that you will not have to move your neck when looking at the documents and then the screen.

- Adjust your chair to the right height for you. Do not simply accept the position it is in when you sit down.

- Alter the brightness and contrast of the monitor to suit you.

- Sit up straight. Do not slouch in your chair as this can lead to back problems in the future.

- Use special keyboards and wrist guards to minimise the likelihood of developing RSI.

- Make sure that your screen is clean.

There is little evidence to suggest that the radiation given out by a computer screen is dangerous

Research sites

The Health and Safety Executive is a government body responsible for enforcing the Health and Safety Regulations.

Further information about health and safety aspects of using computer screens can be found at:

http://www.hse.gov.uk

Case study

The dangers of viruses

Here is an article which appeared in the *Liverpool Echo* on 18 September 2002.

Techno Virus Hits Hospital

Royal's computer system down for three weeks

Liverpool's main hospital had no electronic communication for three weeks after a computer virus crashed its IT system.

It meant that the 5,000 staff at Royal Liverpool and Broadgreen Hospitals had to rely on phone, fax or letter.

Hospital officials have insisted patients were not put at risk and the medical equipment was not affected by the computer chaos.

It took the trust's IT department almost three weeks to rebuild the computer system, as well as carry out an upgrade to prevent a repeat of last month's disruption.

The NHS Trust was unable to say how much the computer shutdown cost but it is likely to run into many thousands of pounds.

A trust spokesman said: "We are beginning to rely on IT as a means of keeping records and internal communication.

"It was a damaging and contagious virus which slipped through our checking system and spread quickly.

"The effect of it was that our internal communication was shut down and we also had no electronic contact with the outside world.

"This meant staff had to resort to the old methods of conveying messages, such as picking up a phone or walking down a corridor and telling people.

"While it would be wrong to say it didn't affect patients' services, patient care wasn't compromised and the main effect was to make communication between departments that much more difficult.

"It would have delayed things such as getting blood test results to doctors, for example, but it's difficult to know by how much.

"There are other messages which the e-mail is used for which are just as important, such as requests for a particular item from another department."

---

1 Explain what is meant by a 'computer virus'.

2 There is a law which makes it illegal to place a computer virus on a computer. Give the full name of this law.

continued over page

3 Explain why a computer virus is more dangerous on a network of computers than a stand-alone machine.

4 The computer virus that caused computers to crash wasted a lot of money for the hospital. Give two reasons why the virus cost the hospital money.

5 To prevent viruses from entering a network via a connection to the Internet, a firewall is usually installed. Describe two things that a firewall does.

6 The hospital is keen that there is no repeat of a virus attack. Describe three things that the hospital can do to make a virus attack less likely.

Build your notes

Here are some notes that summarise this chapter. The notes are incomplete because they have words missing.

Using the words in the list below, copy out and complete the sentences A to I, underlining the words that you have inserted. Each word may be used more than once.

> misuse register patents piracy hacking data protection
> hack up-to-date privacy information principles

A _____ is about keeping aspects of your personal life private.

B The _____ _____ Act 1998 was passed to protect individuals from the misuse of data.

C The Data Protection Act is enforced by the _____ Commissioner.

D The people who use personal data have to _____ their use of data and they have to make sure that the data is kept _____.

E There are eight Data Protection _____, one of which says that personal data must be accurate and kept up to date.

F Illegal copying of software is called software _____.

G Copying of software is an offence under the Copyright, Designs and _____ Act of 1989.

H The Computer _____ Act of 1990 makes it an offence to _____ into a computer system.

I _____ means gaining access to private data using communication systems.

1 The main purpose of the Data Protection Act is:

   a to give rights to data

   b to make sure that everyone protects their data

   c to place obligations on people who record and process personal data

   d to make it illegal to copy data.

2 The person responsible for the enforcement of the 1998 Data Protection Act is:

   a the Information Commissioner

   b the Data Protection Controller

   c the Data Subject

   d the Data User.

3 A program whose purpose is to do damage to other people's data is called a:

   a bug

   b virus

   c bacteria

   d antivirus.

4 Software piracy involves which one of these?

   a illegally copying computer software

   b downloading pornography off the Internet

   c introducing a computer virus into a computer system

   d hacking into computer systems

5 The Computer Misuse Act 1990 does not involve which one of the following?

   a hacking

   b deliberately planting computer viruses

   c copying computer programs illegally

   d privacy

6 The secret number that needs to be input before a debit card can be used in a cash machine is called a:

a PIN

b PGP

c PIP

d CPU.

7 The Copyright, Designs and Patents Act 1989 is concerned mainly with which one of the following?

a hacking

b privacy

c copying software or manuals illegally without permission or a licence

d planting computer viruses

8 One of these is not an advantage of using computers. Which one is it?

a gives some people the opportunity of working from home

b makes life easier (e.g. you can use credit cards, shop and bank from home)

c creates plenty of interesting jobs in IT

d may increase unemployment

9 The Internet is a great source of information if used correctly. Unfortunately there are some social problems caused by IT. Which one of the following is considered to be a social problem?

a using the computer to send e-mail rather than use the traditional post

b using e-commerce for shopping

c being addicted to chat-rooms

d using the Internet to research a topic for a school project

10 A job that can be replaced by IT is:

a a paint sprayer in a car factory

b a pharmacist in a chemist shop

c a dentist

d a secretary.

1 There are many health problems that may be caused by the use of computers.

   a Give the names of **three** health problems associated with the use of computers.

   b For **one** of the health problems you have written in your answer for part a, describe **one** step that can be taken to prevent the problem from occurring.

2 Here is a list of health problems. Write down the ones that could be caused by computer use.

Health problem
■ backache
■ toothache
■ stress
■ sprained ankle
■ eyestrain
■ repetitive strain injury (RSI)

3 You are choosing some equipment for an office where everyone uses computers. Write **one** requirement for each of the following:

   a office chair
   b office desk
   c office lighting

4 A person makes the following statement. 'Electronically stored information is much easier to misuse than the same information kept on paper.'

Write down the statements that are true when comparing data on a computer with that stored on paper.

Statements about data on a computer
■ It is easier to cross-reference.
■ Alterations to the data are difficult to see.
■ It is easier for people to see the data.
■ There is the danger of hacking.
■ Copying large amounts of data from a computer takes less time.

5 a Give the name of the act that covers the way that organisations may use personal information.

b The act named in part a refers to data controllers and data subjects. Write a sentence about
(i) data controllers, and
(ii) data subjects
to explain what they mean.

c The act mentions 'sensitive personal data'. One of the following pieces of data is classed as sensitive personal data:
◼ home address
◼ middle name
◼ racial or ethnic origin
◼ number of cars in the household
Write down the item in the list that is classed as personal data.

d Give the name of the person who is responsible for the enforcement of the Data Protection Act.

6 Write down the statements from the list below that are one of the Principles of the Data Protection Act 1998.
◼ Data is adequate, relevant and not excessive.
◼ Personal data should be adequate and kept up to date.
◼ Software should not be copied.
◼ Personal data should only be used for one or more specified and lawful purposes.
◼ There must be enough security to cover the personal data.
◼ Hacking is illegal.

7 A student intends to use the Internet at home to help with research for schoolwork.
a Give **one** device that the student will need if the family's ordinary telephone line is to be used to connect the computer to the Internet.
b Give **three** reasons why using the Internet for research might be better than using textbooks.
c Give **two** ways that the student could misuse the family's connection to the Internet.
d Give **two** methods that the student's parents could use to try to prevent any misuse of the Internet.

(NEAB Tier F, June 2000, p2, q3)

F Questions

1 A mail-order company's computer system holds personal data about its customers.

a The data held by the company must be registered under the 1998 Data Protection Act. Give **two** rights the act gives to the customer.

b Personal information stored by a mail order company may be inaccurate. Give **two** examples of inaccuracies which could occur and, for each, describe a possible consequence for the customer.

c Say which **two** of the following have partial exemption from the 1998 Data Protection Act:

- wordprocessed documents
- insurance companies' data
- a database of friends' names and addresses
- all police information, stored on a computer
- a database of doctor's patients
- files stored on paper

(AQA Specification A Tier H short course, specimen paper, q7)

2 A small company that manufactures sportswear is planning to buy a computer system to help with the administration in the office. As a first step it is planning to buy four computers and four printers. A local IT company has advised the company to buy wordprocessing, spreadsheet and antivirus software for each of the computers.

Below is the office manager's estimate for the new system.

Item	Unit cost	No. needed	Total cost
Computer with operating system	£1000	4	£4000
Printer	£500	4	£2000
Wordprocessing package	£250	1	£250
Spreadsheet package	£200	1	£200
Antivirus software	£50	1	£50
		Total	£6500

a The company buys only one copy of each piece of software. It then copies and runs the software on all four computers. Which law has been broken?

b Give **one** possible legal consequence of the company breaking the law.

c In an attempt to improve the security of the stored data, the company is looking into the use of passwords and encryption. Explain what is meant by:
  (i) passwords
  (ii) encryption.

d (i) What is a computer virus?
  (ii) Give **one** way in which a virus could be introduced into a computer system.

(NEAB Tier F, June 2000, p1, q16)

H Questions

1 a Explain how the copyright law applies to computer software.

b What is meant by a **hacker**?

c What dangers do hackers present to other computer users?

(AQA Specification A Tier H full course, specimen paper, q6)

2 Mail-order companies store personal data about their customers on computer files. The Data Protection Act is designed to protect customers from data misuse.

a Give **three** rights that this act gives to the customer.

b Give **five** requirements that the company must meet to comply with the act.

c Some data is granted exemption from some of the provisions of the act. Give **three** grounds for partial exemption, stating the type of exemption allowed.

(AQA Specification A Tier H full course, specimen paper, q10)

3 a The Internet is of great benefit to everyone. There are some negative aspects of Internet use. Describe **three** negative aspects of Internet use.

b Internet misuse concerns employers and parents. Describe what can be done to prevent this misuse of the Internet by:
  (i) employees
  (ii) young children

What is a system?

A system is a way of doing things. For example you may have a system of getting ready for school in the morning. You probably did not sit down and work out the steps – they probably just evolved. Your system may have to fit in with other people in the house. For example, they may need to use the bathroom first.

Some of the systems used in a business could have been developed when the business was small but need to be improved as the business expands to cope with the extra work.

Businesses and other organisations need to have systems. They need a system to cope with customer orders, and another system to cope with returned goods and refunds. An average business can have many systems. Here is a list of some systems a shop might have:

- customer orders – keeping track of the goods customers have ordered
- stock control – knowing when to buy more goods
- purchasing – sending out orders to suppliers for goods
- accounts – making payments
- payroll – paying staff
- personnel – keeping details of staff, staff rotas, sickness records, etc.

Just like people, systems have a life cycle:

- they are created
- they have a useful life
- they get old and are retired when no longer useful.

A new system is then created and the steps are repeated.

Systems analysis – what is it?

Systems analysis is a series of steps performed by a person called a **systems analyst** when creating a new system. There are many different methods of systems analysis. Here we will look at just one.

Key Jargon

systems analyst – a person who studies the overall organisation and implementation of an ICT system.

Systems analysis is done when:

- a brand new system is needed
- an existing system needs to be improved.

There are a number of steps or stages in systems analysis. These steps are carried out in order, but sometimes not all the steps are needed.

How an ICT system is developed

The system life cycle

Key Jargon

system life cycle – the series of steps carried out during the creation of a new system.

The **system life cycle** (sometimes called the system development life cycle) describes the stages that are worked through when a new computer system is being developed. Figure 10.1 shows the stages of the system life cycle.

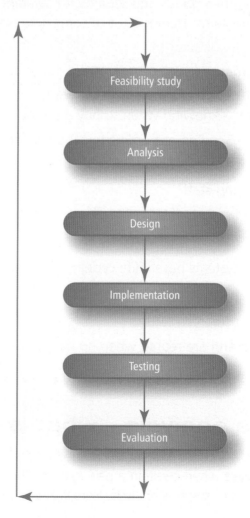

Figure 10.1

The system life cycle

The feasibility study

The **feasibility study** can be the first stage in the system life cycle. The purpose of the feasibility study is to see if it is worth going ahead with the new system. To make this decision it is necessary to do some analysis to understand the problem further.

New projects cost money and take time and effort, so there is no point in starting a project only to abandon it half way through.

The feasibility study looks at the following questions:

- What are the problems with the existing system?
- Can the problem be solved?
- How much will it cost, approximately?
- What is the scope of the project (i.e. what will the new system do and not do)?
- What are the objectives of the project (i.e. what must the new system do)?
- Are there other ways of solving the problem? If so, what are they?
- What are the benefits of the new system?
- What are the recommendations (i.e. what does the project developer/systems analyst think they should do)?

The findings of the feasibility study are summarised in a document called a **feasibility report**. This report is submitted to the senior managers of the organisation, who use it to decide about whether or not to go ahead with the new system.

Sometimes a feasibility study is not needed because there is an obvious need for a new system. This might be the case if a doctor's surgery needs to computerise its patient records. Many surgeries do this, so it would be a waste of time seeing if it was feasible.

The analysis stage

Once it has been decided to go ahead with a new system, the analysis can start. To be able to perform the analysis, the developer needs to understand the existing system (i.e. the way the job is being done now). If it is a completely new system, they will need to find out what the users want the system to do. In order to find out how the existing system works, the developer will perform a **fact find**.

Key Jargon

fact find – the investigation of a system to understand how it works or should work.

feasibility report – a report/document containing the summarised findings of a feasibility study which the decision makers can use to decide whether or not to go ahead with the new system.

feasibility study – a study carried out by experts to see what type of system is needed before a new system is developed.

Methods of fact finding

There are several ways that fact finding can be done:

● **Questionnaires** – a questionnaire could be given to each user. The questions on the questionnaire should be about how the job is done now and not about the overall running of the business.

● **Interviews** – interviews take longer than questionnaires. You could interview the different levels of staff who will use the system, from the managers down.

● **Observation** – here you watch someone who is actually doing the job using the existing system. You then see what problems are encountered with the old system, and chat to the user about what the new system should be able to do.

● **Inspection of records** – this involves looking at any of the paperwork involved with the current system. This would include documents such as order forms, application forms, lists of stock and so on. You can also look at the records that are kept in filing cabinets.

Most of the fact finding takes place in the analysis stage, although some fact finding would need to be completed before the feasibility report could be produced.

Questionnaires

Interviews

Inspection of records

"I'd better look busy or I'll be replaced ..."

Figure 10.2

Fact-finding methods

Observation

Analysis is all about understanding the problem, and includes:

- identifying the problems with the current system
- identifying the needs of users
- investigating similar systems used elsewhere
- investigating what input, processing and output are needed by the new system
- establishing what tasks need to be completed
- establishing deadlines for completion of tasks.

> I keep six honest serving men
> (They taught me all I knew)
> Their names are what and why and when
> And how and where and who
>
> Rudyard Kipling

What is done? How is it done?
Why is it done? Where is it done?
When is it done? Who does it?

Figure 10.3

Things to ask about an existing system

What would you say your main problem was?

What do you think your main problem is?

The design stage

The design stage looks at how the new system will be built. All ICT systems can be broken down into input, process and output, so this stage needs to look at the design of all three.

Once the system has been designed, the developer needs to draw up a document called the design specification. The design specification is then shown to the users for their comments. It is always important to ask the users for their opinions as you need to design the system that they want not the one you think they want.

The design specification

The design specification contains all the details of the design under the headings given below. The design specification should be shown to the user so that they know exactly what you are producing for them. Any changes they suggest can be added to the design before the next stage, which is when you produce the actual solution using the computer.

Here is what is normally in the design specification:

Graphical representations of the system

Diagrams are drawn to help the developer/analyst and others understand the design of the system. These diagrams can also be produced during the analysis stages.

The diagrams might include:

- flowcharts
- system flowcharts
- structure diagrams
- dataflow diagrams.

Each of these diagrams will be looked at later in this chapter.

Input

This part of the design specification will cover:

- the form of data capture used
- the hardware devices used for the input
- the design of any forms (application forms, order forms, etc.)
- the design of the input screens (forms in the case of databases, spreadsheet layouts, etc.).

Process

This part of the design specification describes what processing is performed. (Processing can be putting data into a structure as well as any calculations that need to be done.)

Output

This part of the design specification will cover:

- the hardware devices used for the output
- the type of output to be used (i.e. a printout, a screen display, a warning message for a control system, etc.)

- how the output is to be displayed
- what information is to be output
- designs for the output.

Storage methods

The developer also needs to consider:

- what methods of storage should be used (e.g. magnetic hard disk, magnetic floppy disk, magnetic tape, CD-RW, etc.)
- the storage method used for backing up data and programs.

Hardware and software

The software for the system can be written specifically by programmers. This is an expensive and time-consuming option. Instead, software can be bought and then configured (altered slightly) to work in the way the user wants it to work.

Once the software has been developed, the hardware to run the software is chosen.

File and record structure

This is:

- the files/tables that are needed
- the fields in each record/table.

The user interface

The users of the system may not have the computing skills that you have, so the system you develop needs to be easy for them to use.

Security and back-up procedures

This consists of:

- how unauthorised access is prevented
- how data is backed up.

Test plans

Here you need to consider how you are going to test your solution. You need to determine that what you have developed is what the user actually wants.

The implementation stage

In the **implementation** stage, the working version of the solution to the problem is produced. This involves making the real thing based on the system design. The design specification should be followed closely since the finished solution needs to match it.

What is involved in the implementation stage? This varies according to the type of problem.

For a database solution you might have the following steps:

● create the tables/files
● set up the validation checks for those fields where it is sensible to have them
● link the tables/files
● create input forms
● input sample data
● create queries
● create output forms or reports
● set up the user interface.

Here are some of the tasks performed during the implementation phase:

● installing hardware and software
● testing – the whole system needs to be tested rather than just the individual parts
● transferring data from the old system to the new system
● training users actually to use the system (not just the software).

There are three ways to implement a new system and these are shown in Figure 10.4.

The testing stage

As soon as a system is developed it should be checked against the user requirements to make sure that the system does everything the user wants. To do this, you can produce a list of the user requirements, and tick them off if they have been met by the system you have developed.

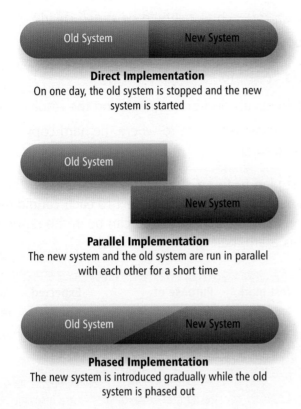

Direct Implementation
On one day, the old system is stopped and the new system is started

Parallel Implementation
The new system and the old system are run in parallel with each other for a short time

Phased Implementation
The new system is introduced gradually while the old system is phased out

Figure 10.4

The three ways of implementing a system

Testing the system

Before a new system is used, it must be thoroughly tested. The testing of a system can be broken down into four stages:

1   The system is tested with data that contains no errors to see if it produces the correct results.

2   Known errors are introduced into the data to see how the computer processes it. It is important to know what should happen, and compare this with what actually happens.

3   The output is produced and checked to make sure that the results are as expected.

4   Extreme data is entered to make sure that the range checks included as part of the validation checks are working.

Test plans

To make sure that the testing is thorough, a test plan is produced during the design stage. To ensure that the test plan is as comprehensive as possible:

● each test should be numbered

● the data to be used in each test should be specified

- the reason for each test should be stated clearly
- the expected results of each test should be given.

Space should be left for:

- the actual results and/or comments on the results
- a page number reference to where the hard copy evidence can be found.

Here is a test plan to test a spreadsheet for analysing the marks in an examination. A mark is input next to each candidate's name. The mark is a percentage and can be in the range 0% to 100%. In this exam, half marks are possible.

Test no.	Test mark entered	Purpose of test	Expected result	Actual result
1	45.5	test valid data	accept	
2	100	test extreme data	accept	
3	0	test extreme data	accept	
4	123	test out-of-range data	error message	
5	−3	test out-of-range data	error message	
6	45D	test invalid characters	error message	

The 'actual result' column is filled in when the test mark is entered. If the expected results and the actual results are all the same, then the validation checks are working. If they do not agree, then the validation checks will need to be modified and re-tested.

Producing user documentation

A user guide or manual is **documentation** that the user can turn to for learning how to use the system. It should also allow them to learn a new procedure or to deal with any problems that crop up. The guide should cover advice like how to load the software, how to perform certain functions, how to save and how to print. More information on user documentation is provided later in this chapter.

Key Jargon

documentation – the paperwork that accompanies a system explaining how the system works.

The evaluation stage

Systems are monitored to make sure that they are performing to the users' satisfaction. For example, a networked computer system may start to run slowly after more users are added than originally anticipated. Steps can then be taken to try to solve any problems that crop up.

Evaluation involves looking at a system to check it is doing its job properly. The demands of a business change and after a time it may be better to think about designing a new system rather than improving the existing one and then the whole system life cycle starts over again.

Evaluating the design and implementation of the system

After a project has been implemented it should be reviewed periodically to make sure that it is still meeting its objectives.

A good way of evaluating a solution is to ask the users of the system. They will be able to tell you if a system does what they want it to do, or if any improvements are needed. It is a good idea to produce a user questionnaire that can be used to find out what the users think of the system. You could ask them how easy they found it to use. You can use the answers to the questionnaire to make modifications or improvements to the system.

The form below is designed to get the users' opinions about a template for producing leaflets on conferences at a country house hotel. The main aim of the template is to look good and to make it easy to change the information in the leaflet such as the title of conference, date, room, etc.

Feature of template	User's comment
Do you think that the template is easy to use?	
Did you find it quick to produce a final leaflet?	
Do you think that the information is easy enough to change?	
Did you find the user guide easy to understand?	

There are always constraints placed on the system and these might include time, money and a lack of qualified staff involved in the project. All solutions have some limitations placed on them. For example, you may have been limited by the hardware or software that your school/college has. It is important to describe how you could have improved on the system had the resources been available.

Maintenance

Systems need to be updated to keep pace with changes in the users' requirements. Changes made to a system during its useful life are called maintenance.

Maintenance can include:

- providing support for users – usually in the form of a help desk that they can ring with their problems
- providing enhancements – these are things that are added to the system to make it better
- creating patches (small bits of programming code) to correct bugs in software
- improving software – the software producer may provide updated versions of software with improved features.

Documentation

There are two types of documentation: user documentation and technical documentation.

User documentation

A user guide or manual is documentation that the user can turn to for guidance when learning a new procedure or dealing with a problem that has cropped up. The guide should cover:

- minimum hardware and software requirements
- how to load the software
- how to perform certain functions
- how to save
- how to print
- frequently asked questions (FAQs)
- how to deal with error messages and troubleshooting.

It is a good idea to include examples and exercises to help the user understand the system. Since users are often non-technical, any specialist, technical language should be avoided.

The user guide should explain what to do in exceptional circumstances. For instance, if the system fails to read a disk, or data is sent to the printer without it being switched on and the machine is locked, the user will need to know what they have to do. The guide should also include backing-up and closing-down instructions.

As always, users have the best view of a system, and so should be asked to evaluate any proposed user guide. Their comments should be incorporated into the guide. You have probably tried to look things up in manuals yourself so you will realise just how important they are.

Technical documentation

It is important that systems are fully documented because the person who designed and implemented the system may not always be around to help with problems. Someone else, who may not be as familiar with the system, may have to maintain it. In order to do this they will need to understand the technical workings of the system, and it is for this purpose that technical documentation is produced. In technical documentation you would expect to find:

- a copy of the system design specification
- all the diagrams used to represent the system (flowcharts, system flowcharts, structure diagrams and dataflow diagrams)
- macro designs, spreadsheet formulae or program listings
- screen layout designs
- user interface designs
- test plan.

Explaining how an ICT system works
Graphical representation of systems

In ICT, diagrams are often drawn to help explain how ICT systems work. These diagrams include block diagrams and flowcharts. The simplest way any ICT system can be represented is as three boxes representing input, process and output.

Flowcharts

When you are planning how to solve a particular problem, a good way to start is to break the problem down into a series of small steps placed in the correct order. Rather than just listing the steps, you can show them in a diagram. This type of diagram is called a **flowchart**.

Key Jargon

flowchart – a chart or diagram used to break down a task into smaller parts. It can also show the order of the tasks and any decisions which need to be made.

	Terminator (start or end)
	Process (done by the computer)
	Input or output
	Decision
	Connector

Figure 10.5

The main flowchart symbols

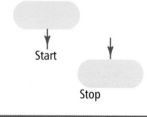

Start

Stop

Figure 10.6

Stop and start boxes

Figure 10.7

Examples of process boxes

Flowcharts are made up of boxes connected by lines, and the steps are written inside the boxes. The main flowchart symbols (i.e. the boxes) are shown in Figure 10.5.

Stop or start boxes

These symbols are used at the start and end of the flowchart. Notice the way that the flow lines go into or out of the boxes and that the name of the box is placed inside.

Process boxes

A process is something that is done. This could be:

- a calculation (e.g. calculate VAT)
- finding some data (e.g. on a disk, in a file, etc.)
- an activity that someone has to do (e.g. contact a customer, fill in a form, etc.)
- an activity that may be performed automatically (e.g. measure temperature, open a window, etc.)
- storing data (either manually or using the computer).

Figure 10.7 shows some process boxes with the names of the processes inside.

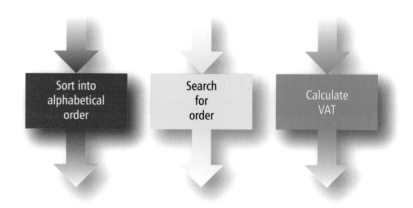

Sort into alphabetical order

Search for order

Calculate VAT

Input and output boxes

Data needs to be put into a system before it can be processed. If a calculation needs to be performed then the input will need to be some numbers. If you are replying to a job advertisement, then the input could be the job advert itself.

The output is the result of processing. A printed list of all the pupils in a certain class is an example of an output.

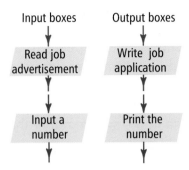

Figure 10.8

Input and output boxes

Decision boxes

These boxes are used to ask questions to which there are only two possible answers: yes or no. One flow line goes into the decision box and two lines leave it (see Figure 10.9). 'Yes' and 'no' must be written next to the lines leaving the box to show which path is to be taken in each case. Some examples of decision boxes are shown in Figure 10.10.

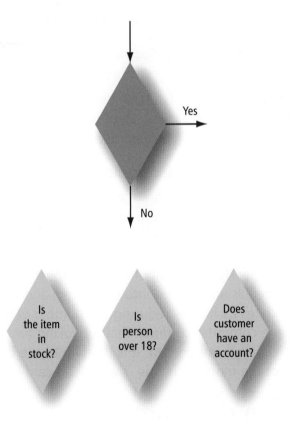

Figure 10.9

You need to decide between two routes depending on whether the decision inside the box is true or false

Figure 10.10

Examples of decision boxes. A question is asked inside the box that has a yes or no answer

In decision boxes one of the flow lines can come out of the decision box to either the right or the left. The line coming out of the right or the left of the flowchart eventually joins up at a place further along the flow line.

System flowcharts

A system flowchart shows what happens to data when it is input, processed and output by a computer system. It gives a more general view of a whole system than a flowchart that looks in detail at a particular area. The flow lines in a system flowchart show the flow of data in the system rather than the order in which the steps should be carried out.

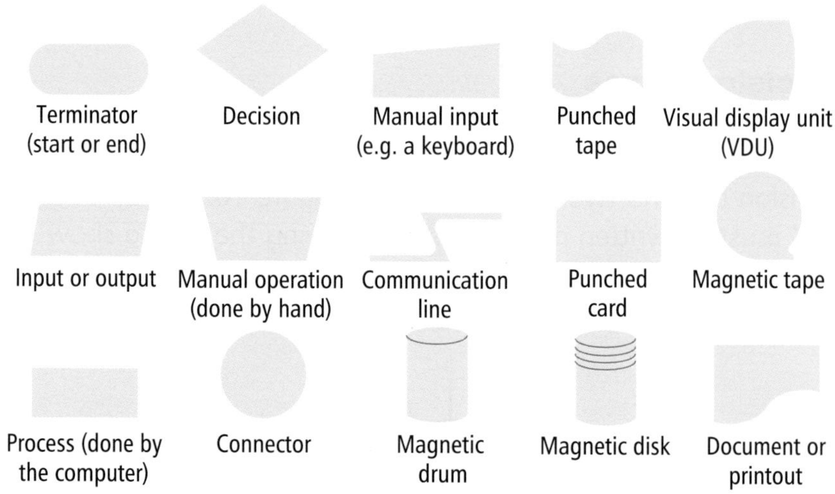

Terminator (start or end)   Decision   Manual input (e.g. a keyboard)   Punched tape   Visual display unit (VDU)

Input or output   Manual operation (done by hand)   Communication line   Punched card   Magnetic tape

Process (done by the computer)   Connector   Magnetic drum   Magnetic disk   Document or printout

Figure 10.11

Symbols used in system flowcharts

System flowcharts show the types of input and output methods used and also the type of backing store used. The process boxes show what is happening to the data during processing.

A computerised concert booking system

In a typical system (see the diagram in Figure 10.12), the booking agent types into the computer the venue number, concert date and concert time. Records of all the concerts are held on disk and, because they are on-line, these can be accessed by computer very quickly. The computer then outputs the availability of seats. The details are entered into the system and the computer updates its files by reducing the number of available seats. Then the computer confirms that a booking has been made and the tickets are printed. It is then up to the booking clerk to collect the money (cheque, credit/debit card or cash).

Structure diagrams

Structure diagrams can be used to describe information systems. An overall task is broken down into smaller, more manageable tasks. These may then be broken down further into smaller tasks. This way of describing tasks is described as the '**top-down**' approach.

Key Jargon

top-down design – a way of describing a problem where you start off with the problem and then break it down into a few smaller problems. Each of these smaller problems may then be broken down further. As you break the problem down, you look at it in more and more detail.

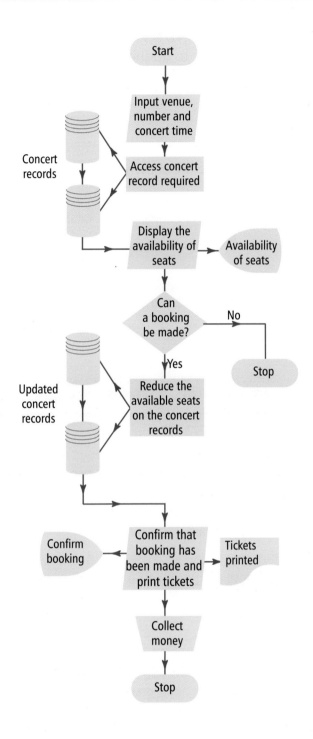

The system flowchart for a concert booking system

Top-down design

Let's take a look at drawing a structure diagram for a task we are probably all familiar with: doing the weekly shopping.

First we place the overall task at the top (i.e. doing the weekly shopping) and write a brief description of it. This is shown in Figure 10.13.

The overall task

This task is then divided up into a series of tasks that make up the main task. For instance, to do the shopping we may have to:

- prepare a shopping list
- do the shopping
- put the shopping away.

So, we now have the structure shown in Figure 10.14.

Figure 10.14

Main task divisions

Prepare list   Do weekly shopping   Put shopping away

Again, this second set of tasks may be split up as shown in Figure 10.15.

| Check cupboards | Look in fridge | Write down items needed | Drive to shops | Select items | Pay for items | Unpack shopping | Put some food in fridge | Put some food in cupboard |

We write these in the order in which they are performed ⟶

Figure 10.15

Further task divisions

We can now put all the stages together to produce the final structure diagram as shown in Figure 10.16. When drawing structure diagrams, don't worry if yours looks different from other people's. They are rarely the same.

Figure 10.16

Final structure diagram

As you can see, the purpose of a structure diagram is to show the tasks in more detail as you move down the diagram. The top box is the overall view (doing the weekly shopping), hence the term 'top-down' approach. You could break each task down still further, but there comes a point when you have enough detail for your needs.

Dataflow diagrams

Dataflow diagrams are used to look at the data without considering the equipment used to store it. They are used as a first step in describing a system. They show where the data comes from and what data is needed for the processes in the system. Four symbols are used in these diagrams and these are described below.

The box
The box is either a source of data, such as an order form from a customer, or a part of the system which uses or consumes the data, called a sink. We are not concerned with what happens to the data before it reaches the box (if it is a source) or what happens to it after it goes past the box (if it is a sink).

The sausage
The sausage is sometimes replaced by a circle on dataflow diagrams and is used to denote a process. A process is something that is done to the data, like a calculation. The process might be sorting the data or combining it with some other data. A brief description of the process should be placed inside this box.

The open rectangle
The open rectangle represents a data store. This is where data is held. It could represent the data being held manually or on a computer. Basically, a data store is a logical collection of data. A description of the store should be placed inside the box.

The arrows
The arrows are used to show how the other symbols are connected. They show the flow of data around the system.

A video library system

We will now draw a series of dataflow diagrams for a video library system. The first diagram follows the data flow that takes place when a new member joins the library. To join the library a person needs to fill in an application form and to show certain documents to provide proof of their identity. If the potential member does not have this documentation, then the library manager will refuse them membership. After the membership details have been checked (or validated) a membership card is produced and given to the new member and the member's details are recorded. If the member borrows a video, or if the manager wants to know whether a particular person is a member, then the details can be found easily. Figure 10.17 shows the dataflow diagram for this part of the system.

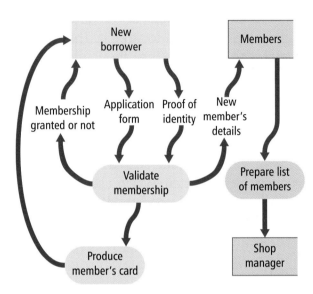

Figure 10.17

Dataflow diagram for a video library

Now we can look at the dataflow diagram for a video being added to the library. This is a simple system, with the details of the video such as name, price, etc. being recorded and then stored. Figure 10.18 shows this part of the system.

```
        New
        video
          |
       Video
       details
          |
   Record video   →   Videos
     details
```

Figure 10.18

The dataflow diagram for adding a new video to the library

Figure 10.19 shows the dataflow diagram for the process of borrowing a video. Notice that the member data and video data are needed because the loans store of data will only contain the video number and the membership number. This is done to save space. By storing the video and member number together it is possible to find out a member's details and the video details if they are needed.

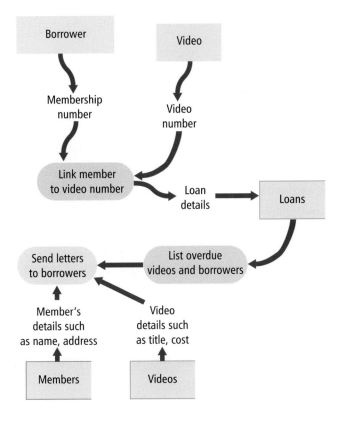

Figure 10.19

The dataflow diagram for borrowing a video

If we wanted to get an overall view of the system, we could join these diagrams together. However, it is much easier to draw a diagram for each part of the system and then to draw another diagram with them all joined.

Activity 1

A college needs to keep records of the students on all of the courses it runs. The data is collected when the students come to the college to enrol on courses. Here are the procedures that take place when a student enrols on a course.

1 The student fills in an enrolment form.
2 The course tutor fills in details about the course such as the course number (each course has its own unique number), the length of the course, etc.
3 The student takes the enrolment form to the college office.

continued over page

4 The student is allocated a unique number, called the student number, by the college office.

5 The details such as name, address, telephone number, date of birth and National Insurance number are keyed in by the enrolment officer.

6 The enrolment officer looks to see if the course is free. If not they look in a course fee booklet to find out the fee for the course. The student pays the course fee if applicable (many courses are free).

7 A photograph is taken of the student using a small digital camera.

8 A plastic card with a photograph of the student, the student's name, student number and expiry date on it is printed. This is called the student ID card. There is also a barcode on the card that can be used to input the student number into any of the college systems. This card can also act as a library card or to gain entry to certain college rooms.

9 A receipt is printed and given to the student with their student number printed on it.

Draw a dataflow diagram to illustrate this part of the enrolment system.

Build your notes

Here are some notes that summarise this chapter. The notes are incomplete because they have words missing.

Using the words in the list below, copy out and complete the sentences A to J, underlining the words that you have inserted. Each word may be used more than once.

> system life cycle   feasibility study   testing   systems analyst
> fact find   feasibility report   outputs   implementation   design
> parallel   design specification   evaluation

A _____ _____ is the person who looks at the existing system to see how it could be improved.

B The series of stages worked through when a new system is introduced is called the _____ _____ _____.

C The system life cycle consists of the following stages: feasibility study, analysis, _____, implementation, testing and evaluation.

D To assess a project's feasibility, a _____ _____ is performed after which a _____ _____ is produced.

E During the analysis stage, the systems analyst will perform a _____ _____ in order to find out a variety of facts about the business.

F The design of the system would look at the inputs, processes and _____ and would be outlined in a document called the _____ _____.

G Once the design stage has been completed, the working version of the solution can be produced. This is called the _____ stage.

H Thorough testing is then undertaken to make sure that the solution works properly. This is called the _____ stage.

I The final stage, called the _____ stage, makes sure that the system is performing to the user's satisfaction.

J There are three ways that a system can be implemented: _____ implementation, phased implementation and direct implementation.

1 **In order to find out about the existing system used by an organisation, fact finding is performed. Which one of the following would not be performed during fact finding?**

a   interviewing staff
b   observing staff at work
c   inspecting files, invoices, stock lists, etc.
d   performing a cost-benefit analysis

2 **For what reason is systems analysis performed?**

a   to look at the existing system and make improvements to it
b   to identify staff who are no longer needed
c   to give work to the systems analyst
d   to replace the existing system with a manual system

3 **User documentation will normally contain:**

a   programming flowcharts
b   lists of program instructions
c   details about how to load the software
d   a systems flowchart.

4 **Which one of the following is not a way of implementing a system?**

a   direct
b   phased
c   parallel
d   vertical

5 **The purpose of the feasibility study is:**

a   to test the system thoroughly
b   to train the users
c   to decide whether to go ahead with the new system
d   to convert the manual files to computer files.

6 **Which one of the following would a feasibility study not look at?**

a   whether the problem can be solved
b   how much the solution will probably cost
c   the benefits of the new system
d   the training of the users

7 **The design stage of the system life cycle would not consider:**

a   the form of data capture to be used
b   the processing that is done on the data
c   the reports to be outputted
d   whether to go ahead with the new system.

8 **Which one of the following tasks would not be performed during the implementation of a new system?**

a   creating the structure of a database
b   installing the hardware and software
c   training the users
d   designing the user interface

9 **Top-down design:**

a   is a design where the overall problem is broken down
b   is a design where only the senior managers are involved in the design
c   is only used for developing systems for managers
d   is a method of training users.

10 **Which one of the following would not be considered to be maintenance of the system?**

a   providing a help desk for users
b   correcting bugs in the software
c   providing new versions of the software
d   designing the database

1 During systems analysis it is important to understand how the old system works. Finding out about an existing system is called fact finding.

   a Name and briefly describe **three** different ways of collecting facts about a system.

   b In order to decide whether to go ahead with a new system a feasibility study is carried out. The findings of the study are outlined in a report called a feasibility report. Briefly describe **three** things that this feasibility report should contain.

2 Here is a list of the steps that are normally taken when producing a new information system. At present these are in the wrong order. Copy out the steps, putting them in the correct order.

   ■ evaluation
   ■ analysis
   ■ testing
   ■ implementation
   ■ design

3 Here are some of the steps that should be completed when creating a new computer system:

   ■ evaluation
   ■ analysis
   ■ testing
   ■ implementation
   ■ design

For each of the tasks given below, write down the name of the step at which it would be carried out.

   a Getting the user to answer a questionnaire to find out what they want from the new system.

   b Working out accurate costs for the new system.

   c Deciding what outputs are needed from the new system.

   d Typing information from the paper-based records into the new system.

   e Asking users what they think of the new system that has been developed.

   f Putting data into the computer to see if the output is the same as expected.

4 When a new system is developed, documentation is produced.

   a Briefly describe **two** items that would be recorded as part of the user documentation.

   b Briefly describe **two** items that would be recorded as part of the technical documentation.

F Questions

1 In solving problems using IT, there are five distinct stages. The first two stages are Analysis and Design. Name the other three stages.

(AQA Specification A Tier F short course, specimen paper, q12)

2 The partners of a doctors' surgery are considering using a computer system to store patient records and handle appointments. A systems analyst is called in to carry out a feasibility study.

   a Explain why a feasibility study is carried out.

   b After the feasibility study, the decision is made to go ahead with the introduction of the computer system. The systems analyst then carries out a detailed analysis of the existing system.

      Give **three** ways that the systems analyst could find out about the existing system.

   c After the analysis, the systems analyst then produces a design specification for the new system.

      Give **four** items that should be included in the design specification.

(NEAB Tier F, June 2000, p2, q9)

3 The system life cycle describes the stages that are worked through when a new computer system is being developed.

   a List the stages of the system life cycle given below in the correct order. The first one has been done for you.

      Design
      Implementation
      Analysis
      Feasibility study

Evaluation
Testing

Stage 1: Feasibility study

b Give **two** activities that would take place during the analysis stage of the system life cycle.

c Give **two** activities that would take place during the design stage of the system life cycle.

d Give **three** different types of test data that should be used during the testing stage of the system life cycle.

e Give **three** topics that should be included in the user documentation for a new computer system.

f Give **two** items that should be included in the technical documentation for a new computer system.

(AQA Tier F, June 2001, p2, q10)

 Questions

1 A new computer system is to be produced to handle ticket sales for a sports stadium. The stages in production of this system include Analysis, Design, Implementation, Testing and Evaluation.

At which stage does each of the following tasks take place?
a considering how well the system works
b working out a testing plan
c finding out how the present booking system works
d deciding how to store the data
e setting up the ticket sales database
f finding out if it is possible to sell two tickets for one seat at an event

(AQA Specification A Tier H full course, specimen paper, q9)

2 When a new computerised system is suggested, a full analysis of user requirements has to be carried out. Describe the methods which can be used to find out about an existing system and what will be needed in the new system. Discuss the advantages of the methods used.

(NEAB Tier H, June 98, p2)

Mimicking real situations using a computer
Modelling

What is a model?

Have you ever made a model of a car or plane? If it was one of those plastic kits where you glue the parts together, then what you end up with is a scale model. If you made a working model that could fly with its own engine, then you would have a model that is more realistic (i.e. nearer to the real thing).

What is a computer model?

A computer model is used to mimic a real situation. Models are usually constructed using specialist modelling software, but there are many models that can be produced using an ordinary spreadsheet.

What are models used for?

Models are used to provide answers to questions such as 'what would happen if I did this? For example, an economist could look at the effects raising interest rates would have on the economy.

Making a simple computer model

Simple models can be produced using spreadsheet software. In Activity 1 you will create a simple model using spreadsheet software.

Activity 1

When you drive a new car out of the showroom it immediately goes down in price. If you tried to sell it back to a garage or privately, you

continued over page

would get less than you paid for it. As you use the car and it gets older its value goes down. This is called depreciation.

Cars depreciate at different rates depending on the make and model. BMWs and Mercedes depreciate less than Fords or Vauxhalls, although they generally cost more to buy in the first place.

In this activity you will try to produce a model for the depreciation of two different new cars over a four-year period.

Car A has a depreciation of 40% per year, while car B has a depreciation of only 25% per year.

The costs of each car when new is:
Car A: £13,000
Car B: £18,500

Follow the steps below to set up the model.

1 Load the spreadsheet software until you see the blank grid. Now type in the data exactly in the positions shown here.

	A	B	C	D	E	F	G	H
1	A model showing car depreciation							
2				Year 1	Year 2	Year 3	Year 4	
3	Car A	£13,000						
4	Car B	£18,500						
5								
6								

2 In cell D3 type in the formula =0.6*B3
This will calculate 60% of the original price (i.e. 100% − 40%= 60% depreciation, which can be written 60/100 or 0.6)
Check that it now looks like this:

	A	B	C	D	E	F	G	H
1	A model showing car depreciation							
2				Year 1	Year 2	Year 3	Year 4	
3	Car A	£13,000		£7,800.0				
4	Car B	£18,500						
5								
6								

3 In cell E3 type in the formula =0.6*D3
This works out 60% of the price after Year 1.
In cell F3 type in the formula =0.6*E3
In cell G3 type in the formula = 0.6*F3
Check that the spreadsheet now looks like this:

	A	B	C	D	E	F	G	H
1	A model showing car depreciation							
2				Year 1	Year 2	Year 3	Year 4	
3	Car A	£13,000		£7,800.0	£4,680.0	£2,808.0	£1,684.80	
4	Car B	£18,500						
5								

4 For Car B, the depreciation is 25%. This means that the car is worth 100% − 25% = 75% of its price the previous year.

You have to construct the formulae in a similar way to step 3 using the figure 0.75 to fill in the amounts for Year 1, Year 2, etc.

Your spreadsheet should now look like this:

	A	B	C	D	E	F	G	H
1	A model showing car depreciation							
2				Year 1	Year 2	Year 3	Year 4	
3	Car A	£13,000		£7,800.0	£4,680.0	£2,808.0	£1,684.80	
4	Car B	£18,500		£13,875.00	£10,406.25	£7,804.69	£5,853.52	

5 You can now work out how much the cars have depreciated in total over the four years. In cell H4 put the heading 'Depreciation' (you will need to widen the column to fit in the text).

To work out the total depreciation for Car A, subtract the figure in cell G3 from the figure in cell B3. Put the formula =B3−G3 in cell H3.

Put a similar formula =B4−G4 in cell H4.

The final model should look like this:

	A	B	C	D	E	F	G	H
1	A model showing car depreciation							
2				Year 1	Year 2	Year 3	Year 4	Depreciation
3	Car A	£13,000		£7,800.0	£4,680.0	£2,808.0	£1,684.80	£11,315.20
4	Car B	£18,500		£13,875.00	£10,406.25	£7,804.69	£5,853.52	£12,646.48
5								
6								

6 You can now alter the prices and see what happens to the depreciation. Suppose both cars cost exactly the same price but still had the same rate of depreciation. What would happen if they both cost £15,000?

Put the value £15,000 into cells B3 and B4.

The model should now look like this:

	A	B	C	D	E	F	G	H
1	A model showing car depreciation							
2				Year 1	Year 2	Year 3	Year 4	Depreciation
3	Car A	£15,000		£9,000.0	£5,400.0	£3,240.0	£1,944.00	£13,056.00
4	Car B	£15,000		£11,250.00	£8,437.50	£6,328.13	£4,746.09	£10,253.91
5								

continued over page

This car depreciation model is fairly simple. You can alter the prices of the cars fairly easily but it is quite difficult to change the depreciation rate because it is part of each formula. What you need is two cells where you input the depreciation rate for each car.

Different cars have different depreciation rates. Try to work out the depreciation rates for different cars using accurate data. You can get data about prices for cars from the following website:

www.parkers.co.uk

You may also like to look into whether the depreciation rate changes from one year to the next. If this could be built into the model it would make it reflect the real situation more closely.

Creating a model

The rules of a model

All models are based on certain rules. These rules are expressed as formulae. It is important that these formulae are accurate so that the model mimics the real situation. For example, the stopping distance of a car depends on many things such as the state of the tyres or the road conditions (i.e. dry, icy or wet). All these factors would need to be taken into account in the formulae.

The variables

Variables are those inputs to the system that you would like to change. You can change the variables and see the effect on the model. In the car depreciation model above, the variables were the prices of the cars. It was also decided that it was possible to vary the percentage depreciation rate.

The importance of getting the rules right

When you first start building a model, you make a lot of assumptions and simplifications. For example, if you are considering the stopping distance of a car you may think of it as just the thinking distance of the driver added to the braking distance of the car. However, other factors also affect stopping distance, such as the condition of the road, the tiredness of the driver, the condition of the brakes, the condition of the tyres and the make of car.

It is hard to get all the rules right first time, so the best approach is to create a simple model to start with and then make it more complex by including more factors. Only when you have considered all the rules and have the correct formulae for them will the model properly mimic the real thing.

How can you test check a model?

To test a model you can input the variables from a real situation and then compare the results obtained from the model with what happened in real life.

Specialist modelling software

Model Builder is the name of a specialist modelling package. The model shown in Figure 11.1 is set up to show how the concentration of carbon dioxide in the atmosphere stays almost constant. You can increase the concentration of carbon dioxide by burning more fossil fuel and seeing the effect it has.

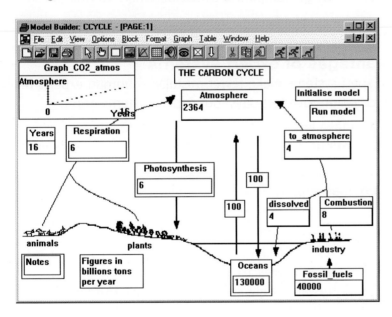

Figure 11.1

Model of the carbon cycle, created in Model Builder

You may come across this software in your science or geography lessons. Here are some of the other models that can be built:

- showing heat losses in a home and how to reduce them
- mimicking the water cycle
- planning the route of a new motorway that is cost effective and environmentally friendly
- human population growth
- a traffic calming scheme outside a school.

Expert systems

Expert systems are programs that mimic human experts. The system acts in the same way a human expert would act. Like models, expert systems use a set of rules, such as:

- "If the meal includes red meat
- Then choose red wine".

Like human experts, they can make decisions using past experience. This means that they can become more expert in their area as time goes on.

Applications of expert systems

Expert systems are specialist software. Here are three uses for this software:

- for making medical diagnoses or giving medical advice
- for use by oil companies to decide where to drill for oil
- for giving tax advice to individuals and companies.

Advantages of expert systems
- Expert systems make fewer mistakes – human experts may forget or have 'off days' but expert systems don't.
- They take less time to train – it is easy to copy an expert system but it takes many years to train a human expert.
- They are cheaper – it costs less to use an expert system than a human expert.

Disadvantages of expert systems
- Expert systems lack common sense – humans are able to decide if an answer to a question is sensible or not; computers aren't always able to do this. Humans can make judgements based on their life experiences, and not just on a limited set of rules as in the case of computers.
- Expert systems lack senses – they can only react to information entered by the user. Human experts have other senses they can use to make judgements. For example, a person describing a type of pain might use body language as well that would not be detected by an expert system.

Expert Builder is a program that you can use to build your own expert system. The example shown in Figure 11.2 was built by a group of 10- and 11-year-old pupils studying Medieval History.

They decided to construct a system which gives the sort of advice a medieval doctor might have given.

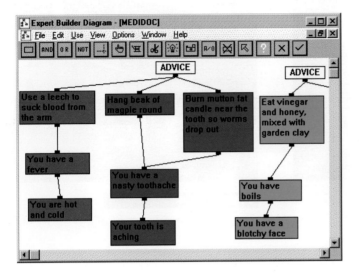

Figure 11.2

An expert system built using Expert Builder to show the advice given by a medieval doctor

Using computer models

Simulations

Doing something with a model is called a **simulation**. Models consist of a set of equations that are used to describe how a real thing behaves. When you perform a simulation you put values into these equations to see what happens. Some models, such as a flight simulator, require continual interaction with the user.

Flight simulators

Flight simulators are used to train pilots.

You can buy flight simulator software for your computer. Obviously you will not experience the feel of a real plane but it will give you some idea of what the controls are. Real flight simulators move in the same way as a plane, so you can get the feel of the plane accelerating along the runway, climbing and descending, etc.

As well as the rules which make up the models, there are also some inputs needed to the system.

Key Jargon

simulation – an imitation of a system (e.g. aircraft flight) using a computer model. Any phenomenon that can be described mathematically (e.g. how the economy of the country works) can be simulated.

Figure 11.3

A flight simulator used to train Boeing 737 pilots

Figure 11.4

Inside a flight simulator

Inputs to a flight simulator

The following are inputs to a flight simulator:

- type of weather (fine, snow, fog, thunderstorms, rain, etc.)
- type of aircraft
- total weight of the aircraft, as this will affect the plane's performance
- any problems with the aircraft (e.g. loss of power from an engine, undercarriage not coming down, etc.)
- the terrain (i.e. what the ground looks like from the plane)
- time of day – whether it is day or night
- the approach scenery to the airport.

For a simulation used for crash testing a car, the inputs might be:

- speed of the car
- road conditions (rain, ice, snow, etc.)
- condition of the brakes and tyres
- make of car (some cars can withstand crashes better than others)
- direction of the collision
- number of occupants in the car.

Other types of computer simulation include games, and animated weather maps showing the path of a storm.

Using computers to control things

Control systems

Computers are often used to control things. If you have a new central heating system then it will probably be controlled by a small computer. In order for a computer to control a device it needs some data to process. The computer gets this data from the outside world using **sensors**. The measurements obtained from the sensors allow the computer to determine what to do next. It might operate a switch to turn a heater on or off, or open or close a window.

In order to understand this section better, it would be a good idea to look back at the section on sensors in Chapter 3 before carrying on.

Key Jargon

LOGO – a simple programming language which enables a 'turtle' to move according to the instructions given to it.

sensors – devices which measure physical quantities such as temperature, pressure, etc.

LOGO

LOGO is a simple programming language that can be used to control the movement of a 'turtle' on a screen. You have to supply the instructions to move the turtle.

Here are the commands used to move the turtle:

- PENUP raises the pen so that when the turtle moves, it does not draw a line.
- PENDOWN puts the pen down so that a line is drawn behind the turtle.
- FORWARD 30 moves the turtle 30 units forward.
- BACKWARD 10 moves the turtle 10 units backward.

You can turn the turtle through any angle. The angle is measured from the line the turtle would take if it carried on moving in the same direction. As well as the angle turned through, you have to also say whether it is LEFT or RIGHT.

Here are the commands to turn the turtle:

- LEFT 90 turns the turtle to the left by 90 degrees.
- RIGHT 60 turns the turtle to the right by 60 degrees.
- CLEARSCREEN clears the screen.

Making a simple program

A program is a list of instructions arranged in a logical order that can be obeyed by a computer. Here are some commands put together to draw a square.

FORWARD 20

RIGHT 90

FORWARD 20

RIGHT 90

FORWARD 20

RIGHT 90

FORWARD 20

This method is a bit tedious, so there is a quicker way of drawing a square, like this:

REPEAT 4 (FORWARD 20 RIGHT 90)

The above instruction tells LOGO to repeat the steps in the brackets four times.

To check that a series of steps works you should try obeying the instructions using a piece of paper. Make sure that at the end of each line, you know which way the turtle is pointing.

Activity 2

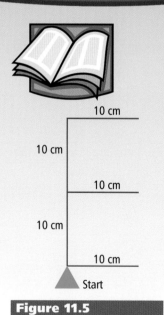

A turtle robot is placed on a piece of paper on the floor. Here is the set of instructions that the robot uses:

FORWARD n	Move n cm forward
BACKWARD n	Move n cm backward
LEFT t	Turn left t degrees
RIGHT t	Turn right t degrees
PENUP	Lift the pen off the paper
PENDOWN	Place the pen on the paper

10 cm

10 cm

10 cm

10 cm

10 cm

10 cm

Start

Figure 11.5

Write a set of instructions to make the turtle draw the shape shown in Figure 11.5 on the paper, starting in the position shown with the pen up.

Activity 3

Your teacher will show you how to load the LOGO software.

Once this has loaded, write a program to draw an equilateral triangle on the screen with sides of length 50. (In an equilateral triangle, all the sides are the same length and all the angles are 60°).

Activity 4

See if you can work out, using pen, paper and a protractor, what happens in the following program written using LOGO.

> FORWARD 50
> RIGHT 150
> FORWARD 60
> RIGHT 100
> FORWARD 30
> RIGHT 90

A computer-controlled central heating system

Central heating systems are often computer controlled. A temperature sensor measures the temperature in one room. If the temperature is below a certain value the heater is turned on. If the temperature is above a certain level the heater is turned off. The temperature is monitored continuously so as soon as the heating has been altered in response to one value, the temperature is measured again and the process repeated. This looping back to the beginning is called feedback (see page 277).

Figure 11.6 shows how we can put this information into a flowchart. The parallelogram box represents either input or output (input in this case), the rectangle represents a process and the diamonds represent decisions to be made.

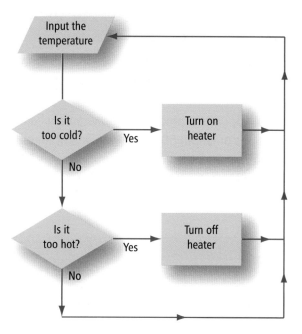

Figure 11.6

A flowchart showing how a computer-controlled heating system can control the temperature in a room

Why is a computer-controlled heating system more efficient than a manually controlled one?

There are two main reasons:

- the heating is only on when it is needed, so no fuel is wasted
- each room can be maintained at a set temperature at set times.

Robots

Robots are often seen in factories doing routine jobs such as assembling, welding and paint spraying.

Why use robots?

Robots, unlike people, don't take time off sick, they don't have tea or lunch breaks and they don't go on strike for more pay. They are able to work continuously to the same standard all the time. Robots are used for building cars and household goods such as washing machines.

Robots are used in hazardous situations and in places that are inaccessible to humans. Here are some situations where they might be used:

- investigating bombs to make them safe
- searching for aircraft wreckage in the sea
- investigating underwater structures such as the feet on drilling platforms.

Does the use of robots cause unemployment?

Robots in factories do replace people; however, people are needed to build, program and repair them. So, overall, they probably have no effect on the level of unemployment.

Process control

Computers are used for the control of industrial processes, such as making beer, paint, chemicals and food. Process control is also used in the oil and nuclear industries.

Why use process control?

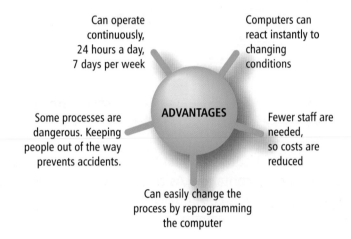

Can operate continuously, 24 hours a day, 7 days per week

Computers can react instantly to changing conditions

Some processes are dangerous. Keeping people out of the way prevents accidents.

ADVANTAGES

Fewer staff are needed, so costs are reduced

Can easily change the process by reprogramming the computer

Computers are expensive to introduce initially

DISADVANTAGES

Fewer people needed, so leads to unemployment

The importance of feedback

Feedback is an essential part of any computer-controlled system. The following example shows how important feedback is.

A computer can be used to control a robot arm. If you wanted the robot arm to move through a certain angle, you can give an instruction to a special motor that moves in small steps at a time. When the command has been issued, the arm will move to the required position. However, if there is an object in the way, it will stop. The problem is that if this happens the computer will not know whether it has reached its desired position or not.

What is needed is a way in which the arm can relay its actual position back to the computer. It can do this making use of sensors. The sensors continually send data about the position of the arm back to the computer. If the robot arm is not in the correct position then remedial action can be taken to put it in the correct position. Here, output from the system directly affects the input. Such a system is said to use **feedback**.

Figure 11.7

The advantages and disadvantages of using computers for process control

Key Jargon

feedback – where the output from a system directly affects the input.

Example of process control

Here is a simple example of process control.

In a chemical process, a container is filled with water to a certain level and heated up to a temperature of 70°C.

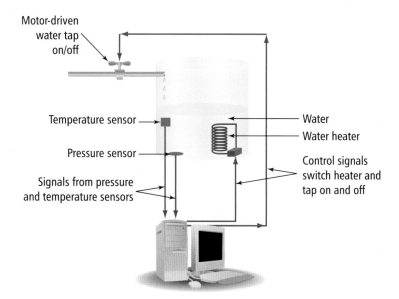

Figure 11.8

Using a computer to control a chemical process

The computer issues a control signal to turn on the motorised tap and let water into the container. As the water enters and the level rises, the water pressure is continually fed back to the computer. As soon as the pressure reaches a certain value, signifying that the water is at the correct level, a control signal is sent back to the tap to turn the water off.

At the same time, a signal is fed back to the computer from the temperature sensor. If the temperature of the water is less than 70°C, a control signal is sent to the heater to turn it on. The temperature is continually measured and fed back to the computer. As soon as the temperature reaches 70°C, a control signal is issued to the heater to turn it off. If at any time the temperature drops below 70°C, the heater is switched on again. In this way the temperature remains more or less constant at 70°C.

Activity 5

Produce a flowchart to show how the process control system described above works.

Activity 6

Once you have produced your hand-drawn flowchart in Activity 5, and have had it checked by your teacher, load the wordprocessing software Word.

1 Click on A̲utoshapes in the menu bar at the bottom of the screen.

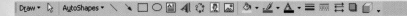

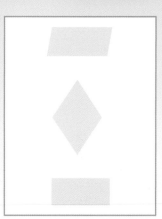

2 Click on F̲lowchart on the menu that drops down.

You will see a series of flowchart boxes. By clicking on them you can get them to appear in your wordprocessed document.

The main ones you will need are shown opposite: the first box is for input/output, the second box for decisions and the third box for processes.

See if you can use the computer to make the same flowchart as in Activity 5.

Build your notes

Here are some notes that summarise this chapter. The notes are incomplete because they have words missing.

Using the words in the list below, copy out and complete the sentences A to H, underlining the words that you have inserted. Each word may be used more than once.

> rules   simulator   sensors   process control   test
> flight   spreadsheet   feedback

A Models can be produced using specialist modelling software or _____ software.

B When making a model you need to think about the _____ of the model and then describe these as equations (formulae).

C When a model is used in the same way as the real thing it is called a _____.

D Examples of simulations include games and _____ simulators used to train pilots.

continued over page

E To _____ a model you can compare the results from the model with the results obtained from the real thing.

F Computers are often used to control a process in a factory. This is called _____ _____.

G Control often makes use of _____ where the output has some influence on the input.

H The input to control systems is usually obtained from _____.

1 **Flight simulator software can be used to train pilots. Why is simulator software used?**

a   It is cheaper and safer to use a simulator than the real thing.
b   Pilots need to practise using computers.
c   A simulation is better than the real thing.
d   Pilots enjoy using the simulator more than flying aeroplanes.

2 **Here is a short program written in the programming language LOGO:**

FORWARD 10
RIGHT 90
FORWARD 10
RIGHT 90
FORWARD 10
RIGHT 90
FORWARD 10

The shape drawn by this program is:

a   a rectangle
b   a triangle
c   a cube
d   a square.

3 **A model is produced of a supermarket queue. Which one of the following is not an input to the model?**

a   the number of shoppers waiting
b   the number of EPOS terminals open
c   the average time for each shopper to be served
d   the average age of each shopper

4 **Which one of the following is an advantage of the supermarket queue model?**

a   It allows the supermarket to have the right number of EPOS terminals.
b   It makes the shoppers spend more money.
c   It records all the shoppers' purchases.
d   It produces an itemised bill.

5 Which one of the following is not one of the steps in producing a model?

a evaluate
b implement
c design
d DTP

6 A program that is designed to behave like a human expert in a specialist field is called:

a a professional program
b an expert system
c a game
d an executive information system.

7 In which of these applications are you least likely to see a robot being used?

a welding car panels in a car factory
b spraying paint onto car bodies in a car factory
c moving stock around in a frozen-food warehouse
d painting a house

8 What is represented by a rectangle in a flowchart?

a a process
b an input/output
c a decision
d a disk drive

9 How is a model tested?

a by giving the developer a multiple-choice test
b by comparing the results from the model with the results from the real thing
c by performing a spellcheck
d by using a test meter

10 In a control system for a greenhouse, too much humidity is controlled by the system opening a window. What output device would be used to open the window?

a printer

b motor

c light

d speaker

1 Write a set of instructions to control the central heating system in a house where the temperature in the house needs to be kept between 20°C and 25°C.

2 Here is a set of commands that can be used to move an arrow on the screen of a computer. When the arrow moves, it leaves a line.

FORWARD distance
LEFT angle
RIGHT angle

Hence, using the command FORWARD 5 would move the arrow forward five units and LEFT 90 would turn the arrow left through an angle of 90°.

a Here is a shape that was drawn on the screen. The numbers represent the lengths of the lines.

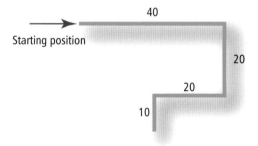

Using only the commands in the following list, write the set of instructions that need to be issued to draw the shape shown above. You may need to use some of the commands in the list more than once.

LEFT 90
FORWARD 10
FORWARD 20
FORWARD 40
RIGHT 90

b

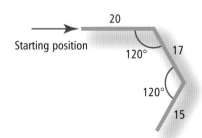

Write down a list of commands that would draw this shape.

---

3 **a** Explain what is meant by an expert system.

b Name **two** jobs that are likely to use an expert system.

c For each of the jobs you have mentioned in part b, explain how the expert system would be used.

---

4 Airlines use flight simulators to train airline pilots.

a Explain briefly what a flight simulator is.

b Give **two** reasons why a flight simulator is used rather than a real plane.

F Questions

1 A computer system controls a robot turtle. The turtle holds a pen. When the turtle moves, the pen leaves a line on the paper beneath it. The turtle is moved by typing commands into the computer system.

The commands which are used to move the turtle are as follows:

FORWARD distance (in mm)
LEFT angle (in degrees)
RIGHT angle (in degrees)

So FORWARD 30 would move the turtle forward 30 mm and RIGHT 45 would turn the turtle right through an angle of 45 degrees.

Using only the commands in the list below, write down a set of instructions needed to draw the shape shown on the next page.

Command list
FORWARD 20
FORWARD 40
FORWARD 60
FORWARD 80
LEFT 90
RIGHT 90

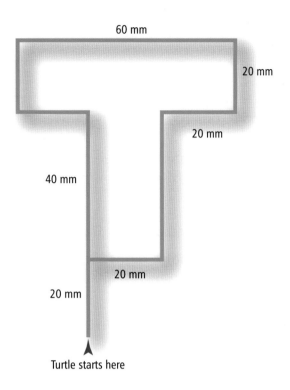

60 mm

20 mm

20 mm

40 mm

20 mm

20 mm

Turtle starts here

You may need to use some of the commands in the list more than once.

(AQA Specification A Tier F full course, specimen paper, q3)

2   A computer system is used to control a crane that puts boxes onto ships. A grip at the end of the crane is used to pick up and put down the boxes. The grip is moved by typing commands into the computer system. The commands which are used to move the grip are as follows:

Command list	Meaning of the command
RIGHT 3	Move the grip right 3 units
LEFT 2	Move the grip left 2 units
UP 4	Move the grip up by 4 units
DOWN 5	Move the grip down by 5 units
CLOSE	Close the grip to pick up the box
OPEN	Open the grip to release the box

Write down the instructions needed for the grip to pick up box A and stack it on top of box B, which is already on the ship. The grip must then be returned to its original starting position.

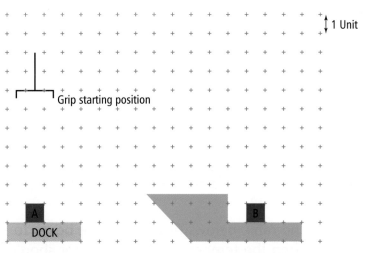

Grip starting position

1 Unit

A

DOCK

B

(NEAB Tier F, June 2000, p1, q10)

3 a A swimming pool uses a feedback and monitoring system to control the temperature of the water.

Using only phrases from the list given below the diagram, copy and complete the flowchart to show how this system works. The first box has been completed for you.

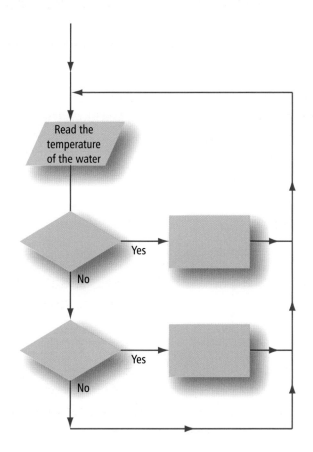

Read the temperature of the water

Yes

No

Yes

No

Turn off the heaters
Add more chlorine
Read the temperature of the water
Is the temperature too hot?
Swimming session ends
Add more water
Is the temperature too cold?
Turn on the heaters

b What device would be used to read the temperature of the water?

c Copy the table below. Tick **one** of the boxes to show how often the temperature of the water should be read.

	Tick one box
Every minute	
Every hour	
Every three hours	
Every day	

(AQA Tier F, June 2001, p1, q8)

4 a Using the words from the list, copy and complete the flow diagram to show how the temperature in a **fridge** is controlled.

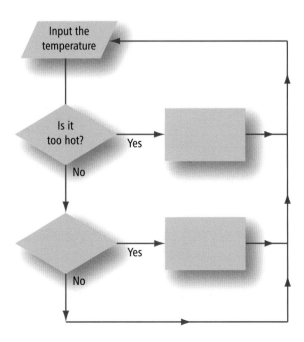

Is it too wet?

Turn on the cooler.

Turn off the cooler.

Open the door.

Is it too cold?

b Draw a flow diagram to show how a computer-controlled **central heating system** can control the temperature in a room.

c The program below is used in a computer-controlled central heating system.

The program controls the temperature in a room.

The program does not work correctly because line 2 and line 3 are wrong.

Line	Instruction
1	INPUT THE TEMPERATURE
2	IF THE TEMPERATURE IS MORE THAN 18°C THEN TURN ON THE HEATER
3	IF THE TEMPERATURE IS LESS THAN 18°C THEN TURN OFF THE HEATER
4	GO TO LINE 1

(i) The statements below describe the possible effects of the incorrect program on the temperature in a room. Copy out the **two** that are correct.

If the temperature is below 18°C then the heater is turned on and the room gets warmer.
If the temperature is above 18°C then the heater is turned off and the room gets colder.
If the temperature is 18°C then the heater is turned on for 10 seconds, then turned off for 10 seconds, then turned on for 10 seconds, and so on.
If the temperature is below 18°C then the heater is turned off and the room gets colder.
If the temperature is 18°C then no action is taken.

(ii) Rewrite line 2 and line 3 so that the program works correctly.

(iii) Write down **three** tests from the list below which would be carried out to make sure that the program is working correctly.

When the temperature of the room is 200°C, the operation of the heater is checked.
When the temperature of the room is 20°C, the operation of the heater is checked.
When the temperature of the room is –100°C, the operation of the heater is checked.
When the temperature of the room is 16°C, the heater is turned on manually.
When the temperature of the room is 18°C, the operation of the heater is checked.
When the temperature of the room is 16°C, the operation of the heater is checked.)

d   Write down **two** reasons from the list below that show why a computer-controlled heating system is more efficient than a manually controlled system.

No fuel is wasted.
Gas is more economic than oil.
The set temperature is maintained in every room at set times.
A computer-controlled system is easier to set up.
As the temperature falls, fuel is wasted keeping the rooms warm.

(AQA Specification B Tier F full course, specimen paper, q6)

 Questions

1   Simulators can be used to gain experience of driving cars at high speeds.

a   Give **one** example of people who may need to use such a simulator as part of their job.

b   Give **two** reasons why a simulator would be used in this situation.

c   All simulators rely on rules built into the controlling software. Write down **three** rules from the list below that could reasonably be built into this driving simulator.

Motorway driving must be fast.
Cars take longer to stop on wet roads than on dry roads.
Cars over three years old must have a valid MOT certificate.

The faster a car is travelling, the greater the distance needed to stop.

Cars should stop at red traffic lights.

Younger drivers pay more for car insurance.

d Name and briefly describe **two** other situations in which computer simulation might reasonably be used.

(AQA Specification A Tier H full course, specimen paper, q2)

---

2 A computer-controlled hopper is used to fill bottles.

The bottles are placed on the conveyer, which moves them under the hopper where they are filled.

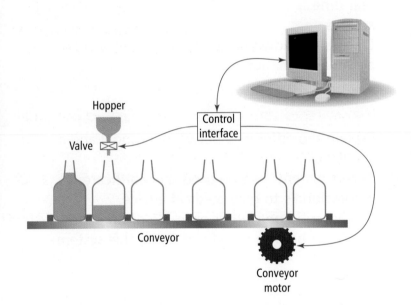

The operator can use these instructions:

MOVE   Moves the conveyer belt one position.

FILL   Opens the valve, fills the bottle, and closes the valve.

START   Indicates the beginning of the program.

END   Indicates the end of the program.

a Write the instructions to fill these **three** bottles.

b (i) Explain why the computer system shown **cannot** be used to fill the bottles **automatically**.

(ii) Describe the additional **hardware** needed so that the computer system could fill the bottles automatically.

(iii) In this context, explain what is meant by **feedback**.

c What **type** of operating method should be used? Choose **one** from the list below.

multi-user
virtual
joystick
real time
serious

d Discuss the advantages and disadvantages of automated manufacturing.

(AQA Specification B Tier H full course, specimen paper, q5)

---

3 a Explain the difference between a model and a simulation.

b Expert systems can be used by healthcare professionals to give medical advice.

(i) Describe **one** other example of an expert system.

(ii) Describe **one** benefit of using this system.

Spreadsheets

The basics

You will probably have used spreadsheets before, so this is a reminder.

The grid into which you put your data is often referred to as a worksheet. The words 'spreadsheet' and 'worksheet' are often used to mean the same thing. The worksheet is the working area of the spreadsheet and is arranged as follows:

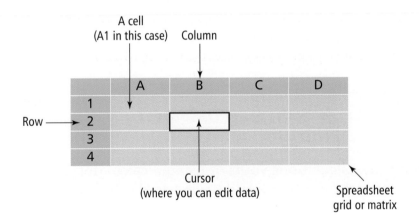

Figure 12.1

The basic structure of a worksheet

Cells

In Figure 12.1, the rectangles are called **cells**. If a particular cell needs to be referred to, we use the column letter followed by the row number. Cell C3 is the cell where column C intersects row 3. In other words, cells are referred to like this:

COLUMN (letter) and then ROW (number)

Hence S4 is a cell reference whereas 3E is not. It does not matter whether large (called upper case) or small (lower case) letters are used. This means that b3 is the same as B3.

cell – an area on a spreadsheet produced by the intersection of a column and a row in which data can be placed.

What can you put into a cell?

You can put the following into a cell:

- words (titles, row headings, column headings, etc.)
- numbers (ordinary numbers, currency, dates, etc.)
- formulae (used to perform calculations with the numbers).

Using spreadsheet software

Excel

Excel is the most popular spreadsheet software package in use. You can buy it either on its own, or as part of the integrated software package Microsoft Office. The version used in this book is Excel XP or Office XP.

Excel is ideal if you want to produce tables (though Microsoft Word can also be used to produce tables). Spreadsheets are especially useful for doing repetitive sums. Excel is also excellent for producing graphs and charts from a set of data.

TIPS when using a spreadsheet for the first time

1. Do not work out any of the calculations yourself using a calculator. The whole point in using a spreadsheet is to avoid having to do this.

2. Use formulae wherever possible. This means that if you change any of the numbers in any of the cells then the spreadsheet will automatically update the rest of the values in the spreadsheet.

3. Make sure that any formulae you enter start with an '=' sign.

4. If the result of a calculation appears like this – ####### – it means that the number is too big to fit in the current column width. You can correct this by widening the column.

5. Plan the layout of the spreadsheet first on paper. It is easier to get it right at the start than to try to change it later.

6. Do not worry too much about the appearance of the spreadsheet. It is more important that it works. You will learn about improving the appearance of a spreadsheet later on.

The menu bar and toolbars

When you load Excel the screen below appears.

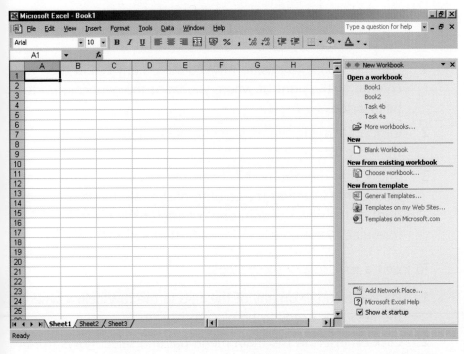

Figure 12.2

The opening screen of Excel

There are many different toolbars and you can choose which are displayed by clicking on <u>V</u>iew and then <u>T</u>oolbars. A tick is shown beside the toolbars to be displayed.

Using Undo

It is easy to issue the wrong command. The spreadsheet may then do something you did not expect. As well as issuing the wrong commands, you can also accidentally press the wrong buttons. Suddenly something unexpected happens or the screen goes blank. What can you do if this happens?

First thing is don't panic!

You can undo the last command in this way:

● In the menu bar click on <u>E</u>dit and then select <u>U</u>ndo from the list.

If more than one command has been issued, then you can do this several times.

Undo is very useful if you delete something by mistake.

Inserting rows and columns

When you are designing a spreadsheet of your own, you may find you need to insert a column between two columns that already contain data. You also might need to insert an extra row.

To insert a column, follow these steps:

1   Use the mouse to position the cursor on any cell in the column to the right of where you want the new column to be inserted.

2   Click on Insert in the main menu bar and select Columns from the list.

3   Check that the column has been inserted in the correct place. Notice that inserting the column pushes all the data to the right of the new column, one column to the right. Any formulae in these cells will be adjusted automatically.

To insert a row, follow these steps:

1   Place the cursor on any of the cells in the row below where the new row needs to be placed.

2   Click on Insert in the main menu bar and select Rows from the list.

3   Check that the row has been inserted in the correct place.

Deleting rows and columns

1   Move the cursor to the row or column that you want to delete.

2   Select Edit from the main menu bar and then choose Delete.

3   The box shown in Figure 12.3 will appear (this box is called a dialogue box).

4   Select either the Entire row or Entire column and click on OK.

If a column is being deleted, those cells in columns to the right of it will move and fill the gap.

If a row is being deleted, those cells in the rows below the one being deleted will move up to fill the gap.

Figure 12.3

The Delete dialogue box

Mathematical operators

You will not find the divide sign ÷ or the multiplication sign × on the computer keyboard. Instead * is used for multiply and / is used for divide. Mathematical operators are summarised in the table shown opposite.

Operator	Use
+	Addition
−	Subtraction
*	Multiplication
/	Division
%	Percentage

Formulae

If you type in a formula to add two cells together like this: C3 + C4 then the spreadsheet will just enter 'C3 + C4' in the cell where the cursor is. 'C3 + C4' will therefore be treated as text. In order to distinguish between text and formulae a '=' symbol needs to be typed in first.

Here are some calculations and what they do. Notice that you can use upper or lower case letters (i.e. capital or small letters).

=C3+C4 (adds the numbers in cells C3 and C4 together)

=A1*B4 (multiplies the numbers in cells A1 and B4 together)

=3*G4 (multiplies cell G4 by 3)

=sum(b3:b10) (adds up all the cells from b1 to b10 inclusive)

=C4/D1 (divides the number in cell C4 by the number in cell D1)

=30/100*A2 (finds 30% of cell A2)

Producing graphs and charts

Activity 1

In this activity you will learn how to:

- select data for charting
- select a chart type
- give the chart a title
- put the chart with the data
- size a chart.

Charts and graphs make it easier to understand numerical information. Take the following information, for example. The table shows the temperatures and rainfall for a British seaside resort for the first eight months of 2001.

continued over page

Month	Mean temperature (°C)	Mean rainfall (inches)
January	5.8	3.3
February	7.0	2.1
March	7.3	3.0
April	9.3	2.2
May	13.7	0.4
June	16.0	0.6
July	17.4	0.6
August	17.6	0.5

To see if there are patterns or trends in this data, you can draw a line graph using a spreadsheet package.

1 Type the data accurately into the worksheet like this:

	A	B	C
	Month	Mean Temperature (°C)	Mean Rainfall (inches)
1			
2	January	5.8	3.3
3	February	7	2.1
4	March	7.3	3
5	April	9.3	2.2
6	May	13.7	0.4
7	June	16	0.6
8	July	17.4	0.6
9	Aug	17.6	0.5

2 Highlight the area where all the cells contain data.

3 Click on Insert and then Chart….

This menu pops up:

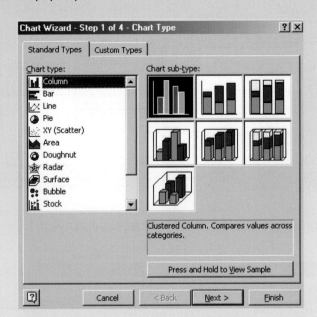

4 Choose Line as the chart type.

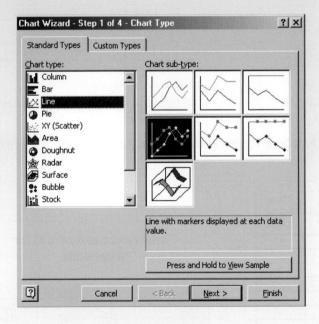

5 Click on Next>. (For each step of the Chart Wizard just click on Next>.)

6 For Step 3 of the Chart Wizard type in the text **Temperature and rainfall for Weymouth** in the Chart title box.

Notice that the title is displayed. You can also add X- and Y-axis titles, but none are needed here.

continued over page

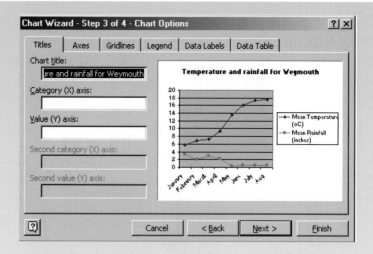

7 Click on Next> and the following screen is displayed:

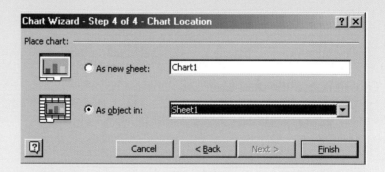

You can place the chart with the data in the worksheet. Make sure that As object in: is selected and then click on Finish.

8 The chart now appears next to the data in the worksheet like this:

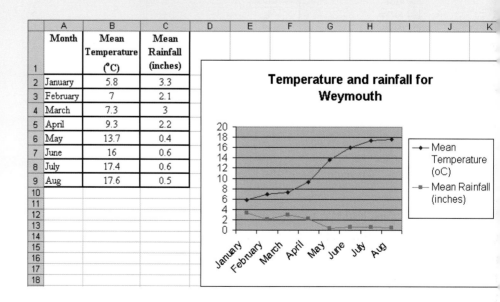

The size of the chart can be altered by clicking on the corners to get the handles. By dragging the handles you can alter the size.

Using graphs like this one you can see trends and make forecasts. For example, you can see easily that the temperature increases from January to August. This increase is greater in May than in the other months. The rainfall in the months January, February, March and April is fairly constant. There is then quite a decrease in May, after which it is steady.

It is much easier to make comments like this by looking at the graph rather than the numerical data in the table.

Cut and paste

To cut cells, select them (the selected cells will be highlighted) then click on Edit and then Cut. The cells will be placed in a temporary storage (called the clipboard) by the computer. You can now move the cursor to another part of your worksheet where you want the cell or cells to be moved to and then click on Edit and then Paste. Using this method, you can move cells to a different position in the same worksheet or to a different worksheet.

If the worksheet contains cells with formulae that refer to the cells you are moving, then do not worry because the formulae will be adjusted to take into account the moved cells' new positions.

Copy and paste

When you cut cells, they are taken out of the worksheet. Suppose instead you wanted to use the same cells in a different worksheet without having to type them in. You can use Copy. Copy is similar to cut, except that a **copy** of the cells is put onto the clipboard. The spreadsheet from which the cells are copied remains unaltered. Once copied, the cells can be pasted anywhere in the same worksheet, or a different one.

Printing formulae

When you print out a worksheet, it will always print out the results of any formulae along with any text or numbers. In order to check the spreadsheet, it is useful sometimes to be able to see these formulae so that they can be checked. Here is a simple activity to show how to display the formulae on the screen and then print them out.

Printing a selected area of a spreadsheet

Activity 2

In this activity you will learn how to:

- use the AutoSum button
- copy formulae
- show the formulae in a worksheet.

1 Set up a worksheet and enter the following data:

	A	B	C	D	E	F
1	Item	June	July	August	September	Total
2	Swimwear	600	150	142	112	
3	Ski-Wear	50	35	60	98	
4	Shorts	85	87	82	50	
5	Golf Clubs	104	69	75	82	
6	Football	20	32	146	292	
7	T-Racquets	85	90	50	80	
8	Totals					
9						

2 Total column B and put the result in cell B8. The quick way to do this is to press the AutoSum button on the toolbar with the cursor on cell B8. The AutoSum button can be found on the standard toolbar, and it looks like this: Σ

If the AutoSum button is not there, then you will need to display the standard toolbar. To do this click on <u>V</u>iew and then <u>T</u>oolbars, then select the standard toolbar.

Be careful how you use AutoSum. Check that the cell range indicated by the dotted rectangle is correct.

3 Total row 2 and put the result in cell F2. Again this can be done by positioning the cursor on cell F2 and then pressing the AutoSum button.

4 Copy the formula in cell F2 down the column to cell F7. You do this by moving the cursor to cell F2 containing the formula. Now click on the bottom right-hand corner of the cell and you should get a black cross shape. Hold the left mouse button down and move the mouse down the column until you reach cell F7. You will see a dotted rectangle around the area where the copied formula is to be inserted.

Now take your finger off the button and all the results of the calculation will appear. This is called **relative copying** because the formula is changed slightly to take account of the altered positions of the two numbers which are to be added together.

Copy the formula in cell B8 across the row to cell F8.

Your worksheet will now look like this:

Key Jargon

relative copying – copying a formula so that the formula changes to take account of its new position.

	A	B	C	D	E	F
1	Item	June	July	August	September	Total
2	Swimwear	600	150	142	112	1004
3	Ski-Wear	50	35	60	98	243
4	Shorts	85	87	82	50	304
5	Golf Clubs	104	69	75	82	330
6	Football	20	32	146	292	490
7	T-Racquets	85	90	50	80	305
8	Totals	944	463	555	714	2676

Now you are going to insert the formulae wherever there are calculations.

Select the Tools menu and then click on Options.

The following screen will appear:

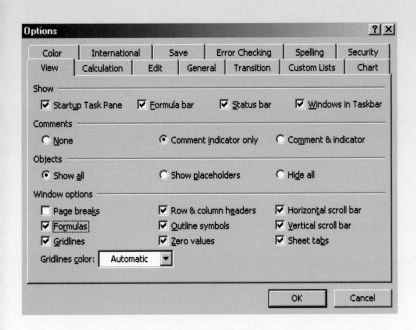

In the bottom part of this screen you will see a box marked Formulas. Click on this box and a tick will appear indicating that the formulae will be displayed. The following screen containing the formulae now appears:

continued over page

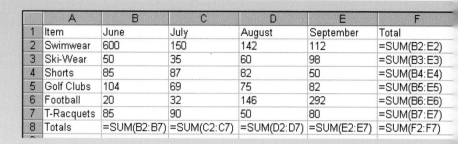

	A	B	C	D	E	F
1	Item	June	July	August	September	Total
2	Swimwear	600	150	142	112	=SUM(B2:E2)
3	Ski-Wear	50	35	60	98	=SUM(B3:E3)
4	Shorts	85	87	82	50	=SUM(B4:E4)
5	Golf Clubs	104	69	75	82	=SUM(B5:E5)
6	Football	20	32	146	292	=SUM(B6:E6)
7	T-Racquets	85	90	50	80	=SUM(B7:E7)
8	Totals	=SUM(B2:B7)	=SUM(C2:C7)	=SUM(D2:D7)	=SUM(E2:E7)	=SUM(F2:F7)

8 When you try to display the formulae, they often require more space than the current column width, so you may need to widen some of the columns. Do this and save, then print a copy of the worksheet containing the formulae on a single sheet. To do this click on File and then Page Setup... and make sure that the settings are the same as those shown on the following screen:

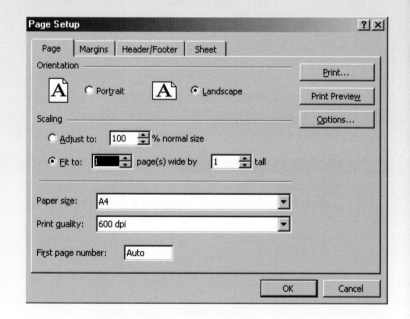

Notice that 'Landscape' has been selected and also 'Fit to 1 page'. Click on OK.

Producing a scattergraph

In this activity you will learn how to:

- produce a scattergraph
- give a title to the chart
- label axes
- print in landscape.

Jenny Ray is a mobile hairdresser. She advertises in the local paper. She spends different amounts on advertising and she records the number of appointments booked as a result of the different adverts. The details are shown in this table:

Amount spent on advertising	Number of appointments booked from adverts
£30	34
£65	28
£105	33
£145	39
£235	49
£250	54
£310	120

Jennie thinks that the more she spends on advertising, the more bookings she will get. It is hard to see if this is true from the numbers in the table. To see if there is a pattern, she decides to use the computer to draw a scattergraph.

1 First, enter the data into the worksheet like this:

	A	B
1	Amount spent on advertising	Number of appointments booked from adverts
2	£30	34
3	£65	28
4	£105	33
5	£145	39
6	£235	49
7	£250	54
8	£310	120

continued over page

2 Select the data by clicking and dragging the mouse from cells A1 to B8. The selected area will be shaded like this.

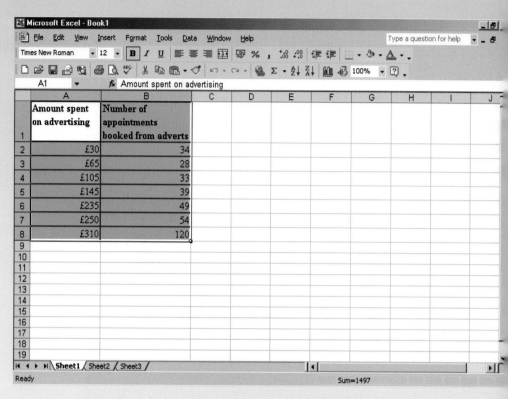

3 Click on the chart icon in the standard toolbar (it is the button with the picture of a bar graph on it).

4 Step 1 of the Chart Wizard appears. Select the Chart type XY (Scatter) and the Chart sub-type as shown here:

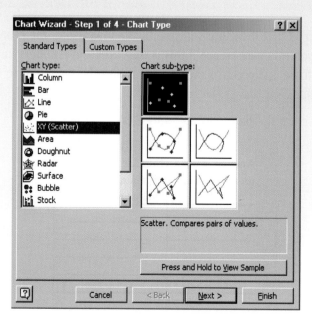

Click on <u>N</u>ext >. Step 2 of the Chart Wizard appears. Check that Series in Columns is selected. The screen should be the same as this one:

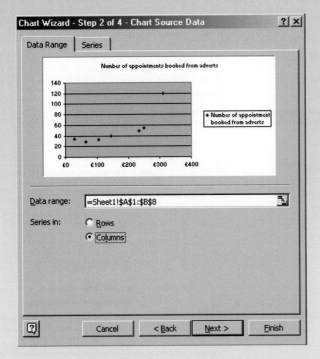

6 Click on <u>N</u>ext>. Step 3 of the Chart Wizard is shown.

In the Chart <u>t</u>itle box enter:

Graph to see any correlation between the amount spent on advertising and the appointments booked.

In the 'Va<u>l</u>ue (X) axis' box type in **Amount spent on advertising.**

In the 'Va<u>l</u>ue (Y) axis' box type in **Appointments booked.**

The screen in Step 3 of the Chart Wizard should now look like this:

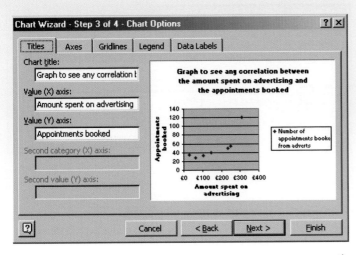

continued over page

7 In Step 3 of the Chart Wizard click on the tab for Legend. The screen will change.

Here you can position the legend (this is the box next to the graph that explains the data). In this case we will remove the legend. To do this, make sure that the box Show legend is left blank. The legend now disappears.

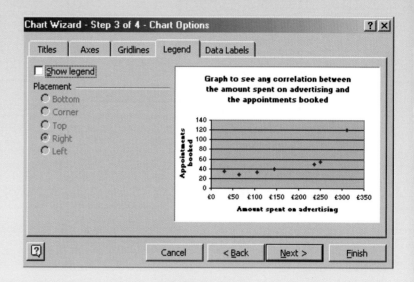

8 Click on Next> to go onto the next step of the Chart Wizard. Step 4 asks you if you want the chart on the same sheet as the data, or to put it into its own worksheet. Click on 'As new sheet' to put it into its own worksheet.

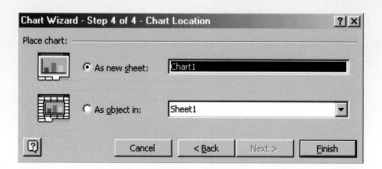

9 Click on Finish. The chart is now displayed.

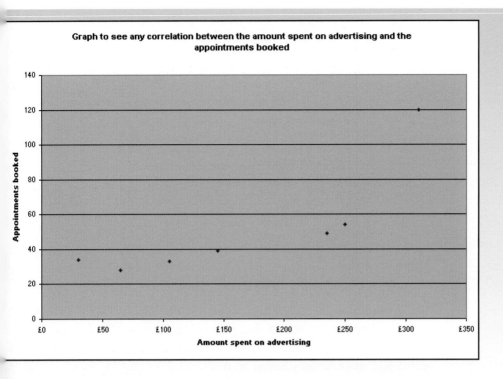

Using simple functions

In this activity you will learn how to:

- set numbers to a certain number of decimal places
- use a function to calculate averages
- test each mark using an IF function and print a message on who did best, boys or girls.

Here are some examination results. They show the percentage of girls and the percentage of boys who got A grades in various subjects. We are going to find out from this data whether the boys or the girls did best.

1 Type in this data exactly as it is shown here. Check to make sure your data is typed in accurately. You will need to widen column A to fit in the subject names. Make the text bold where it is shown in bold below. To do this, highlight the text and then click on the bold button on the toolbar.

	A	B	C
1	**Advanced Level exam results 2001**		
2	Percentage pass rate with 'A' grades		
3			
4	**Subject**	**Boys**	**Girls**
5	Art and design	23.5	28.4
6	Biology	16.8	20
7	Business Studies	10	11.3
8	Chemistry	25.6	27.7
9	Computing	8.9	7.5
10	Economics	22.7	22.6
11	English	17.3	16.2
12	French	26.4	23.9
13	Geography	15.8	23
14	German	32.9	26.8
15	History	17.9	19.1
16	Mathematics	28.9	30
17	Physics	24.1	27.4
18	Psychology	8.1	13.7

2   Notice that the numbers do not line up neatly. This is because whole numbers do not have a decimal point after them. For example, if you enter 30.0, just 30 appears. You can set the numbers to one decimal place, then 30 appears as 30.0.

Highlight all the numbers.

Click on F<u>o</u>rmat and then C<u>e</u>lls....

This screen appears:

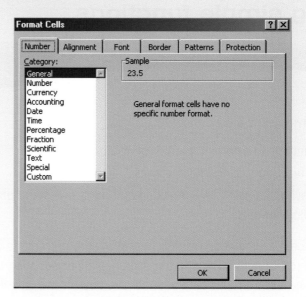

3   Set the <u>C</u>ategory to Number.

Then click on the down arrow of the Decimal places box so that it is set to 1.

One decimal place will now be shown for all the numbers you have selected.

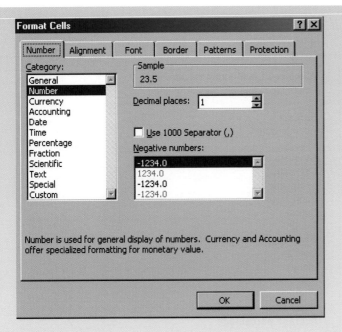

4 Click on the OK button.

Your worksheet will look like this:

	A	B	C
1	**Advanced Level exam results 2001**		
2	Percentage pass rate with 'A' grades		
3			
4	**Subject**	**Boys**	**Girls**
5	Art and design	23.5	28.4
6	Biology	16.8	20.0
7	Business Studies	10.0	11.3
8	Chemistry	25.6	27.7
9	Computing	8.9	7.5
10	Economics	22.7	22.6
11	English	17.3	16.2
12	French	26.4	23.9
13	Geography	15.8	23.0
14	German	32.9	26.8
15	History	17.9	19.1
16	Mathematics	28.9	30.0
17	Physics	24.1	27.4
18	Psychology	8.1	13.7

5 We will now find the average (or mean) mark for the boys and the girls.

Put the following into cell A19: **Average percentage**.

To give the average of all the numbers in the cells from A5 to A18 and put the answer into cell B19, enter into cell B19 the formula **=AVERAGE(B5:B18)**.

Enter a similar formula into cell C19. This time it is **=AVERAGE(C5:C18)**.

continued over page

Your worksheet will now look like this:

	A	B	C	D
1	**Advanced Level exam results 2001**			
2	Percentage pass rate with 'A' grades			
3				
4	**Subject**	**Boys**	**Girls**	
5	Art and design	23.5	28.4	
6	Biology	16.8	20.0	
7	Business Studies	10.0	11.3	
8	Chemistry	25.6	27.7	
9	Computing	8.9	7.5	
10	Economics	22.7	22.6	
11	English	17.3	16.2	
12	French	26.4	23.9	
13	Geography	15.8	23.0	
14	German	32.9	26.8	
15	History	17.9	19.1	
16	Mathematics	28.9	30.0	
17	Physics	24.1	27.4	
18	Psychology	8.1	13.7	
19	**Average percentage**	15.8	21.3	
20				

You can now see that the girls do better than the boys.

6 Now type the text **Who did best at this subject?** into cell D4.

Now type the formula **=IF(B5>C5,"Boys","Girls")** into cell D5.

This basically says that if the number in cell B5 (i.e. the boy's mark) is greater than the number in cell C5 (i.e. the girl's mark), then the text **'Boys'** will be placed in cell D5. If not, the text **'Girls'** will be displayed in cell D5.

Your screen should now look like this:

SUM	▾ ✕ ✔ *fx* =IF(B5>C5,"Boys","Girls")			
	A	B	C	D
1	**Advanced Level exam results 2001**			
2	Percentage pass rate with 'A' grades			
3				
4	**Subject**	**Boys**	**Girls**	**Who did best at this subject?**
5	Art and design	23.5	28.4	=IF(B5>C5,"Boys","Girls")
6	Biology	16.8	20.0	
7	Business Studies	10.0	11.3	
8	Chemistry	25.6	27.7	
9	Computing	8.9	7.5	
10	Economics	22.7	22.6	
11	English	17.3	16.2	
12	French	26.4	23.9	
13	Geography	15.8	23.0	
14	German	32.9	26.8	
15	History	17.9	19.1	
16	Mathematics	28.9	30.0	
17	Physics	24.1	27.4	
18	Psychology	8.1	13.7	
19	**Average percentage**	15.8	21.3	

Now copy the formula down the column. This saves having to type it in for each row and altering it slightly each time. You do this by moving the cursor to the cell containing the formula. Now click the bottom right-hand corner of the cell and you should get a black cross shape. Hold the left mouse button down and move the mouse down the column until you reach cell D18. You will see a dotted rectangle around the area where the formula is copied. Now take your finger off the button and the results will be inserted. This is called relative copying because the formulae are changed to take account of the altered positions of the marks for each subject.

The completed worksheet now looks like this:

	A	B	C	D
1	Advanced Level exam results 2001			
2	Percentage pass rate with 'A' grades			
3				
4	Subject	Boys	Girls	Who did best at this subject?
5	Art and design	23.5	28.4	Girls
6	Biology	16.8	20.0	Girls
7	Business Studies	10.0	11.3	Girls
8	Chemistry	25.6	27.7	Girls
9	Computing	8.9	7.5	Boys
10	Economics	22.7	22.6	Boys
11	English	17.3	16.2	Boys
12	French	26.4	23.9	Boys
13	Geography	15.8	23.0	Girls
14	German	32.9	26.8	Boys
15	History	17.9	19.1	Girls
16	Mathematics	28.9	30.0	Girls
17	Physics	24.1	27.4	Girls
18	Psychology	8.1	13.7	Girls
19	Average percentage	15.8	21.3	

In the examination results spreadsheet above, you used a simple function called AVERAGE. You need not have used this function because most people know the formula for working out the average of a set of numbers. But functions save us time, and save us having to think, as the formula is already set up. Functions are therefore useful.

A function must start with an equals sign, =, and it must have the range of cells to which it applies in brackets after it.

For example, to find the average of the numbers in a range of cells from A3 to A10 you would use:

=AVERAGE(A3:A10)

Here are some other functions:

- **Maximum:** =MAX(D3:J3) displays the largest number in all the cells from D3 to J3 inclusive.
- **Minimum:** =MIN(D3:J3) displays the smallest number in all the cells from D3 to J3 inclusive.
- **Mode:** =MODE(A3:A15) displays the mode (i.e. the most frequent number) of the cells from A3 to A15 inclusive.
- **Median:** =MEDIAN(B2:W2) displays the median of the cells from cells B2 to W2 inclusive.
- **Sum:** =SUM(E3:P3) displays the total of all the cells from cells E3 to P3 inclusive.

There are many other functions you can use. For a list of them, use the on-line help facility.

Using absolute and relative cell references

There are two ways in which you can make a reference to another cell. They are not the same, and it is important to know the difference if you want to copy or move cells.

An **absolute reference** always refers to a particular cell. It therefore always refers to the same cell.

A **relative reference** refers to a cell that is a certain number of rows and columns away. When a cell containing a relative reference is copied or moved to a new position, all the cells referred to will also change so that it remains the same number of columns and rows away from them, i.e. in the same relative position.

To understand the difference, here are two examples:

The first example shows relative referencing, with cell B4 containing a relative reference to cell A1. This reference tells the spreadsheet that the cell to which it refers is three cells up and one cell to the left of cell B4. If cell B4 is copied to another position, say E5, then the reference will still be to three cells up and one to the left, so the reference will now be to cell D2.

With absolute cell referencing, if cell B4 contains a reference to cell A1, then if the contents of B4 are copied to a new position, the reference will not be adjusted and it will still refer to cell A1.

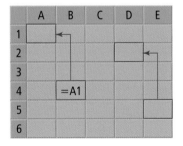

Figure 12.4

Example 1: relative cell referencing in a spreadsheet

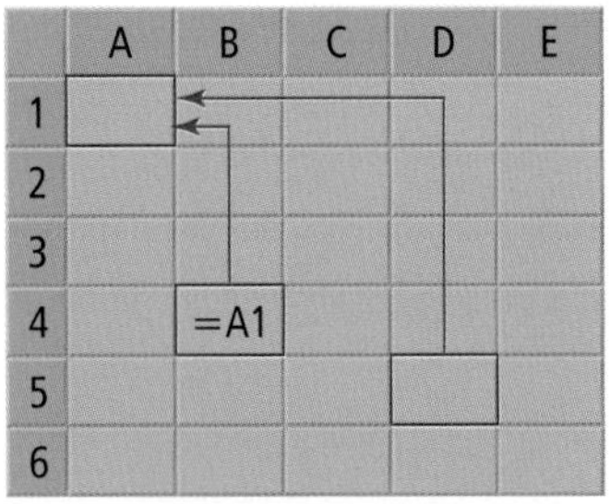

Figure 12.5

Example 2: absolute cell referencing in a spreadsheet

Usually you will want to use relative cell references, and the spreadsheet will assume that all cell references are relative unless you specify otherwise.

Sometimes you may want to refer to the same cell even when the formula referring to the cell is copied to a new position. In this case you must make sure the formula contains an absolute cell reference. To do this, a dollar sign is placed in front of the column and row number.

Cell B6 is a relative cell reference. To change it to an absolute cell reference we would add the dollar signs, like this: B6.

Formatting cells to match data types

There are many different types of data and some of these are shown in the following table:

Type of data	Example of data
Date	12/12/02
Integer number (a whole number)	34
Decimal number	3.14
Percentage	4%
Currency	£3.45
Text	John Smith

If the general number format is used (which it will be, unless you tell Excel otherwise) the numbers will be shown with up to eleven digits (including all the numbers up to and after the decimal point). A cell that has a formula typed in will show the results of the formula rather than the formula itself.

Cells need to be able to hold the data you want to put into them. To do this, you have to tell the cell what type of data you will put in it. In other words you have to **format** it.

A spreadsheet will interpret the data you put into a cell. Although each cell is set to the general number format, it can change automatically depending on the data you type in. If you type in a pound sign followed by a number, the spreadsheet will assume that you are dealing with currency and will format the cell to 'currency' automatically. It will only show the currency to two decimal places, so if you typed in £1.349, '£1.35' would be shown.

For large numbers, you often use commas to make them easier to read (e.g. 3,000,000). As soon as such a number is entered (i.e. with commas), the spreadsheet will apply the number format with the thousands separator and use a maximum of two decimal places.

If a number is entered ending in a % sign (e.g. 4%), then the spreadsheet will set the cell automatically to the percent format with two decimal places.

When does 3 + 3 = 7?

Three plus three can equal seven if you have failed to consider the cell formats.

Suppose we have 3.51 in cell A1 and 2.86 in cell B1 and both cells have been set to integers. If the formula =A1+B1 to add these two cells together is placed in cell C1, and this cell is set to integer, then the result of the calculation will be seven. This is because 3.51 had been set to 4 and 2.86 to 3. In fact, 3.51 + 2.86 = 6.37, which rounded down equals 6.

You can see that you have to be careful with cell formats. Make sure that you match the cell format to the number of decimal places of the numbers being entered. In this example, all the cells should have been set to two decimal places.

Cell presentation formats

Data can be presented in cells in various ways.

Aligning cells

When you enter data into a cell, the spreadsheet automatically aligns (i.e. positions) the cells according to the following rules:

- numbers are aligned to the right
- text is aligned to the left.

Do not put any spaces in front of numbers in order to align them as this will make it impossible for the spreadsheet to use the numbers in calculations.

If you want to align the data differently, you can use the special buttons for alignment on the formatting toolbar. Using this method, you can align them to the left, right or centre.

Figure 12.6

The Excel formatting toolbar

Using cell presentation formats

You can pre-set cells to a certain presentation format using the Format Cells screen.

Setting up a database in Excel

In this activity you will learn how to:

■ set up data so that the spreadsheet package can recognise it as a database

■ enter data into a database

■ sort data into order

■ print a selected area of a database.

You have been asked to set up a database for a job agency. The database will contain information on all the jobs held by the agency.

1 Enter the data into the database exactly as shown below. The first row contains the field names and subsequent rows contain the job records.

Important: Do not leave any blank rows between the data. When setting up a database in Excel, always make sure that the field names are in neighbouring cells along the first row.

	A	B	C	D	E	F
1	Job Number	Job Type	Area	Employer	Pay	
2	1010	Systems Analyst	London	Am Bank	£35,000	
3	1023	Programmer	Blackburn	Minstral Finance	£28,000	
4	1012	Accountant	Liverpool	Mutual Insurance	£42,000	
5	1034	Sales Clerk	Liverpool	Mutual Insurance	£18,000	
6	1011	Sales Manager	Birmingham	DC Switches Ltd	£28,000	
7	1045	Sales Manager	Lancaster	Air Products Ltd	£31,500	
8	1024	Electrical Engineer	Bristol	Manners Ltd	£27,800	
9	1021	Network Manager	Warrington	D&Q Ltd	£19,800	
10	1000	Trainee Programmer	Cardiff	PCSoft	£7,500	
11	1002	Systems Analyst	Liverpool	AmSoft	£24,000	
12	1013	Junior Accountant	Liverpool	AmSoft	£17,000	
13	1018	Accountant	Manchester	DC Switches Ltd	£45,000	
14	1035	Sales Clerk	Preston	FR Venn & Co	£16,900	
15	1078	Shipping Clerk	London	P&R	£21,800	
16	1080	Trainee Programmer	London	Arc Systems	£19,300	
17	1079	Programmer	London	Arc Systems	£35,600	
18						

continued over page

2 You need to sort the database into order according to salary, with the highest paid jobs first. To do this, move the cursor to cell E2 (where the first salary figure is).

Click on <u>D</u>ata and then on <u>S</u>ort... . The following screen appears:

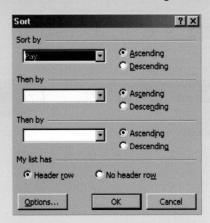

3 Select <u>D</u>escending and then click on the OK button. The pay will now be sorted with the highest pay first.

	A	B	C	D	E
1	**Job Number**	**Job Type**	**Area**	**Employer**	**Pay**
2	1018	Accountant	Manchester	DC Switches Ltd	£45,000
3	1012	Accountant	Liverpool	Mutual Insurance	£42,000
4	1079	Programmer	London	Arc Systems	£35,600
5	1010	Systems Analyst	London	Am Bank	£35,000
6	1045	Sales Manager	Lancaster	Air Products Ltd	£31,500
7	1023	Programmer	Blackburn	Minstral Finance	£28,000
8	1011	Sales Manager	Birmingham	DC Switches Ltd	£28,000
9	1024	Electrical Engineer	Bristol	Manners Ltd	£27,800
10	1002	Systems Analyst	Liverpool	AmSoft	£24,000
11	1078	Shipping Clerk	London	P&R	£21,800
12	1021	Network Manager	Warrington	D&Q Ltd	£19,800
13	1080	Trainee Programmer	London	Arc Systems	£19,300
14	1034	Sales Clerk	Liverpool	Mutual Insurance	£18,000
15	1013	Junior Accountant	Liverpool	AmSoft	£17,000
16	1035	Sales Clerk	Preston	FR Venn & Co	£16,900
17	1000	Trainee Programmer	Cardiff	PCSoft	£7,500

4 A client comes into the job agency and only wants jobs that pay a minimum of £20,000. She would like a list of these jobs. We therefore need to select only part of this spreadsheet for printing. To do this click on <u>V</u>iew. Now click on <u>P</u>age Break Preview.

5 This box appears, explaining what you do. Click on the OK button.

6 The cross can now be used to mark out the area on the spreadsheet that you want to print. Highlight the area from cells A1 to E11. Your spreadsheet will look like this:

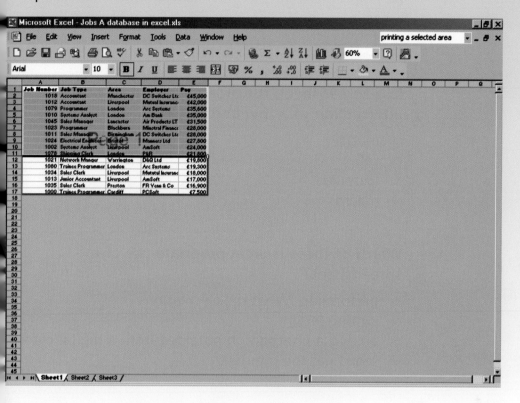

Click on the printer button 🖨 to print the selected area.

Testing a spreadsheet

When you produce your own spreadsheet, it should be tested thoroughly before assuming any of the values taken from the spreadsheet are correct. There are a number of ways a spreadsheet can be tested:

- You can work out the results manually and compare them with the values calculated from the spreadsheet.

- You can print out all the formulae and use this to check that they all refer to the correct cells.

- You can show the spreadsheet to a user for checking and evaluation: they may spot things you have missed.

1 Which one of these is not a mathematical operator?

a *
b /
c %
d $

2 In a spreadsheet, the area produced by the intersection of a row and a column is called a:

a matrix
b cell
c formula
d macro.

3 Which of these is an appropriate use of a spreadsheet?

a performing 'What if?' calculations
b writing letters
c editing a photograph obtained from a digital camera
d searching the Internet

4 Which one of these is not a cell reference?

a D3
b A4
c 2A
d AA1

5 Which one of the following is not a mathematical operator used in spreadsheets?

a /
b *
c @
d +

6 Which one of the following cannot be put into a spreadsheet cell?

a formula
b number

c   words

d   database

7 **Which one of the following is not a cell format?**

a   centre

b   bold

c   underline

d   save

8 **Which one of the following is not an advantage of using a spreadsheet rather than pen and paper?**

a   You can do 'What if?' investigations.

b   You can recalculate if costs change.

c   You can save and use again.

d   You need to understand how to use the software.

9 **In the following worksheet, cell B8 is most likely to contain a:**

a   formula

b   number

c   word

d   graphic.

	A	B	C	D	E	F	G	H	I
1									
2	Car	46							
3	Rent	33							
4	Electricity	12							
5	Gas	9							
6	Clothes	28							
7	Food	32							
8	Total	160							

Microsoft Excel - Book1

File Edit View Insert Format Tools Data Window Help   Type a question for help

Arial   10   B I U

10 **One way of testing a spreadsheet is:**

a   to use a spellchecker

b   to use a grammar checker

c   to work out the results manually and compare them with the results from the spreadsheet

d   to use a validation check.

1 Here are some statements concerning the reasons for putting formulae into spreadsheets.

Write down those reasons that are correct.

Reasons
- If a cell changes, then all those cells that depend on the cell will change.
- A more accurate answer is produced than with a calculator.
- It improves the appearance of the spreadsheet.
- The formulae in the spreadsheet need to be kept secret.

2 Explain the meaning of the following mathematical operators that are used in spreadsheets:

a /
b +
c *
d –

3 The diagram below shows a simple spreadsheet that a student uses to help budget her money.

	A	B	C
1			
2	Rent	£32.50	
3	Food	£13.00	
4	Electricity	£2.50	
5	Phone	£1.50	
6	Gas	£4.00	
7	Entertainment	£15.00	
8	Total		
9			

a Write down the contents of cell A4.
b Write down the contents of cell B7.
c Write down those formulae that would correctly work out the total of her expenditure when placed in cell B8.

Formulae
- +B1+B2+B3+B4+B5+B6+B7
- +A2+A3+A4+A5+A6+A7
- =sum(B2:B7)
- =sum(A2:A7)
- +B2+B3+B4+B5+B6+B7

4 A plumber is using his computer to work out the cost of a new bathroom.

	A	B	C
1	**Activity**	**Materials**	**Labour**
2	Removal of old suite	£45.00	£50.00
3	Removal of old tiles	£10.00	£45.00
4	Installation of bath	£120.00	£64.00
5	Installation of washbasin	£85.00	£42.00
6	Installation of shower tray and cubicle	£286.00	£125.00
7	Installation of electric shower	£145.00	£85.00
8	Tiling	£195.00	£230.00
9	Total	£886.00	£641.00
10	Total Labour and Materials	£1,527.00	
11	VAT at 17.5%	£267.23	
12	Total including VAT	£1,794.23	

a What software is the plumber using to work out the costs?

b Three types of data that can be entered into a cell include:

- numeric
- formula
- text.

(i) Which one of the three types of data is in cell A3?

(ii) Which one of the three types of data is in cell B8?

(iii) Which one of the three types of data is in cell A11?

c Write down the formula that would be entered into cell B9.

d Write down the cell references of **three** cells other than B9 that contain a formula.

e Give **one** advantage to the plumber of using the software.

f Give **one** disadvantage to the plumber of using the software.

F Questions

1 A builder uses a computer to work out the cost of building a conservatory.

	A	B	C
1	**Activity**	**Materials**	**Labour**
2	Excavations	£50.00	£150.00
3	Concrete base	£500.00	£50.00
4	Walls	£1,500.00	£200.00
5	Roof	£1,000.00	£150.00
6	Interior finish	£250.00	£200.00
7	Patio	£550.00	£150.00
8	Totals	£3,850.00	£900.00
9	Total labour and materials	£4,750.00	
10	VAT at 17.5%	£831.25	
11	Total including VAT	£5,581.25	

a What type of software should be used? Choose **one** from the list below.

- ▨ wordprocessor
- ▨ videoconferencing
- ▨ desktop publishing
- ▨ data logging
- ▨ spreadsheet

b Using a word from the list, copy and complete the sentence:

- ▨ numeric
- ▨ formula
- ▨ furniture
- ▨ text
- ▨ a palette

The data in cell A3 is _____.

c (i) Write down the formula that would be in cell B8.
  (ii) Identify **four** other cells that would have this formula in them.

d (i) Write down **two** advantages to the builder in using the software. Choose from the list below.

- If the costs are changed, VAT and the totals are automatically recalculated.
- Labour costs are kept to a minimum.
- VAT is not charged when a conservatory is built.
- The calculations can be sent to the customer.
- The builder knows that the calculations are accurate.

(ii) Write down **two** disadvantages to the builder in using the software.

- The builder can rely on the office staff to prepare the estimates.
- The builder must have a concrete mixer and ladders.
- The builder must know how to use the software or hire someone who does.
- The builder must have the use of a computer.
- The builder must know how to use a database.

e   The software is used to generate this graph.

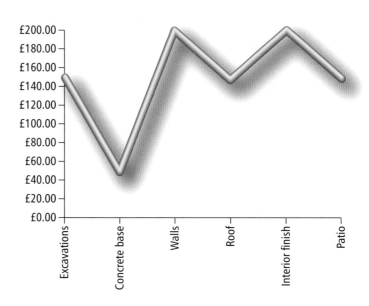

Write down **three** ways the graph could be improved so that it is more accurate and easier to understand. Choose from the list below.

- The axes could be given the labels 'Activities' and 'Cost'.
- The graph could be given the title 'Labour Costs for Building a Conservatory'.

- The graph could be in colour.
- The graph could be a bar graph.
- A picture of the builder could be shown next to the graph.
- The graph could be given the title 'Materials Costs for Building a Conservatory'.

f The builder wants to buy a new desktop computer to run the software. The builder looks in magazines for a suitable computer.

Copy and complete these sentences:

(i) The computer will cost around £_____.

(ii) The computer's processor will run at a speed of around _____ MHz.

(AQA Specification B Tier F full course, specimen paper, q2)

2 A teacher uses a spreadsheet to investigate the cost of a leaving party for Year 11 students. The spreadsheet is shown below.

	A	B	C	D
1	Party Planner			
2	Date of Party	29 June 2000		
3	Number of Students	125		
4				
5	Item		Cost	
6	Entertainment		£150.00	
7	Food (per person)	£3.25	£406.25	
8	Room		£100.00	
9				
10		Total Cost	£656.25	
11				
12				
13	Total Cost per Student	£5.25		
14				

a Give **two** advantages of using a spreadsheet to work out the cost of the party, compared to working out the cost by hand.

b (i) The content of which cell would have to be changed if the cost of the room were increased?

(ii) The contents of which **two** cells would change automatically as a result?

c (i) What formula must be in cell C7 to work out the total cost of food for the party?

(ii) What formula must be in cell C10 to work out the total cost of the party?

d Give **four** cell formats that have been used in this spreadsheet.

(NEAB Tier F, June 2000, p2, q4)

H Questions

1 Joe Robinson is a plumber who works for himself from home. He has recently bought a spreadsheet package to help him work out how much each customer's bill should be. If people ask him to work after 6 p.m. he has an additional call out charge of £15. The unfinished spreadsheet given below was Joe's attempt to calculate one day's bills.

	A	B	C	D	E	F	G
1	Name of customer	Charge	Number of	Cost of	Cost of	Call out charge	Total bill
2		Per hour	Hours worked	Labour	Materials	(after 6pm)	for each
3							customer
4							
5							
6		£12.00	3	£36.00	£4.00	£0.00	
7	Mr Sing	£12.00	2	£24.00	£21.00	£0.00	
8	Ms Brown	£12.00	4	£48.00	£1.00	£0.00	
9	Mrs Yau	£12.00	1	£12.00	£45.00	£15.00	
10	Mr Penrose	£12.00	2	£24.00	£12.00	£15.00	
11							
12						Grand total	for the day

a Joe has decided to change his charge per hour from £12 to £13. Describe how Joe would make this change to the spreadsheet for all his customers.

b State the formula which would be contained in the following cells:

(i) G6

(ii) G12.

c When Joe bought the spreadsheet package he also received some documentation. Choose **three** sections from the list below that should be in this documentation.

- a tutorial guide to help use the spreadsheet
- a price list of parts from suppliers
- a list of customers
- details of how to install the spreadsheet
- how much to charge his customers
- a section explaining how to use formulae

d Give **three** advantages to Joe of using the spreadsheet instead of using a calculator and paper.

(AQA Specification A Tier F short course, specimen paper, q9)

13 Wordprocessing

Software for presenting information is the type of software most people are familiar with. Wordprocessing, desktop publishing and presentation software are all used for presenting information. These types of software offer similar features and it is sometimes difficult to decide which one to choose. An important factor is how easy the software is to use, and many people will choose to use the one they are most familiar with.

If you are using Microsoft Office, you will be using the following:

- wordprocessing: Microsoft Word
- desktop publishing: Microsoft Publisher
- presentation: Microsoft PowerPoint.

By the time you do your GCSE course, most of you will be quite familiar with using wordprocessing software. Rather than starting from the basics, this book will therefore assume some previous knowledge and will concentrate on the less widely used features.

Using wordprocessing software

Microsoft Word

Entering text

Usually, text is entered via the keyboard by typing it in. But this is not the only way of entering text. If there is a lot of text to enter, perhaps from a book or newspaper, then you can scan it in and use optical character recognition software (which usually comes free when you buy a scanner) to put the text into the application you are using.

If there is some text on a web page or website that you want to enter and edit, then you can do this easily as follows. Highlight the text (you can include the diagrams as well if you like) and then click on Edit and then Copy. This will put the text plus any pictures onto the clipboard. You can then load your wordprocessing software, go to a new document or one created already and position the cursor where you want the text to be inserted. Then click on Edit and then Paste. The text will now be inserted. You can now edit (i.e. alter) the text in some way if you want to.

Selecting, cutting, copying, pasting and moving text

You will often have to move a block of text from one place to another. Sometimes you will just want to move a section from one place in a document to a different place in the same document. Other times you may want to move it to a different document.

Selecting text

To select text you move the cursor to the start of the text. Then click on the left mouse button and, keeping your finger on the button, move the cursor across the text. This process will leave the text you have selected highlighted.

Cutting text

Cutting text takes a block of text out of the current document and stores it in an area of memory called the clipboard. When you cut text it no longer remains in the current document. If you want the text to remain then you should copy the text rather than cut it (the next section explains how to do this).

To cut a block of text you follow these steps:

1   Select the block of text to be cut by highlighting it.
2   Click on Edit.
3   In the pull-down menu, select Cut. The text is removed from its current position and stored on the clipboard.

Copying text

A block of text can remain in its current position while it is copied to another position, either in the same document or a different one. Copying text involves storing the text on the clipboard.

To copy a block of text you follow these steps:

1   Select the block of text to be copied by highlighting it.
2   Click on Edit.

3   In the pull-down menu, select Copy. The text is now stored on the clipboard and it also remains in its current position.

The block can now be pasted in the way described in the next section.

Pasting text

Pasting text involves using text that has first been stored on the clipboard. You could copy a section of the text onto the clipboard with the original block of text remaining unaltered, or alternatively you could cut a block of text by taking it from the document and transferring it to the clipboard.

To paste text means taking an item from the clipboard and putting it into a document. You could put it into the same document or a completely different one. To paste text you must first have some text on the clipboard. You then follow these steps:

1   Move to the document where the text is to be pasted.
2   Make sure that the cursor is positioned where you want the block of text to be inserted.
3   Click on Edit.
4   In the pull-down menu, select Paste. The text should now appear in its correct position.

Moving text

Text can be moved by cutting it from its original position and pasting it to a new position. If you make a mistake, then there is an Undo command in the Edit menu which will 'undo' the last action.

Formatting text

Text is formatted to make it stand out. Here are the three main styles you can use:

Bold   **B**

Underline   <u>U</u>

Italics   *I*

To format text, select it and click on the relevant button.

here are other ways to format text. First select the text you want
to format and then, in the Format menu, select Font... from the
list. You will then be presented with the following screen from
which you can format text in a number of different ways.

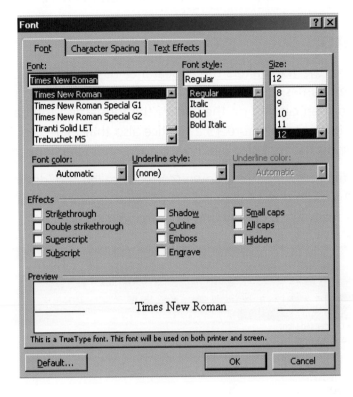

Figure 13.1

Selecting Font in Word

From this menu you can do many other things such as:

- alter the colour of the text
- produce other text effects (emboss, engrave, etc.)
- use different styles for underlining text.

Justifying text

Justifying text means aligning (lining up) the text in some way.
The main buttons for justifying text are shown below.

Align left (left justification)
This lines the text up with the left margin but leaves the right-
hand side ragged. This type of alignment is the most common
and is the one used by wordprocessors unless another is
specified.

Align right (right justification)
This lines the text up with the right margin but leaves the left-
hand margin ragged.

Key Jargon

font – a style of type.

Times New Roman 12

Figure 13.2

Altering the font and font size in Word

Centre ▤

This puts the text in the centre of the page.

Fully justified (justified) ▤

This lines text up with both the right and left margins.

Fonts

Changing the **font** alters the appearance of the characters. Fonts are given names and you can change the font by selecting the text and then clicking on the part of the formatting toolbar shown opposite in Figure 13.2. Notice also that there is a section for altering the font size (i.e. how big the characters appear).

When the arrow pointing down (correctly called the 'down scroll arrow') is clicked the following list of fonts appears for you to choose from. Click on any one to make your choice.

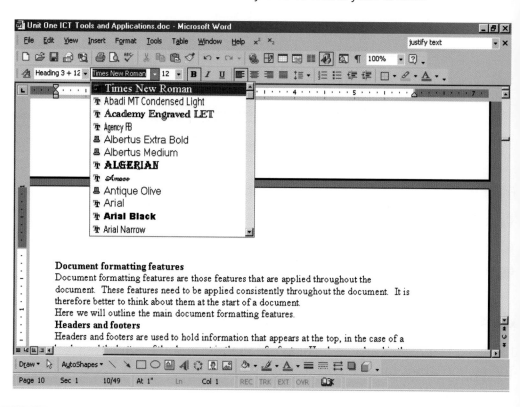

Figure 13.3

The font drop-down menu

Document formatting features

Document formatting features are features that are applied throughout the document. They need to be applied consistently, so it is better to think about them at the start of the document rather than when it is completed. Here are the main document formatting features.

Headers and footers

Headers and **footers** are used to hold information that appears at the top of the page in the case of a header, and at the bottom of the page in the case of a footer. Headers are placed in the top margin and footers are placed in the bottom. You can choose whether they are included on every page or just some of the pages.

Here are some types of information that are often put into headers and footers:

- page numbers
- today's date
- the title of the document
- a company logo (it can be a graphic image)
- the author's name
- the name of the file that is used to hold the document.

footer – text placed at the bottom of a document.

header – text placed at the top of a document.

Figure 13.4

A header and footer in a multi-page document

Bullet points

If you need to put a list of things in a document, you can use **bullet points** to emphasise each item in the list. The 'items' could be the equipment you need to take with you on a camping trip, or the advantages of using a particular piece of software.

bullet point – a line of text or a word that has a symbol placed in front to make it stand out.

Bullet points are used a lot in this book – they help to make important points clearer.

You can choose from many different shapes for the bullet. In this book, red spots and blue squares are used, but you can have triangles, arrows, diamonds, etc. You can even design your own.

The screen shown in Figure 13.5 illustrates the different types of bullet points available.

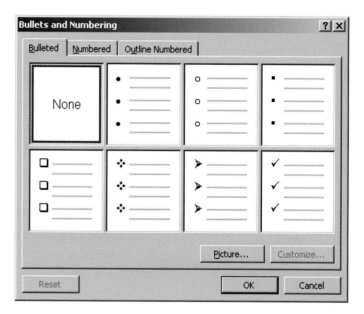

Figure 13.5

The Bullets and Numbering screen in Word

Activity 1

In the first column of the table below there is a picture of a button used in Microsoft Word (the most popular wordprocessing package). The column 'What it does' has been mixed up. Your task it to match each term in the 'What it does' column with the correct button. For each button, write the number of the button, then write the correct term next to it.

Button		What it does
1	B	Applies italic formatting to text or numbers
2	I	Prints out a copy of a document
3	🖨	Applies bold formatting to text or numbers
4	U	Applies underline formatting to text or numbers
5	✓ABC	Saves a document
6	☰	Numbers a list
7	☰	Checks spelling and grammar
8	☰	Puts text into columns
9	?	Cuts selected text
10	💾	Copies text
11	☰	Right justifies text
12	✂	Left justifies text
13	☰	Makes a bulleted list
14	📋	Accesses help
15	🔍	Justifies text
16	☰	Print preview
17	🗋	Opens a new document

Putting tables into a document

Putting data, especially numerical data, into a table makes it look neat and professional. It also makes it easy to read. Tables may also be used to summarise information. In Word, there are many different table types you can insert into a document.

Using a table to provide a summary

Activity 2

In this activity you will learn how to:

- insert a table into a document
- adjust the column widths and row heights
- input data into a table.

You are going to produce a table to show two of the main differences between a wide area network (WAN) and a local area network (LAN).

1 Load Word and start a new document.

2 Click on Table on the menu toolbar and select Insert and then Table. The following menu appears, where you can specify the number of columns and rows. Change the number of columns to 3 and the number of rows to 3 and click on OK.

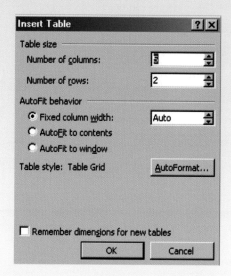

3 The following table will appear at the cursor position. Notice that it spans from one margin to the other.

Adjust the widths of the columns and the heights of the rows in the following way. Move the pointer onto a line and you will notice that the cursor changes to two parallel lines (either vertical or horizontal). Press the left mouse button and drag the line either left or right if it is a vertical line, or up and down if it is a horizontal line. In this way, alter the columns and rows until they look like the ones in the diagram below.

	LAN	WAN
Difference 1	Confined to a small area, usually a single site.	Cover a wide geographical area spanning towns, countries or even continents.
Difference 2	Usually uses simple cable links owned by the company.	Uses expensive telecommunication links not owned by the company.

4 Type in the text shown in the table above. You can centre the headings 'LAN' and 'WAN' by typing them in, highlighting them and then clicking on the centre button on the toolbar. This will centre the headings in the column. Also, embolden the words 'LAN', 'WAN', 'Difference 1' and 'Difference 2'.

5 See how neat this now looks. Save your document using the filename **The differences between a LAN and a WAN**. Print out a copy of your document.

Selecting a table

The table created in Activity 2 was the simplest type of table you can produce in Word. There are some pre-stored tables you can use. Once you have selected the number of rows and columns in the Table menu, click on Table AutoFormat... and the menu in Figure 13.6 appears. By flicking through the sample formats you can select one that will work well with the data you need to present.

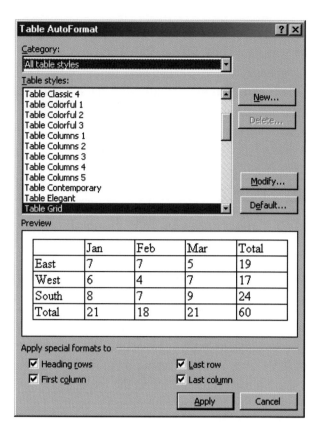

The Table AutoFormat menu in Word

Putting clip art or graphic images into a document

A document's appearance can be improved by adding clip art or graphic images.

Activity 3

In this activity you will learn how to:

■ search for clip art or graphics images
■ insert clip art or graphics images into a document.

To insert clip art, follow these instructions:

1 Open a new document or a saved one.
2 Position the cursor where you want to insert the clip art.
3 Click on Insert.
4 In the pull-down menu, select Picture and then Clip Art....

5 The screen will now split into two. On the right is a search facility that will help you find suitable clip art.

6 Suppose you want some clip art about looking after you teeth. Type in 'dentistry' in the Search text: box and then click on the Search button (see opposite).

7 Thumbnails (small pictures) of the clip art that's available are shown.

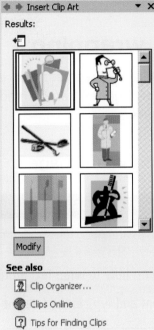

Use the scroll bar at the side to look for a suitable piece of clip art.

8 Double click on one of the pictures to place it in your document.

You may be asked to insert a CD with the clip art on. Alternatively, the clip art may be stored on your hard disk so that it can be accessed immediately.

Activity 4

You have been asked by your dentist to design and produce a poster to encourage young people to take care of their teeth. The poster is to be placed on the wall of the surgery. It must be on an A4-sized piece of paper and in colour.

continued over page

341

Produce three draft designs for the dentist to choose from.

Consider the following:

- different fonts
- different sized text
- using clip art.

wrap – the process by which a computer automatically starts a new line.

Using word wrapping

When an object (table, clip art, spreadsheet, photo, etc.) is inserted into a document the text can be made to 'wrap' around the object in different ways.

Wrapping text around an image

Activity 5

In this activity you will learn how to wrap text around an image.

1 Open a new document and type in the following text:

> **Getting cash from your supermarket**
>
> It is common to see cash dispensers in the walls of out-of-town supermarkets. It is possible to get cash at the same time as paying for the goods using the EPOS terminal.
>
> The service is called 'Cashback' and to get cash, the customer needs to have a card called a Switch card or a similar debit card. Debit cards can be used as an alternative to paying by cheque. When the customer pays for their goods they will be asked if they want 'cashback'. The customer details are read using a card reader and a voucher is produced that the customer then signs for the goods. For cashback, the customer also signs for the amount of cash they have received.
>
> When a debit card is used, the money is transferred from the shopper's account to the store's bank account. This process takes place immediately.

2 Move the cursor to the gap between the two sections of text.

3 Insert an item of clip art or another suitable image into this space. The text with the image should now look like this, but yours will contain a different image (preferably something to do with cash dispensers or supermarkets).

Getting cash from your supermarket

It is common to see cash dispensers in the walls of out-of-town supermarkets. It is possible to get cash at the same time as paying for the goods using the EPOS terminal.

The service is called 'Cashback' and to get cash, the customer needs to have a card called a Switch card or a similar debit card. Debit cards can be used as an alternative to paying by cheque. When the customer pays for their goods they will be asked if they want 'cashback'. The customer details are read using a card reader and a voucher is produced that the customer then signs for the goods. For cashback, the customer also signs for the amount of cash they have received.

When a debit card is used, the money is transferred from the shopper's account to the store's bank account. This process takes place immediately.

---

4 Select the image by clicking on it. You should see some small squares appear.

5 Click on the Format menu and then on Picture. The Format Picture screen will appear.

continued over page

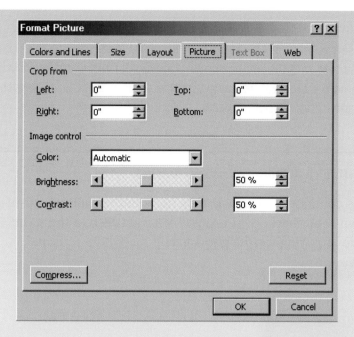

6 Click on the Layout tab. The screen will now change to this:

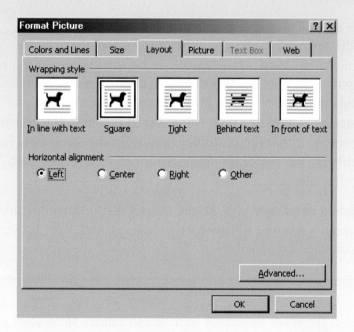

Select Square for the wrapping style and Left for the horizontal alignment. Click on the OK button.

7 The text will now flow around the image like this:

Getting cash from your supermarket

It is common to see cash dispensers in the walls of out-of-town supermarkets. It is possible to get cash at the same time as paying for the goods using the EPOS terminal.

The service is called 'Cashback' and to get cash, the customer needs to have a card called a Switch card or a similar debit card. Debit cards can be used as an alternative to paying by cheque. When the customer pays for their goods they will be asked if they want 'cashback'. The customer details are read using a card reader and a voucher is produced that the customer then signs for the goods. For cashback, the customer also signs for the amount of cash they have received.

When a debit card is used, the money is transferred from the shopper's account to the store's bank account. This process takes place immediately.

3   Use the same text and image to experiment with different wrapping styles. Save each version under a different name and produce printouts of your results.

Mail merge

Mail **merging** involves combining a list of names and addresses with a standard letter so that a series of similar letters is produced, each addressed to a different person. The list is created either by using the wordprocessor or by importing data from a database of names and addresses. The letter is typed, using the wordprocessor, with blanks where the data from the list will be inserted.

merge – to combine data from two different sources.

Performing a mail merge

Activity 6

In this activity you will learn how to:

- create a letter to be sent to different people
- create a name and address list for the recipients of the letter
- insert the variable fields into the letter
- merge the name and address details with the letter to produce personalised letters.

1 Load Word and create a new document. Click on Tools and the menu shown on the left drops down. Move down to Letters and Mailings.

2 The following menu appears. You need to select Mail Merge Wizard....

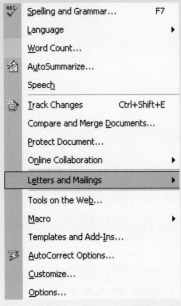

Click on Mail Merge Wizard.

3 The screen divides into two, with the right-hand side containing instructions for you to follow.

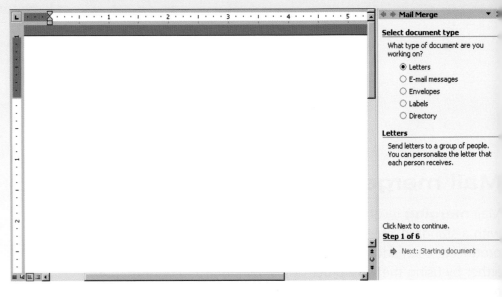

Make sure that Letters is selected. You can then start typing.

4 Type in the following letter, making sure that you leave two lines blank at the top of the page.

Dear

As you know you will soon be taking your end of year examinations. For those of you in year 11, these will be your GCSE exams. We will be holding a revision club on Mondays and Wednesdays from 4 p.m. to 6 p.m. A variety of staff will be on hand to help you with your revision questions. You should take advantage of this as it is completely free.

There will be a meeting on Wednesday 3rd May at 4 p.m. in the hall for any of you interested in taking up the offer.

Happy revision and good luck.

Click on 'Next: Starting document'.

5 Make sure that the option 'Use the current document' has been selected (see figure opposite).

Click on 'Next: Select recipients'.

6 In the following screen, select 'Type a new list'.

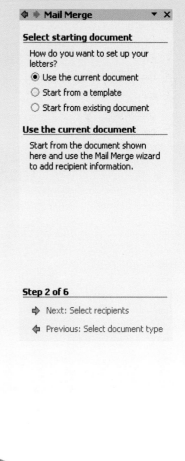

continued over page

Click on Create....

7 The following screen appears. Here you can select the name and address details.

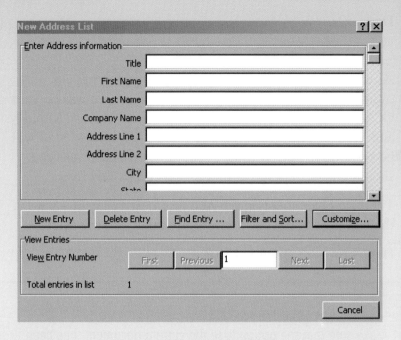

To send the letters to the pupils you need to have the following information for the names and addresses:

Surname

Forename

Street

Town

Postcode

8 Click on the Customi<u>z</u>e… button and the following screen will appear:

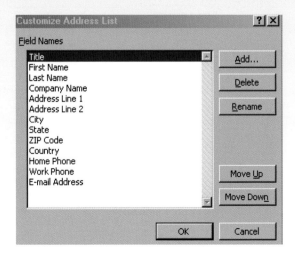

Make sure that Title is highlighted. Click on the <u>D</u>elete button to remove it from the list.

The following confirmation screen appears:

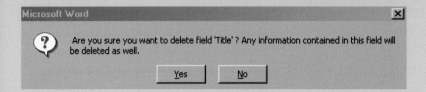

Click on the <u>Y</u>es button to confirm that you want it deleted.

9 Move the cursor to First Name. Change this to Forename by clicking on <u>R</u>ename and then typing in **Forename** (see figure opposite).

Click on the OK button.

In a similar way change Last Name to Surname.

10 Now make the following changes by repeating steps 7 to 9 for each one.

Delete Company Name.

Rename Address Line 1 to **Street**.

Rename Address Line 2 to **Town**.

Rename City to **Postcode**.

Delete the rest of the fields.

Your list will now look like the screen below:

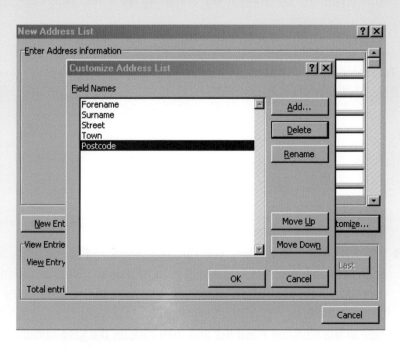

11 Click on the OK button. The following screen appears where you can type in your list of names and addresses:

continued over page

12 You now enter the pupil data (i.e. the pupils' names and addresses) into your list. Enter the details as shown below:

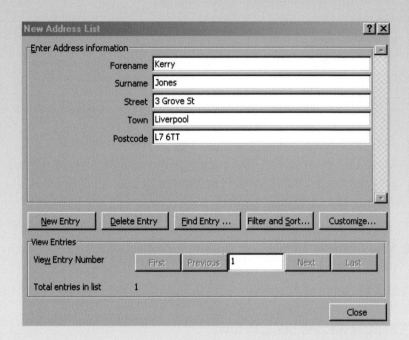

When you have typed in the details, click on New Entry.

Now repeat this by typing in the details for these two pupils:

Forename	Adam	Robin
Surname	Keel	Jackson
Street	12 Moor Grove	34 Fell St
Town	Liverpool	Warrington
Postcode	L13 7YH	WA 4ER

Now click on the Close button.

13 You will see a screen where you can name the file of names and addresses and also specify where it is to be stored. If you are storing your work on a floppy disk, make sure that Save in is altered to the floppy A drive.

Type in the filename **Pupil list** and then click on the Save button.

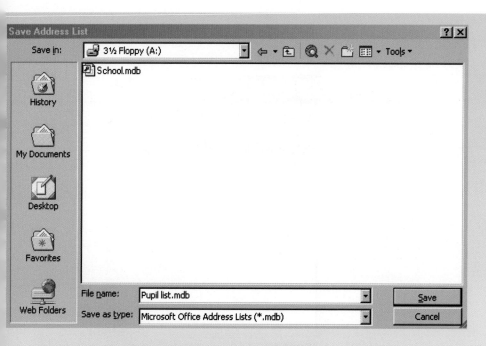

14 The following screen appears:

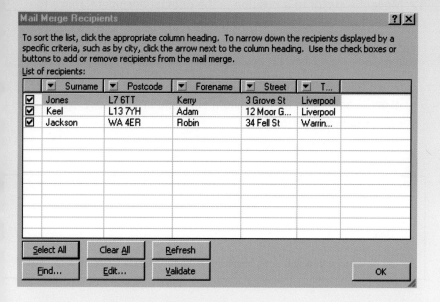

Make sure that there are ticks by the three records. This means that you have selected them for the mail merge.

Now click on the OK button.

15 Near the bottom right of the screen click on 'Next: Write your letter'. Look at the right section of the screen. It should look like the figure on the right.

continued over page

16 Click on More items… .

The following window will be opened:

17 Move the cursor to a position in the original document above the word 'Dear' and then click on the Insert button on the above screen. This will insert the Forename details here. Now click on the Close button.

Leave two spaces by pressing the spacebar twice. Click on More items… again and then highlight Surname in the above screen and press the Insert button.

Your letter will now look like this:

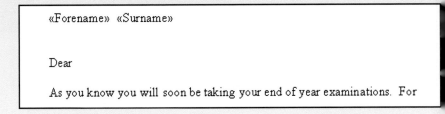

18 Now add the following fields in a similar way until your letter looks like this:

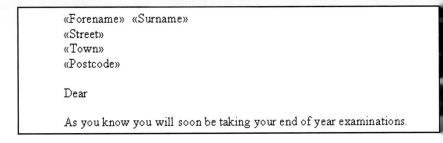

19 Add the Forename field next to Dear like this:

> «Forename» «Surname»
> «Street»
> «Town»
> «Postcode»
>
> Dear «Forename»
>
> As you know you will soon be taking your end of year examinations.

20 You can now get the computer to insert the variable data into these fields to complete the mail merge.

Click on 'Next: Preview your letters'.

The first name and address details will be inserted and your first letter will look like this:

> Kerry Jones
> 3 Grove St
> Liverpool
> L7 6TT
>
> Dear Kerry
>
> As you know you will soon be taking your end of year examinations. For those of you in year 11, these will be your GCSE exams. We will be holding a revision club on Mondays and Wednesdays from 4 p.m. to 6 p.m. A variety of staff will be on hand to help you with your revision questions. You should take advantage of this as it is completely free.
>
> There will be a meeting on Wednesday 3rd May at 4 p.m. in the hall for any of you interested in taking up the offer.
>
> Happy revision and good luck.

21 Click on 'Next: Complete the merge'.

22 Click on Print… to print out the three letters.

23 On closing the windows down, you will come to the screen shown on the next page. Here you can save the letter.

continued over page

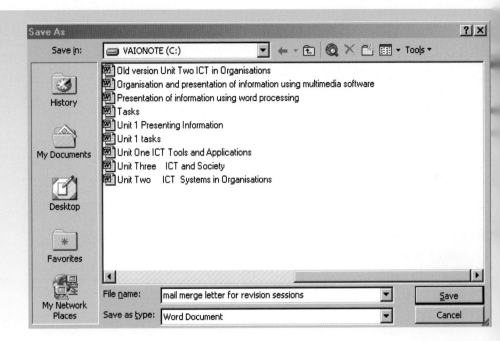

1 **Which one of the following features are you unlikely to find in a wordprocessing package?**

a   the ability to insert a file
b   the ability to store a document
c   a way of centring text or changing margins
d   the ability to play games

2 **Spellcheckers are used in wordprocessing packages to:**

a   proofread a document
b   validate a document
c   check the spelling of words in a document
d   check the grammar in a document.

3 **It is possible to use a single key to replace a series of keystrokes or mouse movements. You can do this using a:**

a   macro
b   grammar checker
c   spellchecker
d   template.

4 **A block of text is to be taken out of one document and put into another. This is an example of:**

a   cut and paste
b   spellchecking
c   grammar checking
d   formatting.

5 **Which one of the following is not an example of justifying text?**

a   align right
b   align left
c   bold
d   centre

6 Text placed at the bottom of a document is called a:

 a header
 b footer
 c note
 d bullet point.

7 A paragraph or line of text that has a symbol placed in front of it to make it stand out is called a:

 a header
 b footer
 c bullet point
 d cut and paste.

8 Combining a list of names and addresses with a standard letter is an example of:

 a electronic mail
 b mail merging
 c copying
 d calculating.

9 A wordprocessor checks all the words you have typed against an on-line dictionary. This is an example of:

 a grammar checking
 b mail merging
 c proofreading
 d spellchecking.

10 Checking the rules for constructing sentences can be done by the computer using a:

 a spellchecker
 b grammar checker
 c spreadsheet
 d database.

1 a List **four** items of hardware that would be needed for a typical wordprocessing system.

b List **two** items of software that would be needed for wordprocessing.

2 Give **three** advantages of using wordprocessing compared to using an ordinary typewriter for producing letters.

3 a Explain the difference between proofreading a document and spellchecking it.

F Questions

1 a Text may be formatted using wordprocessing software. Give **two** examples of text formatting.

b A letter can be made more attractive by putting artwork (pictures, clip art, photographs, etc.) into it. Describe **two** ways that artwork can be put into a wordprocessed document.

c A document can be improved by the use of different fonts. Explain what is meant by the term 'font'.

2 a You are thinking of buying a wordprocessing package. Apart from being able to enter text, edit text, save text and print text, describe **four** features you would look for in this package.

b For each feature you have mentioned, explain why the feature would be useful for you.

H Questions

1 A student is preparing a curriculum vitae using wordprocessing software. The curriculum vitae looks like the one on the following page.

a The student wants to improve the appearance of the curriculum vitae.

> Curriculum vitae
> Adrian Jones
> 23 High Street
> Holmcroft
> Stoke ST23 5TY

Paragraph A

Interests
I am interested in football and rugby, and support my local teams. My other sports are cricket, golf and squash. Sometimes I like to go hill walking as I keep a dog. Also I like to go to the cinema or to music festivals.

Paragraph B

Qualifications
GCSE English (C), Maths (B), Science (C), Design Technology (D), Information Technology (C), French (D), PE (C), RE (D).

Paragraph C

Work experience
July 1998 – Supersave Supermarket – temporary checkout operator – one month full-time.
1997 to 1998 – Khan's Newsagent – paper deliveries – part-time.

Describe **three** features of wordprocessing software that could be used.

b   The student wants to put paragraph A at the end of the curriculum vitae, just after paragraph C. Describe how this could be done.

c   A photograph of the student is to be included in the curriculum vitae before it is printed by the computer. Describe how this could be done.

d   Describe **two** tasks the student should do before printing the curriculum vitae and switching off the computer.

(AQA Specification B Tier H full course, specimen paper, q1)

2 A car dealership sends information about new models, special promotions, etc. using personalised letters. These letters are produced using mail merging.

a   Describe the processes involved in mail merging.

b   Describe **four** features other than mail merging that the staff at the dealership could use to produce advertising leaflets.

Before starting this chapter, you should have read and fully understood Chapter 5 Doing things with data. Make sure that you are familiar with the following terms:

- database
- record
- field
- table
- key field.

Also make sure that you understand:

- the reasons for using a computerised database
- preparing the structure of a database
- linking files/tables
- data types
- picking a key field.

Deciding on the fields in a database

When you are setting up a database, here is some advice when deciding what fields to have in it:

1 **Ask the user.** The user will know what information they need. Ask them what they want to get out of the database and use this to decide what data needs to be put in.

2 **Break fields down into several smaller ones.** For example, don't just have a field called 'Name'. It is better to break the 'Name' field down into 'Title', 'Surname' and 'Forename'. If you just stored 'Name', then it would make it difficult to search for a person's surname without knowing their forename as well. Also, it does not make it clear whether the user is to type in a forename as well as a surname or just an initial and a surname. Similarly, the 'Address' field should be broken down into 'Street', 'Town' and 'Postcode' or something similar.

3 **Do not have a field for age.** Use 'Date of birth' instead as the computer is able to calculate an age using date of birth and today's date. If you store age then the data will go out of date at the person's next birthday.

4 **Be consistent in the way you name fields.** For example, don't start by using 'Student number' and then 'Student No.'. Also, if you have used 'Student number' then to be consistent you should use 'Teacher number' rather than 'Teacher No.'.

Activity 1

Below are some fields that have been suggested for a student database in a school. There are various problems with this database. How many can you spot?

Student Number
Name
Address
Telephone number
AGE

Using databases

Creating a database for a school

Let us return to the database created in Chapter 5 to hold details about the pupils, forms and form teachers at a school.

Using more than one table

Single tables are not really databases, and they are of limited use. If you put two or more tables together and have links between the tables, you have created a really useful database called a **relational database**.

In the school database, three tables are used; these are called Pupils, Forms and Teachers.

Key Jargon

relational database – a database that consists of several files/tables with links between them so that the data can be combined.

The Pupils table

The Pupils table contains all the pupil details. Each pupil on joining the school is given a unique Pupil number. This prevents confusion with other pupils who may have the same name or live at the same address.

The Forms table

The Forms table combines teacher and form information so that you can identify the teacher of each form.

The Teachers table

This table contains the details of all the teachers in the school.

The database developer has spoken to the headteacher and other staff in the school and has come up with the following fields for each table:

Pupils table	Forms table	Teachers table
Pupil number	Form	Teacher number
Surname	Teacher number	Teacher title
Forename		Teacher surname
Date of birth		Teacher initial
Street		
Town		
Postcode		
Contact phone number		
Home phone number		
Form		

The key field in each of the tables is underlined.

Notice that the Form field appears in two tables: the Pupils table and the Forms table. This is the common field (i.e. it is the one that appears in both tables) and it forms a link between the two tables. If we wanted to know form details for a particular pupil then these can be obtained via this link.

The links between the tables are called the **relationships** and these make relational databases very powerful tools.

Deciding on the relationships between tables

After the fields have been placed into different tables, we need to think about the relationships between the tables. Relationships

Key Jargon

relationships – the ways in which tables are related to each other in a relational database.

between tables can be one-to-one, one-to-many or many-to-many. Many-to-many relationships can cause problems, but we need not be concerned with these here.

One-to-many relationships

If we look at the relationship between the Pupils and the Forms tables we can see that one form in the Forms table can appear many times in the Pupils table.

We also need to look at the relationship from the other end (i.e. from the Pupils table to the Forms table). Each form in the Pupils table corresponds to a single occurrence of the Form field in the Forms table.

The relationship between the Forms table and the Pupils table is therefore a one-to-many relationship.

One-to-one relationships

With a one-to-one relationship, one record in one table has only one matching record in another table.

Many-to-many relationships

Here one record in a table matches many records in another table. When the tables are looked at from the other end, then one record again matches many. This type of relationship is called a many-to-many relationship. If you think you have a many-to-many relationship, then you will need to see your teacher since you cannot link tables with this kind of relationship.

Activity 2

Here are some items of data which are to be stored in tables in a database. Your task is to identify whether they should be stored as text or numbers. Examples of the data to be entered are shown in brackets.

- the number of units in stock (234)
- an invoice number (0001 to 9999)
- a telephone number (0161 876 2302)
- a tax code (488H)
- an employee number (00234442)
- the rate of VAT (17.5%)
- the rate of pay (£10 per hour)
- a National Insurance number (TT232965A)

The relational database

With a relational database, data from different subject areas is first placed in tables and relationships which link the tables are then constructed. Creating separate tables rather than combining all the information in a single table avoids duplicating data. This saves storage space on the computer and increases the speed at which data is accessed.

Linking tables

You cannot link two tables together unless there is a common field. This means one of the fields has to be present in each table.

- The common field has to have an identical name in each table (not just the same spelling, but also the same use of capitals, spaces, dashes etc.).
- The common field has to be set to the same data type in each table. (You can link a numeric field to another numeric field and a character field to another character field.)

Important note

AutoNumber and Number data types are both numbers. This means if two fields have identical names and have data types AutoNumber and Number, they can still be linked.

Key Jargon

AutoNumber – a unique number that is given automatically by the computer. It always gives the next number in the sequence.

Activity 3

Here are two different tables: Tables 1 and 2. These tables need to be linked. Questions 1 to 6 give the name of the common field in each table. Your task is to say whether the tables can be linked using this common field. If they can't, you need to say why they cannot be liked.

	Table 1	Table 2
1	Pupil number	Pupil Number
2	Date of birth	Date-of-birth
3	Teacher Number	Teacher No
4	Form	Forn
5	Patient_ID	Patient-ID
6	Video_ID	Video_No

Activity 4

Table 1 and Table 2 need to be linked. For each table, the name of each field in the table and its data type are shown. For questions 1 to 5, you have to decide if it is possible to link the two tables using the fields shown.

	Table 1		Table 2	
	Field	**Data type**	**Field**	**Data type**
1	Pupil number	Number	Pupil number	AutoNumber
2	Teacher number	Number	Teacher number	Text
3	Video_ID	Text	Video_ID	Text
4	Order no	Text	Order no	Text
5	Supplier code	Number	Supplier code	Number

Key Jargon

query – used to extract specific information from a database.

Searching and sorting

Because the three tables in the school database are related, you can extract and combine data from any of the tables. This is done using a **query**. A query is used to extract specific information from a database. Queries are used to ask databases questions.

Creating the Pupils table

Activity 5

In this activity you will learn how to:

■ load the database software
■ set where to save the database
■ set up the structure of the table
■ save the table.

1 Load the database software Access. Ask your teacher to explain how this is done. You will get a screen like this:

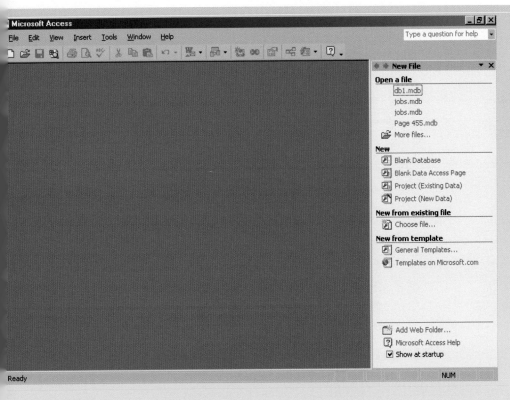

Click on New then Blank Database.

2 You must now decide where you want to save the database that you are creating.

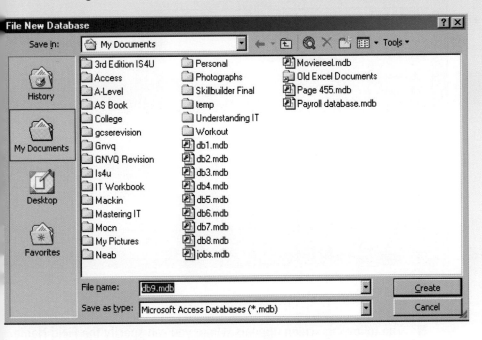

Your teacher will tell you where to save your database. Change the drive so that it is saved on the floppy disk (i.e. the A: drive).

continued over page

3 Type in the filename **School**.

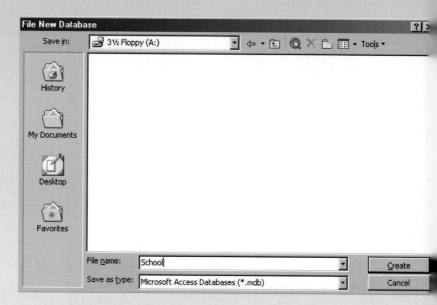

4 Click on the Create button.

The following screen appears:

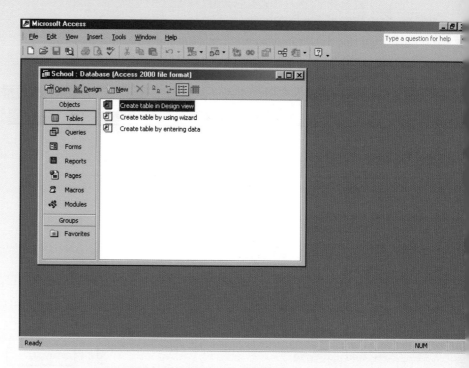

Click on 'Create table in Design view'.

5 The following screen appears where you can specify the Field Name, Data Type and Description. It is on this screen that you set out the structure for the table.

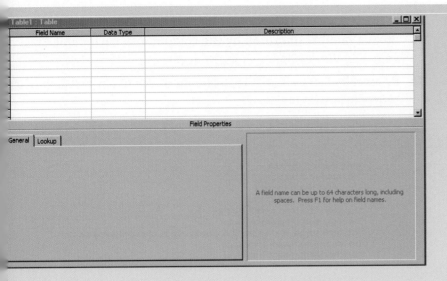

Where the cursor is positioned (i.e. in the first row of the table and in the column headed Field Name) enter the name of the first field: **Pupil number**. Press Enter.

The cursor now moves onto the Data Type column. Double click on this and a list of data types will appear. Select AutoNumber from this list. This tells the computer to allocate a unique number to each pupil. The first Pupil number will be 1, the second Pupil number will be 2 and so on. Because the computer does this automatically you do not have to remember what the next number should be.

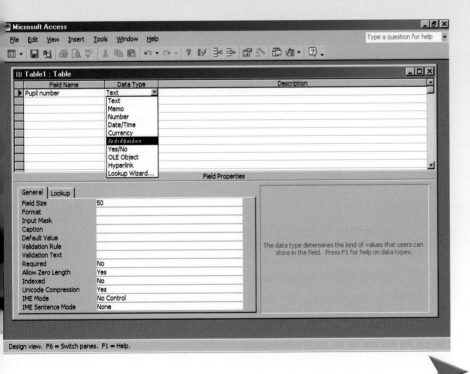

continued over page

7 In the Description column, type in the description for the field: **A unique number allocated by the computer to each pupil**. Press Enter and the cursor moves to the next line.

8 By repeating steps 5 to 7, complete the structure of the database as shown below.

Field Name	Data Type	Description
Pupil number	AutoNumber	A unique number allocated by the computer.
Surname	Text	The surname of the pupil.
Forename	Text	The forename of the pupil.
Date of birth	Date/Time	The date of birth of the pupil.
Street	Text	The first line of the pupil's address.
Town	Text	The name of the town in which the pupil lives.
Postcode	Text	The postcode of the pupil's residence.
Contact phone number	Text	The phone number where a parent or guardian can be contacted during the day.
Home phone number	Text	The home phone number of the pupil.
Form	Text	The form that the pupil is in at school.

9 A key field now has to be set for this table. Pupil number is a unique field for this table, and is therefore chosen as the key field.

Move the cursor to anywhere on the Pupil number field and then clic on the button with the key on it on the toolbar to set this as the key field.

Make sure that a picture of a key is shown next to the Pupil number field (as in the database above).

10 Now save the table by clicking on the Save button 🖫 on the toolbar.

You will be asked for a Table <u>N</u>ame. Type in the table name **Pupils**.

Click on OK. The table is now saved.

11 Click on the Datasheet button ▦ on the toolbar.

A blank datasheet appears into which you can enter data.

12 Enter the data shown at the top of the next page into the datasheet.

When all the data has been entered, click on Close (the cross at the top right of the window).

Pupil number	Surname	Forename	Date of birth	Street	Town	Postcode	Contact phone	Home phone	Form
1	Jones	Kerry	01/12/1989	3 Grove St	Liverpool	L7 6TT	234-0121	221-1098	7A
2	Keel	Adam	23/07/1986	12 Moor Grove	Liverpool	L13 7YH	254-0911	230-0343	11B
3	Jackson	Robin	12/01/1990	34 Fell St	Warrington	WA 4ER	01925-19191	230-0098	7B
4	Green	Amy	01/01/1989	121 Pat St	Liverpool	L13 6RT	254-0087	254-0087	8C
5	Black	John	08/09/1990	12 Pine Grove	Liverpool	L7 9YT	927-3856	221-2312	7A
6	Hughes	Jane	03/09/1990	15 Lire St	Liverpool	L8 6GH	232-9540	230-3422	7B
7	Green	Emma	01/09/1986	10 Moor Lane	Warrington	WA 5FT	01925-12000	01925-20202	11A
8	Keel	John	01/02/1988	12 Moor Grove	Liverpool	L13 7YH	254-0911	230-0343	10C
9	Black	Jenny	30/12/1986	34 High St	Liverpool	L7 6GF	927-8999	221-9034	11B
10	Hughes	James	17/12/1986	5 Bankfield Rd	Liverpool	L12 7TY	945-3493	230-0921	11A
11	Adams	Tracy	02/09/1990	12 Manor Rd	Liverpool	L23 5TG	927-2929	432-8929	7B
12	Jackson	Jordan	04/01/1989	15 Beech St	Liverpool	L7 6RF	487-0387	221-0098	8C
13	Green	Sarah	25/12/1989	45 Teck St	Liverpool	L9 6ED	487-6398	234-9273	7A
14	Crowley	John	30/09/1990	12 Green Lane	Liverpool	L3 6FD	487-0293	235-8193	7B
15	Turton	Brian	12/09/1990	1 Beech Rd	Liverpool	L6 6YH	254-0111	323-3030	7C
16	Forton	Julie	09/09/1990	34 Cedar Drive	Liverpool	L9 6DC	320-3423	324-0101	7B

You will now see the name of the table listed like this:

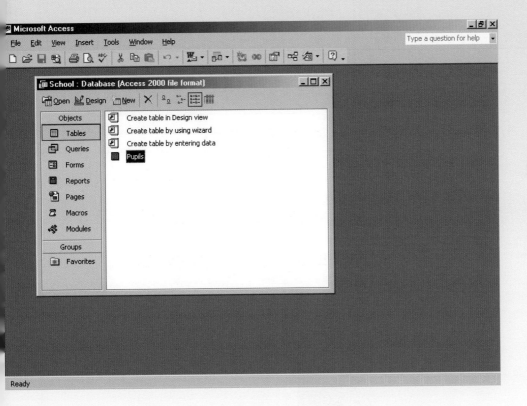

Opening the Pupils table

Activity 6

In this activity you will learn how to open a previously saved database.

1 Load Access. Change the drive to the A: drive (i.e. the floppy drive). The following screen will appear:

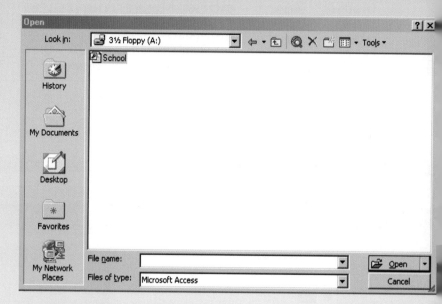

2 Either double click on the file School or move the cursor to School and then click on the Open button.

You will now be shown a list of the tables.

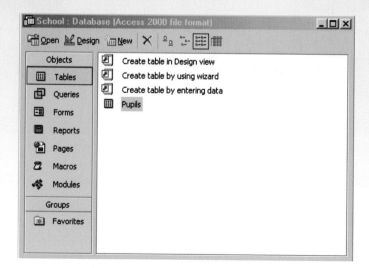

Double click on the table Pupils.

The table is now opened in the datasheet view as shown below.

Pupils : Table

Pupil number	Surname	Forename	Date of birth	Street	Town	Postcode	Contact phone	Home phone	F
1	Jones	Kerry	01/12/1989	3 Grove St	Liverpool	L7 6TT	234-0121	221-1098	7A
2	Keel	Adam	23/07/1986	12 Moor Grove	Liverpool	L13 7YH	254-0911	230-0343	11E
3	Jackson	Robin	12/01/1990	34 Fell St	Warrington	WA 4ER	01925-19191	230-0098	7B
4	Green	Amy	01/01/1989	121 Pat St	Liverpool	L13 6RT	254-0087	254-0087	8C
5	Black	John	08/09/1990	12 Pine Grove	Liverpool	L7 9YT	927-3856	221-2312	7A
6	Hughes	Jane	03/09/1990	15 Lire St	Liverpool	L8 6GH	232-9540	230-3422	7B
7	Green	Emma	01/09/1986	10 Moor Lane	Warrington	WA 5FT	01925-12000	01925-20202	11A
8	Keel	John	01/02/1988	12 Moor Grove	Liverpool	L13 7YH	254-0911	230-0343	10C
9	Black	Jenny	30/12/1986	34 High St	Liverpool	L7 6GF	927-8999	221-9034	11E
10	Hughes	James	17/12/1986	5 Bankfield Rd	Liverpool	L12 7TY	945-3493	230-0921	11A
11	Adams	Tracy	02/09/1990	12 Manor Rd	Liverpool	L23 5TG	927-2929	432-8929	7B
12	Jackson	Jordan	04/01/1989	15 Beech St	Liverpool	L7 6RF	487-0387	221-0098	8C
13	Green	Sarah	25/12/1989	45 Teck St	Liverpool	L9 6ED	487-6398	234-9273	7A
14	Crowley	John	30/09/1990	12 Green Lane	Liverpool	L3 6FD	487-0293	235-8193	7B
15	Turton	Brian	12/09/1990	1 Beech Rd	Liverpool	L6 6YH	254-0111	323-3030	7C
16	Forton	Julie	09/09/1990	34 Cedar Drive	Liverpool	L9 6DC	320-3423	324-0101	7B
* (AutoNumber)									

Record: 1 of 16

Creating the Forms table

Activity 7

In this activity you will set up a table.

The Forms table needs to be created in a similar way to the Pupils table.

1 First make sure that the Forms table has the following structure:

Table1 : Table

Field Name	Data Type	Description
Form	Text	The form that the pupil is a member of (e.g. 7A, 11C etc.).
Teacher number	Number	The number of the teacher who is the form teacher.

Make Form the key field/primary key.

2 Close this window. You will now be asked to give the table a name.

continued over page

371

Give it the name Forms by typing **Forms** in the following window:

3 Click on OK.

You will now see the Forms table listed like this:

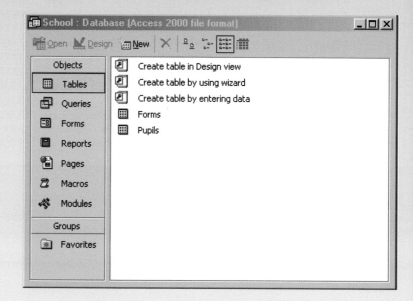

4 Enter the following data into the Forms table:

Form	Teacher number
7A	3
7B	1
7C	2
8A	5
8B	4
8C	10
9A	8
9B	9
9C	13
10A	12
10B	15
10C	6
11A	11
11B	17
11C	7
	0

5 Save the data in your table.

Creating the Teachers table

In a similar way to the other two tables, create the Teachers table. Make sure that you make Teacher number the primary key.

1 The structure of this table should be as follows:

Field Name	Data Type	Description
Teacher number	AutoNumber	A unique number allocated to each teacher when they join the course.
Teacher title	Text	The title of the teacher (e.g. Ms, Miss, Mrs, Dr or Mr)
Teacher surname	Text	The surname of the teacher.
Teacher initial	Text	One initial for the teacher.

Save this structure and give the table the name **Teachers**.

2 Open the Teachers table and enter the following details:

Teacher number	Teacher title	Teacher surname	Teacher initial
1	Mr	Hughes	H
2	Ms	Frampton	G
3	Dr	Chan	H
4	Miss	Hughes	J
5	Mr	Hughes	W
6	Mrs	Jackson	Y
7	Mrs	Green	D
8	Miss	Jones	G
9	Mr	Doyle	R
10	Mr	Poole	G
11	Mrs	Hopper	C
12	Mr	Kendrick	A
13	Miss	Adams	N
14	Miss	Stringer	P
15	Mr	Tarrant	H
16	Ms	Green	E
17	Miss	Ellen	S
18	Dr	Dolby	T
19	Miss	Harrington	G

Validation checks

When data is being entered into a database it is important that the program is able to spot certain types of error. The user can then be alerted to check the data and, if necessary, to re-enter it. The different kinds of checks you can do are called **validation checks**.

Key Jargon

validation check – a check performed by a computer program to make sure that the data being entered is allowable.

When designing the structure of a database, you need to devise a series of validation rules to govern what can and cannot be entered into each field. If data is entered that doesn't match these rules, then an error message appears. It is impossible to trap every type of error; if someone's address is 4 Bankfield Drive and the user incorrectly types in 40 Bankfield Drive, then no simple validation check would detect this.

The easiest validation checks are on numbers and dates. For example, a database can check that a number being entered is above a certain value, below a certain value or within a range of values.

Data type checks

Databases automatically check to make sure the data being entered into a field is of the type specified for that field, so text, for example, cannot be entered into a field that has a numeric data type. This type of check is called a data type check.

If a field is given the data type 'text', you can enter any characters from the keyboard into this field. You can, therefore, enter numbers into a text field but you cannot perform any calculations on them. Always try to specify the most appropriate data type when setting up the structure of a database.

Range checks

As well as checks on data type, you can devise other kinds of checks. Range checks are performed on numbers to make sure that they lie within a specified range. Range checks will only pick up errors that lie outside the range. For example, if you typed in the number of children in a household as '50' rather than '5' then a range check would spot the error; if you typed in '7' instead of '5' then the range check would not pick it up (assuming '7' lies within the specified range for number of children).

Presence checks

You can specify that some fields must always have data entered into them. For example, every pupil must have a pupil number, since it is allocated to them automatically when they join the school. Some fields, such as Telephone number, can be left blank since it is possible for someone not to have a telephone. Checks such as this are called presence checks.

n Microsoft Access you have to decide on two things when you want to validate data: the validation rule and the validation text.

- The **validation rule** decides whether a piece of data is valid or not.
- The **validation text** is a message that appears if the data breaks the validation rule.

Here is an example:

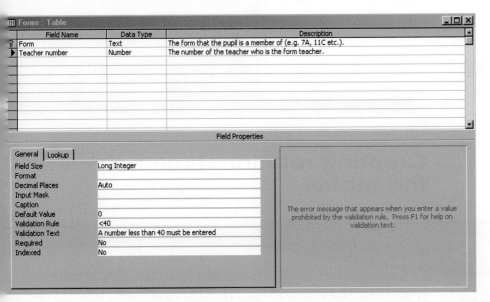

Figure 14.1

Screen showing Validation Rule and Validation Text in Access

This screen shows the table structure being set up for the Forms table. The cursor is on the field Teacher number. Because there are less than 40 teachers in the whole school, you do not want the user to be able to type in a number of 40 or more.

Notice that the Validation Rule line is in the Field Properties box. The validation rule is: **<40**.

You also need to specify the validation text, i.e. a message that will appear should the user enter any value that is 40 or more. Rather than just tell the user that they are wrong, it is better to tell them what values they can enter.

The validation text in the example above is: **A number less than 40 must be entered**.

The validation rule should be tested by entering data into the table. Data that passes the validation check should be entered along with some data that will fail the test. Figure 14.2 shows the message appearing when the Teacher number for Form 9C is changed to 40.

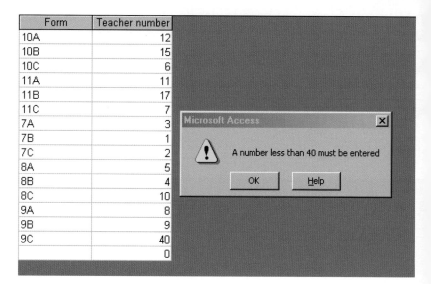

Form	Teacher number
10A	12
10B	15
10C	6
11A	11
11B	17
11C	7
7A	3
7B	1
7C	2
8A	5
8B	4
8C	10
9A	8
9B	9
9C	40
	0

Figure 14.2

Checking the validation rule in Access

Creating relationships between the tables

Activity 9

In this activity you will learn how to create relationships between tables.

1 Load Access and open the School database. You will see a screen like the one below. Notice the three names of the tables listed.

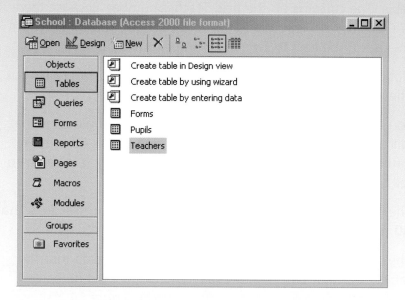

2 Click on the relationships button ⬚⬚ on the toolbar

The following screen appears. This is where you tell the computer what tables you want to use.

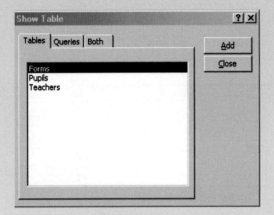

Make sure that Forms is highlighted and then press the Add button.

Click on Pupils and then press Add.

Click on Teachers and then press Add.

Then click on the Close button.

The three tables are shown below. Notice the names of the tables at the top and also the names of the primary/key fields in bold.

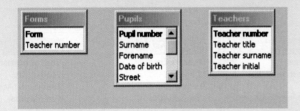

Notice that not all the fields are shown. This is because some of the boxes are too small. To make them bigger move the cursor to the bottom corner of the box. You will see the cursor change to a double-headed arrow. Drag this to enlarge the box. Your boxes will now look like this:

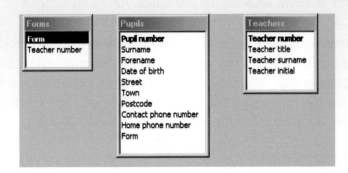

continued over page

5 Click on the Form field in the Forms table and hold down the mouse button. Now drag the small rectangle to the Form field in the Pupils table.

Release the mouse button.

The following window will appear:

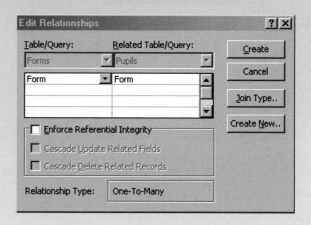

Notice that the Relationship Type is One-To-Many.

Click on the box marked Enforce Referential Integrity.

Click on the Create button.

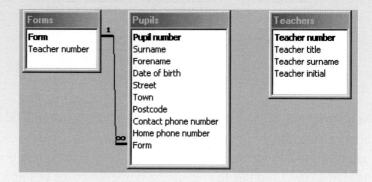

A line is drawn between the two tables. Notice the symbols '1' and '∞' on this line. These indicate the one-to-many relationship.

6 You will now make a similar relationship between the Teachers table and the Forms table. This would have been a one-to-one relationship but due to staff absences a teacher sometimes looks after two forms, so the Teacher number can appear more than once in the Forms table. This means that the relationship is now one-to-many.

In a similar way to that described for step 5, click on Teacher number in the Teachers table and drag it across to Teacher number in the Forms table. Enforce the referential integrity by putting a tick in the box.

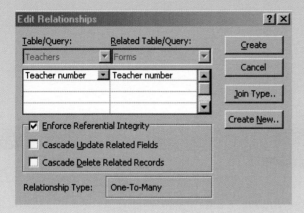

Click on Create.

Your screen showing the relationships will now look like this:

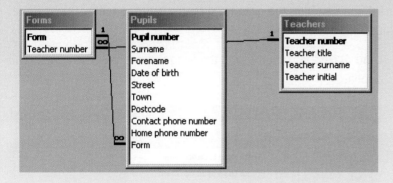

You have now created a relational database.

7 Close the window and you will be asked if you want to save the changes.

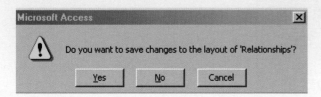

Click on the Yes button.

Extracting data from the database

Activity 10

In this activity you will learn how to:

■ create a query using a wizard
■ run a query.

Now you have set up the relationships between the tables, you can extract and combine the data from more than one table. This is done using a query.

1 Load Access and then select the School database. This screen will appear:

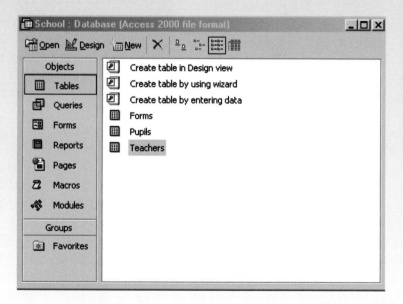

2 Click on the Queries button on the screen above. The queries screen will now appear:

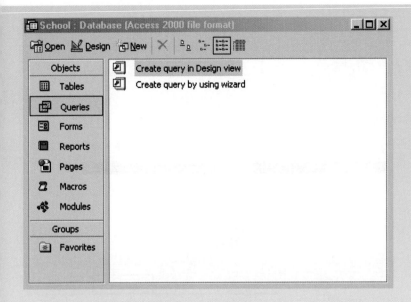

Click on 'Create query by using wizard'.

3 The following screen appears, to guide you through the process of producing a query.

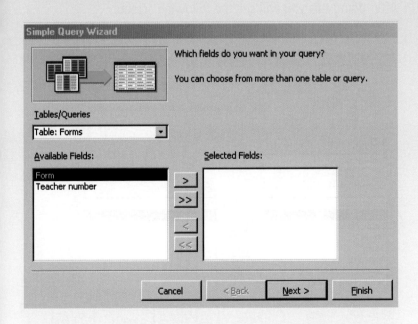

Make sure that Table: Forms appears in the Tables/Queries box.
Click on Form so that it is highlighted in the Available Fields: box.
Form will now appear in the Selected Fields: box. Your screen will look like the one at the top of the next page.

continued over page

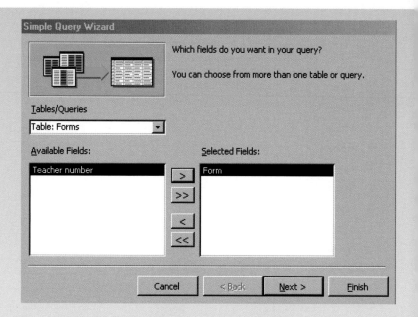

4 Click on the down-pointing arrow in the Tables/Queries box and select Table: Pupils. Add Surname to the selected fields in a similar way to step 3.

After doing this you will see the following screen:

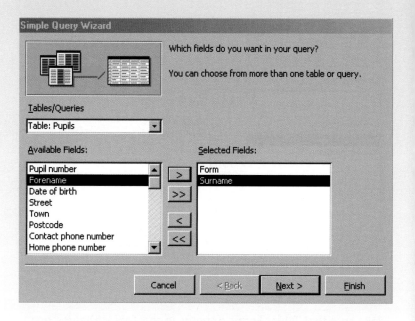

5 Now add the field Surname in the Teachers table in a similar way. Your screen will now look like this:

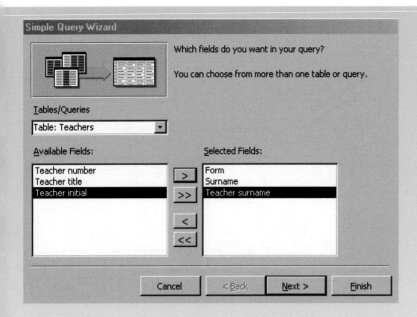

Click on the Next> button.

6 The screen below now appears. Make sure that Detail has been selected and then click on the Next> button.

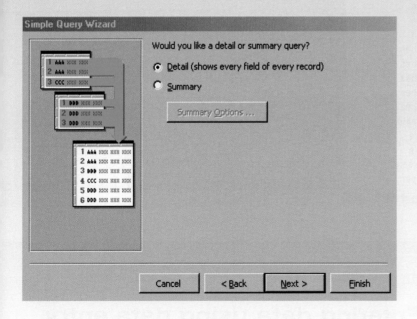

7 Change the name of the query to **List of forms, pupils and form teachers**.

continued over page

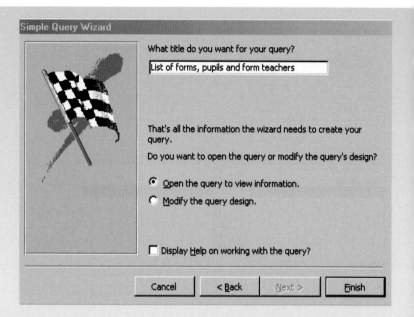

Click on Finish.

8 The query will now run and the results are shown below:

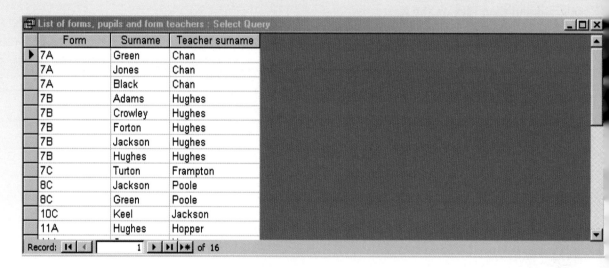

Entering data using data entry forms

So far, whenever data has been entered into a table it has been entered straight into the table using the datasheet view. The datasheet looks a little bit like a spreadsheet, and an inexperienced user may find it intimidating.

To make things easier, you can use a **form**. A form on a computer is just like a form on paper. The title of each field is put next to a box, into which the user can type the data in for that field.

As well as being used to get data into tables, forms can also be used for viewing data one record at a time. While the record is on the screen you can make alterations to the data. You can also delete the record.

The main advantage of using a form to enter data rather than the datasheet view is that the form allows you to see all of the fields for one record, at once.

Creating a data entry form

Key Jargon

form – a screen used to enter data into a database. It can also be a paper document that is used to collect data.

Activity 11

In this activity you will learn how to create a data entry form for putting data into a table.

Here you will create a form for the entry of the pupil details into the Pupils table.

1 Load Access and the School database. Click on Forms and the following screen will appear:

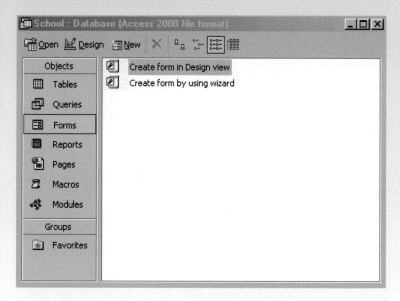

2 Click on 'Create form by using wizard'. This screen will appear:

continued over page

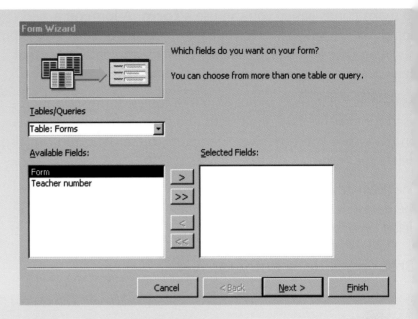

You can see the name of the table in the Tables/Queries box, and a list of all the fields that are available in this table in the box underneath. You can add these fields to the form one by one, by clicking the button with the single arrow on it.

3 Change the table to Pupils.

The following screen will appear:

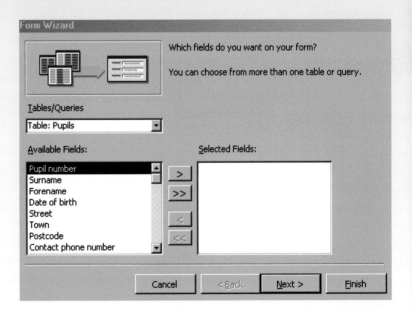

As you want to add all of these fields to the form, you can click on the button with the double arrows on. This will add them all in one go.

Your screen will now look like this:

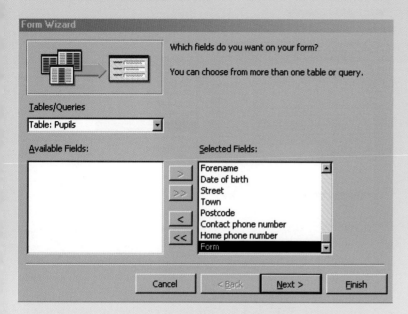

Click on the Next> button. The Form Wizard screen appears:

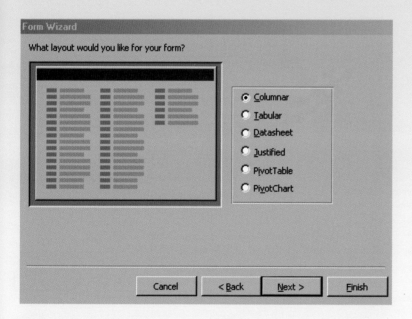

Select Columnar as the layout and then click on Next>. This will arrange the field names and boxes for the data in columns on the form.

The screen below appears, in which you select the style of the form you want to use.

Notice that when you move through the list of styles on the right, a picture of the style appears on the left.

continued over page

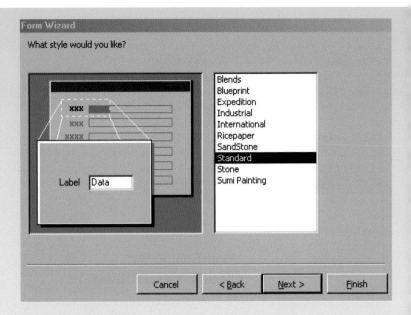

Select Standard as the style and then click on Next>.

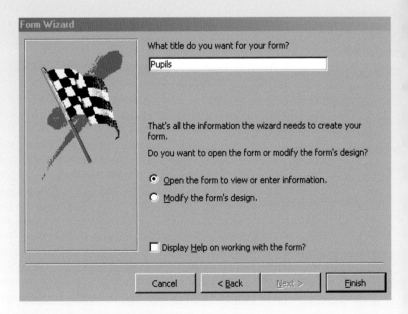

The form has been given the name Pupils. Keep this as the name.
Click on the Finish button.
After a brief wait, the form shown at the top of the next page
appears.
You can use the toolbar at the bottom of the screen to move from
one record to another.

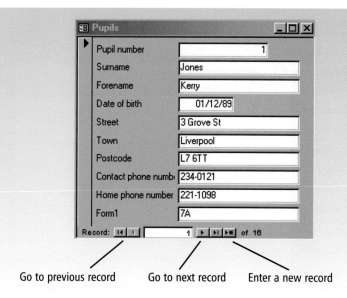

Go to previous record   Go to next record   Enter a new record

Producing reports

A **report** is a printout of the results from a database. Usually a report is printed on paper, but it can also be produced on the screen. If the report is very detailed then it is better to print it out so that it can be looked at more closely.

The person producing the report has control over what information to include in the report and how it is laid out.

In the School database, a report could be produced to show which pupils are in each form.

report – the output from software such as a database in which the results are presented in a way that is controlled by the user.

Producing a report

Activity 12

In this activity you will learn how to:

- select tables and fields to be used for a report
- structure a report
- view and print a report.

1 Load Access and the School database. Click on Report, and the following screen will appear:

continued over page

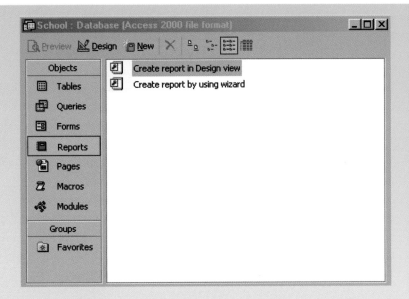

2 Double click on 'Create report by using wizard'. You will now see the following screen:

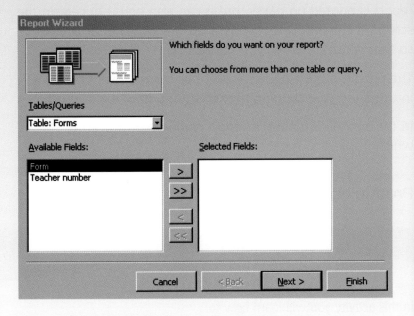

3 Using this screen you can select the table and the fields from each table that you want to include in the report.

Add the following to the Selected fields: Form (from the Forms table) and Teacher surname (from the Teachers table).

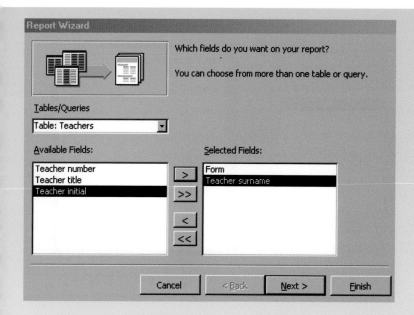

Click on the Next> button.

4 The following screen appears:

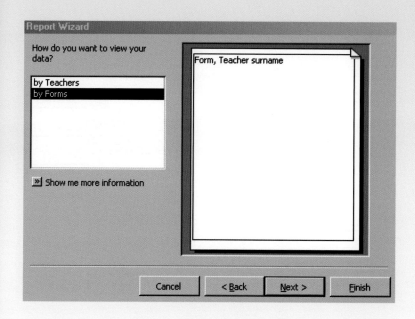

Make sure that 'by Forms' is selected. Click on the Next> button.

5 The grouping level Form is chosen (see the figure at the top of the next page).

Click on the Next> button.

continued over page

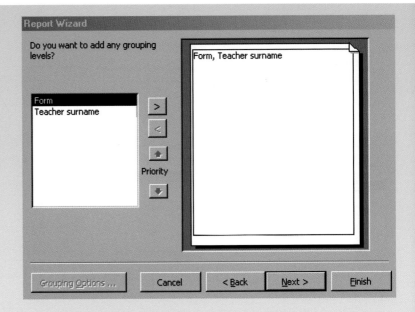

6 This report should be ordered according to Form in ascending order. Click on the arrow to select Form. Make sure that the button is set to Ascending (if you click on it you can change it to Descending).

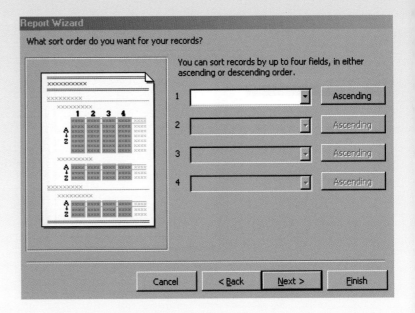

Click on the Next> button.

7 The screen shown at the top of the next page appears.
Make sure that Tabular and Portrait are picked.
Click on the Next> button.

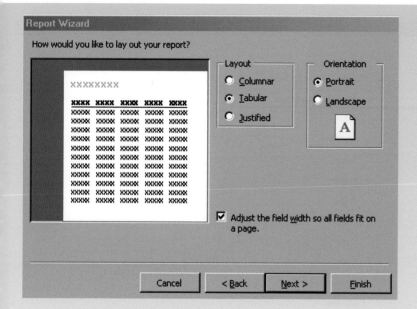

8 The following screen appears:

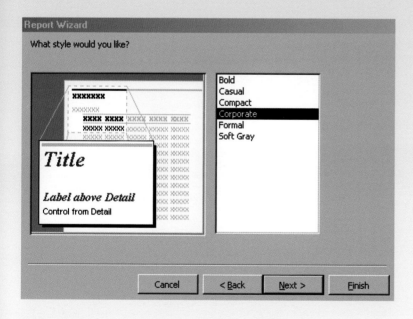

If you highlight other styles you can see what they look like. Select Corporate and then click on the Finish button.

9 The results of the report are now shown as in the figure at the top of the next page.

The report can be printed out by clicking on the printer icon .

continued over page

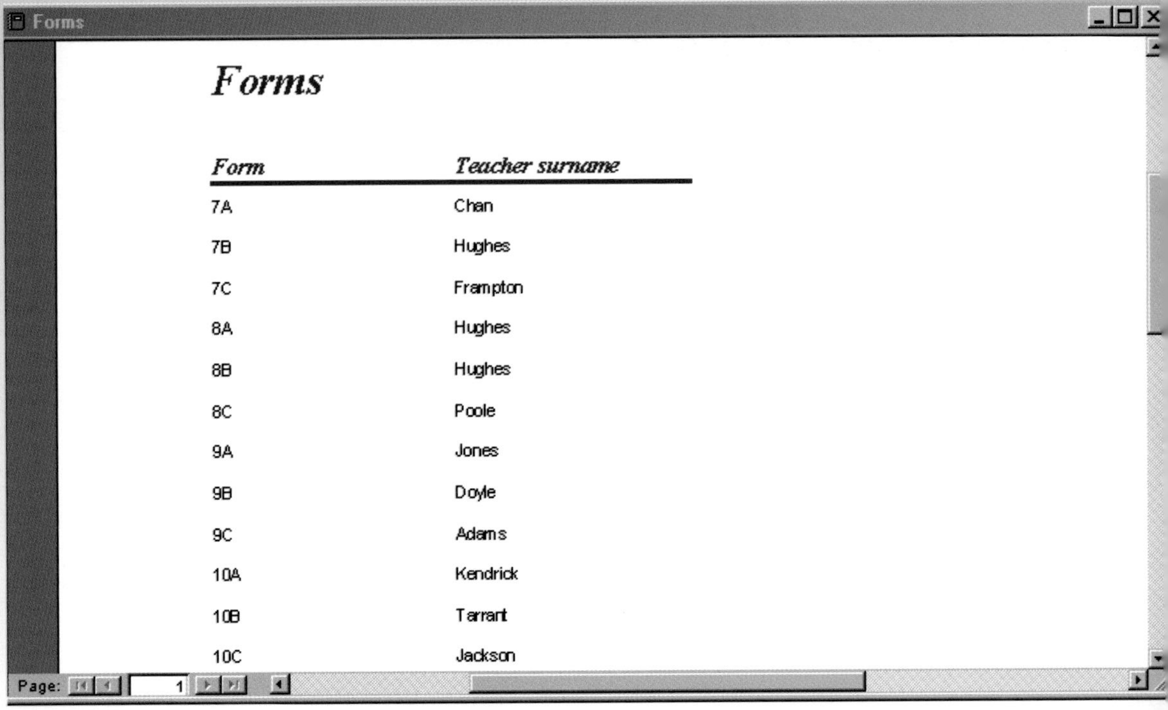

Forms

Forms

Form	Teacher surname
7A	Chan
7B	Hughes
7C	Frampton
8A	Hughes
8B	Hughes
8C	Poole
9A	Jones
9B	Doyle
9C	Adams
10A	Kendrick
10B	Tarrant
10C	Jackson

Page: |◄ ◄ 1 ► ►| ◄

1 A table forms part of what is called a relational database. The main advantage of a relational database is:

a   it reduces data duplication
b   it is easier to understand
c   all the typing of data is done for you
d   there is only one table.

2 In a database, a telephone number should be stored as which data type?

a   number
b   text
c   date/time
d   currency

3 When a pupil joins a school they are given a unique number called the pupil number. The best data type for this field in a database would be:

a   AutoNumber
b   number
c   text
d   date.

4 When choosing a field size for student surname it should always be:

a   the size of the largest surname on the course at the moment
b   the size of a randomly picked student's surname
c   the size of the largest surname you are likely to come across
d   the size of the smallest surname.

5 A key field is:

a   a password used to access a database
b   a unique field used to identify a particular record
c   the key used to access a computer room
d   the name of the most important file.

Multiple-choice questions

6 **A check performed by a database to make sure that data is allowable is called:**

a   verification
b   validation
c   proofreading
d   adding.

7 **A data type check is used to:**

a   make sure that data is entered into a field
b   make sure that the data is in a certain range
c   make sure that data has been entered using a keyboard
d   make sure that data being entered is the right type for that field.

8 **A range check is performed on numbers to:**

a   make sure that they lie within a certain range
b   ensure that not too many records are stored
c   make sure that only letters are entered
d   make sure that only numbers are entered.

9 **The links between tables are called:**

a   strands
b   relationships
c   strings
d   reports.

10 **Asking questions of a database is done by producing a:**

a   form
b   validation check
c   verification check
d   query.

1   A luxury car rental firm keeps the details of the cars it rents out in a table. The structure and contents of this table are shown below.

Reg-number	Make	Model	Year
DB51 AML	Aston Martin	DB7	2001
CAB 360S	Ferrari	360 Modena	2002
X34 FER	Ferrari	355 Spider	2000
N51 MAS	Maserati	3200 GTA	2001
W23 FRT	Porsche	911 Turbo	2000
M3 MMM	BMW	M3 Conv	2002
T433 YTH	Jaguar	XK8	1999

a   Give the names of **two** fields shown in the above table.

b   Give the name of the field that should be chosen as the key field.

c   Explain why the field you have chosen for your answer to part b should be chosen as the key field.

d   The highlighted details in the table are an example of which one of these?
    a record
    a field
    a table
    a file

e   How many records are there in the above table?

2   Data can be valid (i.e. it can pass the validation checks) and yet still be incorrect.

a   Explain, giving an example, how this can be so.

b   Give the name of the check that could be performed to protect against invalid data.

c   Explain how this check could be used to protect against valid but still incorrect data.

3   Explain **one** difference between the database terms 'search' and 'sort'.

4   A validation check is used to check the video hire price in a video hire database. The validation rule for this field is

    = £1.50 or £2.00 or £3.00

Here is some data that is being used to check this validation rule.

For each one say whether it is acceptable (i.e. valid) data or unacceptable (i.e. invalid) data.

a £1.00
b £3.00
c £2.99
d £0.00
e 3.00
f 3 pounds

5 Security is improved with a computerised database compared with a manual database. Give **one** example of how security is improved.

6 Here is a sample of the data that is to be stored in an employee database. The data items shown are the employee's surname, initial, street, postcode and telephone number.

Adams, V, 123 The High Street, L23 6DE, 0151-264-1112
Dolan, N, 64 North Way, L9 8SS, 0151-267-0011
Doyle, B, 12 Crosby Road, L23 2DF, 0151-264-1212
Carrol, A, 15 Barkfield Drive, L23 7YH, 0151-261-0899
Conway, T, 6 Windle Hey, L23 6ER, 0151-289-0899
Harvey, J, 4 Empress Road, L22 7ED, 0151-340-9090
Harvey, J, 4 Empress Road, L22 7ED, 0151-340-9090

a A table is to be set up with four fields. Give names for the four fields that would be suitable for the above set of data items.

b The person who is designing the database looks at the sample of data above and notices that there are two people with the same surname and address.

(i) Explain why the surname would be an unsuitable primary key.

(ii) It is decided that each employee should be given a unique number. What would be a suitable name for this field?

(iii) Rather than have to keep remembering the last number used, it is decided that it would be better if this number were given automatically by the computer. What type of field should be given to this field: text, numeric, AutoNumber or logical?

F Questions

1 a Explain what the word 'database' means.
  b Give **one** advantage of using a computerised database compared with keeping the same data manually.
  c Before data is accepted into the database, it is validated. Explain what the word 'validated' means.

2 The following structure for a database has been set up:

Field name	Field length	Field type	Key field
Surname	30	Character	No
Initial	1	Character	No
Street	35	Character	No
Membership number	6	Numeric	Yes
Date joined	8	Date	No

  a How many fields are shown in the above file?
  b Explain why 'Membership number' is chosen as the key field.
  c Give **one** reason why it is important to specify the field type.

H Questions

1 A dance centre has recently installed a computer system to help run the administration. Data about its members is to be stored on a database.

  a Explain what is meant by the following terms. You may find it helpful to give examples.
    (i) record
    (ii) file
  b Give **two** advantages of the dance centre using a database rather than manual methods for this task.

c   Give **two** disadvantages of the dance centre using a database rather than manual methods for this task.

d   Give **four** fields (other than member's name, address and telephone number) which they may reasonably wish to include in the members database.

e   The dance centre will collect information from members by asking them to fill in a form. This is then used to update the database.
    Using your answers to part d, complete the design of the form below. Follow the examples given on the form.

Surname	
Forename	
Address field 1	
Address field 2	
Address field 3	
Address field 4	
Telephone number	

15 Presenting Text and Graphics

Producing professional documents
Desktop publishing

Desktop publishing (DTP) is used to produce professional documents. Usually, these documents consist of more than just text. For example, they can include diagrams, photographs, tables, worksheets, etc. Most of these items are prepared using different software and are then imported into the DTP software. The DTP software therefore needs to be able to deal with many different types of file.

Key Jargon

desktop publishing – combining text and pictures on a screen to produce posters, newsletters, brochures, etc.

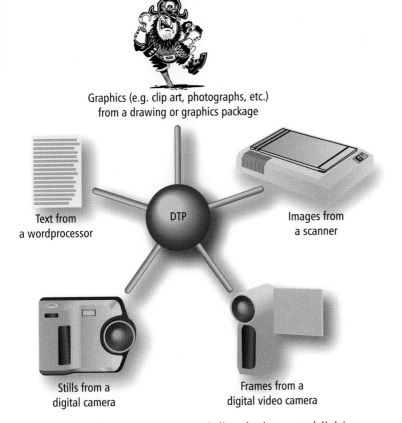

Graphics (e.g. clip art, photographs, etc.) from a drawing or graphics package

Text from a wordprocessor

DTP

Images from a scanner

Stills from a digital camera

Frames from a digital video camera

Figure 15.1

DTP software integrates many different files together in the same document

Professional publishing uses specialist desktop publishing software. However, many wordprocessing packages offer similar features to DTP packages and can be used to produce professional-looking documents at home or at school.

You may find it easier to look at the DTP features of these wordprocessing packages than to use specialist DTP software.

What equipment is needed for desktop publishing?

Computer

A very powerful computer is needed with a lot of memory and a large hard drive. This is because manipulating pictures on the screen takes a lot of computing power.

A large screen should be used so that you can view a whole page on the screen at a time. If the screen is small, then a page will need to be reduced in size a lot to fit on it, and the text will be very small and difficult to read.

Printer

Usually an ink-jet printer is used that is capable of printing in colour. Laser printers produce better quality, but colour laser printers are very expensive.

Scanner

A scanner is used to scan photographs and hand-drawn drawings into a document. If there is a large amount of text to input, this can also be scanned in, provided you have optical character recognition software.

Digital camera

Digital cameras are able to take photographs that are digitised and stored inside the camera. There is no need for film, and you don't need to have the photos developed. Instead the images (i.e. the digitised photos) are transferred direct to a computer. The images can then be altered, sized and incorporated into a DTP-prepared document.

thumbnails – rough, small-scale designs drawn on paper.

Using DTP software

Planning your design: thumbnails

It is a good idea to plan out a design for your document on paper first. **Thumbnails** are small-scale, rough designs on paper. They are used to plan the layout of each page in a document. You can try different layouts and then decide on the best one. Shaded boxes or a number of quickly drawn, horizontal lines are used for columns of text. Darker boxes or boxes with the diagonals drawn in are used for photos or artwork (diagrams, clip art, etc.). 'Squiggly' lines of varying height and thickness are used for headlines and subheadings.

Some tips when planning your design:

- Do not worry about details. Just get the main features in the best place.
- Try to get everything in proportion. If there is a picture that occupies one third of the page, then make it occupy a third on your thumbnail.
- Make lots of sketches. Put things in different places and see if it works or not.
- Don't start using the software until you have decided on your final design.

Templates

Rather than create a design from scratch you can use a design that has already been created. These designs are called **templates**. Some templates allow you to alter them slightly. These templates will often guide you through a series of choices that will tailor the design to your specification.

Some programs include their own set of designer templates for various kinds of document.

Templates determine the structure of a document. They specify things like:

- **fonts:** the style of the letters and numbers used
- **page layout:** margins, justification (how the sentences are lined up), indents, line spacing (i.e. the spacing between lines of text), the number of columns of text on a page, etc.
- **special formatting:** bold, italics, etc.

Here are some advantages of using templates:

- Templates can save you time.
- If everyone in an organisation uses the same template, all the documents produced by the organisation will have a consistent style.

Figure 15.2

Some examples of rough, hand-drawn designs (thumbnails)

Key Jargon

templates – electronic files which hold standardised document layouts.

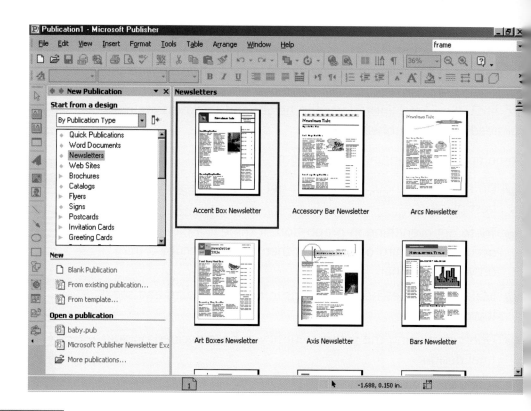

Microsoft Publisher allows you to select a design and put your own content (text, graphics, etc.) into it

Frames

DTP packages often use a frame-based system to produce layouts. This means text and graphics are placed in boxes called frames. These frames can then be moved around the document and repositioned.

Style sheets

Style sheets are used to help make the text, headings and subheadings consistent. It also makes it easier and quicker to apply styles to the document.

Find it out yourself

There is an excellent website that contains advice about drawing pictures and cartoons. Take a look at it on:

http://desktoppub.miningco.com/library/weekly/aa980519.htm?pid=2827&cob=home

is coming up to bonfire night and your local council wants to promote
e local firework display. It is much safer to watch fireworks at an
ganised display than in your garden at home.

u have been asked to produce two posters: one aimed at parents to
t them to attend the council's organised display, and one aimed at the
udents in your school, warning them of the dangers of playing with
reworks.

oth of these posters should be designed using DTP software.

ake sure that the posters are eye-catching and that they get the
essage across.

Giving presentations

Multimedia software

Multimedia software combines more than one medium for
presentation purposes, such as sound, graphics and video. The
implest type of multimedia software is presentation software.

Presentation software

Presentation software can be used when you have to give a talk.
The purpose of the talk could be to give information or advice, or
to sell a product or service.

Presentation software can take the place of an overhead projector
that uses slides. If the audience is small, the presentation can be
done on the screen of the computer. If there is a large audience,
the computer can be connected to a special projector that
projects the image onto a large white screen.

The presentation software used here is Microsoft PowerPoint,
which is included as part of the Microsoft Office set of programs.

Establishing the structure of a presentation

Before using the computer, you need to think about the purpose of your presentation and the type of audience it is aimed at. This will affect the language level and general 'tone' of your presentation.

If the presentation is extremely important – if it is part of your job for instance – or if it is to be used over and over again, then it is worth spending a lot of time thinking about and producing it.

You should consider:

- the number of slides you wish to include
- the design of the slides (it is best to use a design that is set up already – this is called a design template)
- the colour scheme (choose a number of colours that work well with your chosen design template)
- a title for the presentation
- a subtitle, if needed
- animation effects
- whether or not to include other objects such as tables, clip art, drawings, etc.

Templates

A template determines the overall 'look' of a document. Using a template will help make your presentation look more professional. With templates, specialists have already decided what type styles, colours, layouts and so on look right. All you have to do is think about what to put on your slides.

Creating a presentation

Activity 2

In this activity you will learn how to:

- pick a design template
- pick a colour scheme
- prepare the slides
- animate text
- run a presentation
- save a presentation.

Load the PowerPoint software. The opening screen will appear:

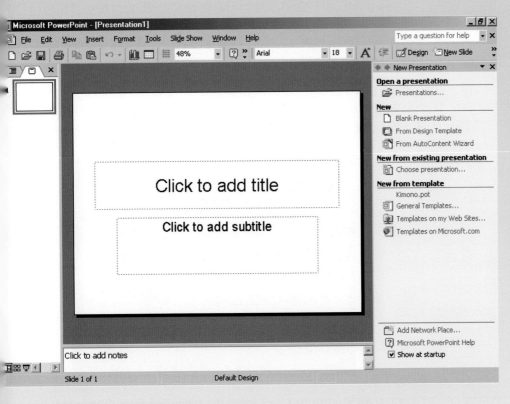

2 Click on From Design Template in the New section of the screen. The
following screen will appear:

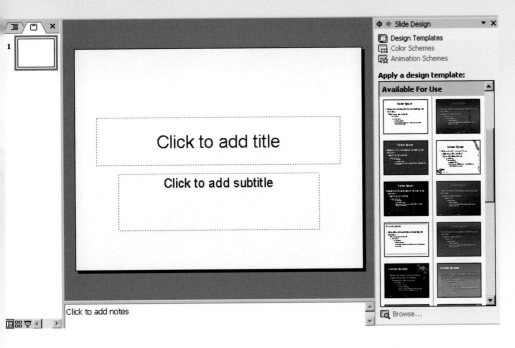

continued over page

You will see a selection of templates, shown as small screenshots, down the right-hand side of the screen. To choose one of them, double click on it.

The main screen will now change and you will see a large version of your chosen template. At this point you may change your mind about using it. To do this you simply double click on the template you prefer.

3 You will now be guided through setting up your slides.

Click on the top box and enter the following title: **Computer Graphics**.

Click on the bottom box and enter: **Advantages of using CAD**.

Your first slide will now look like this:

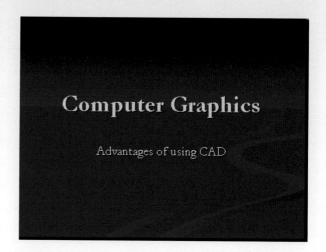

4 To make the title more eye-catching, you can get the text to move. This is called adding animation effects.

Click on Animation Schemes in the Slide Design section of the screen (see opposite).

There are different levels of animation. Move to the Exciting section. Now click on Neutron (see figure opposite).

Try some of the other animation effects by clicking on them to see what happens.

You can change the background colour of the slide by clicking on Color Schemes in the Slide Design section. Again, if you click on each one in turn you can select a colour that you like.

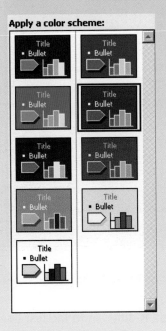

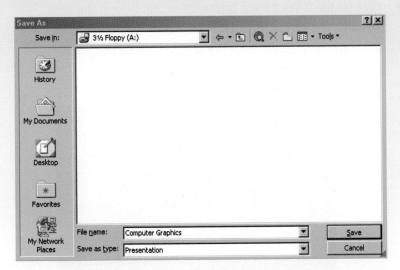

7 To save the slide, click on File and Save As.

Your teacher will tell you where to save your work. Check that the filename **Computer Graphics** is in the File name box. Now click on the Save button.

continued over page

409

8 To create the next slide, click on the following button on the toolbar:

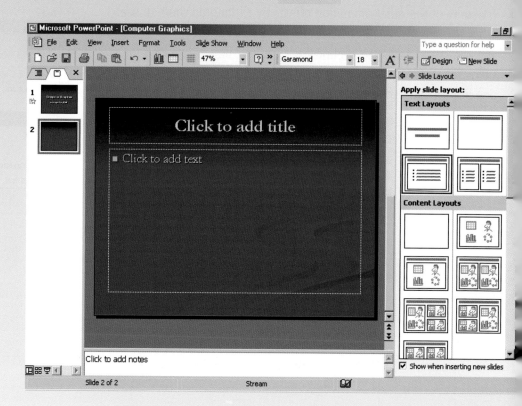

Notice that this slide is different to the first one. This is because the first slide is used to introduce the presentation.

9 Click on the 'Click to add title' section and type in the title: **Advantages of using CAD**.

Move to and click on the 'Click to add text' section.

Key in the text as shown on the following slide:

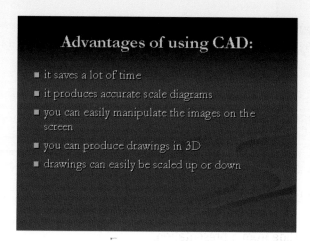

◑ Notice that as you build up the presentation, small versions of the slides are displayed in sequence (see opposite).

◀ Click once on Slide 1 in the above list. To play the presentation, click on 🖵 situated at the bottom left-hand side of the screen. This starts the slide show from the current slide.

2 Save your presentation using the same filename as before.

ips

ere are some tips to help you make a good slide:

○ Keep a constant colour scheme and design throughout the presentation.

○ Only have between five and seven words per line.

○ Only have five to seven bullet points per page.

○ Do not write in complete sentences (only give the main points).

○ Don't overdo the animation and other special effects.

○ Only put one concept on each slide.

above all, use the **KISS** principle (**K**eep **I**t **S**imple and **S**traightforward).

Activity 3

he best way to learn PowerPoint is to experiment with it. In fact this is he best way to learn about any software. Don't worry about making mistakes.

f you want to find out how to do something, then use the help.

Jse the help in PowerPoint to write instructions on how to do each of the following:

◀ change the colour of the text

◀ change the font

◀ increase the size of the font

◀ delete a slide from a presentation.

Activity 4

For this activity, produce a set of slides for a presentation on one of the following topics:

- the Data Protection Act
- the social implications of computers
- keeping your data safe
- the steps involved in systems analysis.

Producing and manipulating graphics
Drawing/graphics packages

Graphics is a word used for all types of artwork, including:

- line diagrams
- coloured drawings
- paintings
- bitmap images
- photographs
- graphs
- charts.

Graphics/drawing packages

Graphics/drawing packages are software that can produce, capture, manipulate and enhance graphic images. The simple Paint package available as part of Windows is a graphics package.

With graphics packages you are able to:

- use pre-defined shapes
- do freehand drawing
- use colour

- add text
- 'flood fill'
- use texture effects
- rotate shapes
- use different types of 'brushes'
- use spray-paint effects
- import images
- move, copy, reflect and scale sections of a picture.

Figure 15.4

The drawing/graphics package Paint provided with the Windows operating system. If you have Windows then you will have this piece of software

Computer-aided design

Computer-aided design (CAD) is a specialist drawing/graphics package used by engineers, architects, etc. to produce high quality technical drawings to scale.

The advantages of using CAD as opposed to traditional drawing techniques include:

- CAD saves a lot of time
- it produces accurate scale diagrams
- you can manipulate or make changes to the images on the screen easily
- you can produce drawings in 3D (useful if you are designing kitchens, gardens, buildings, etc.)

- images can be saved on disk and retrieved at a later date
- drawings can be scaled up and down easily.

Applications of CAD

CAD can be used whenever something needs to be designed and drawn, for example it is used by:

- architects for designing of buildings, etc.
- house builders for designing conservatories, kitchens, bedrooms, bathrooms, etc.
- landscape gardeners for designing gardens
- engineers for designing cars, aircraft, ships, bridges, components, etc.

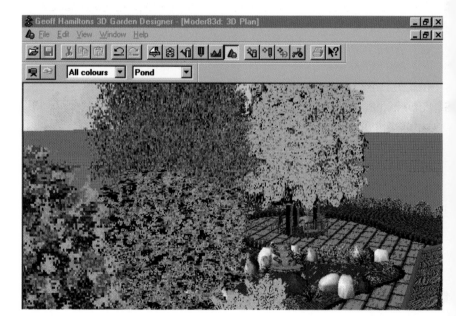

Figure 15.5

Garden design software allows you to design a garden in plan view and then see what it looks like from different angles in 3D

Find it out yourself

Investigate this site at the following address:

www.library.thinkquest.org

It is a good site for finding out about CAD, and includes a free downloadable CAD program.

Activity 5

Drawing packages have many different tools with which you can draw pictures.

a Name **three** tools that are found in a drawing package.

b Describe **two** features of a computer-aided design (CAD) package that would not normally be found in a drawing package.

Explain how a CAD package could be used to design the layout of a new computer room.

A bedroom design company is going to buy a specialist graphics package so that bedroom designs can be printed out and given to customers. Briefly outline **four** features (apart from saving and printing) that you would expect such a package to have.

John is doing a project about space, and to brighten up each page of his project he has imported some clip art into it.

a What is meant by 'clip art'?

b Explain briefly what 'imported' means in the above sentence.

c Describe **two** places where clip art can be found.

Jane is the secretary for her local Girl Guides group, and one of her responsibilities is to produce a quarterly newsletter in colour outlining the group's activities. She wants to use colour photographs, articles and diagrams.

a Outline **two** pieces of hardware she would need, other than the computer, to produce the newsletter.

b Jane receives a photograph that she would like to include in the newsletter. Describe how she could store the photograph as a computer file.

Capturing graphics images

Graphics images often need to be put into documents and websites. Obtaining the image in the first place is called **capturing** the image. Capturing an image can be done in the following ways:

- using a digital camera (if the image is a photo)
- using clip art from a disk; there are also plenty of sites on the internet where you can download free clip art (clip art includes drawings and photos)

Key Jargon

capturing – obtaining an image in a form that enables it to be stored or manipulated (sized, cropped, etc.) by the computer.

- obtaining an image from a website (be aware of the copyright restrictions when doing this)
- scanning an image in (this could be a picture from a magazine, a drawing or a photo).

Manipulating or enhancing graphic images

Once an image has been captured, it may need adjusting in som way. Graphics software is available that allows you to alter (manipulate) images. Here are some of the ways that an image can be manipulated or enhanced:

- it can be sized (i.e. made bigger or smaller)
- the contrast can be altered
- the brightness can be altered
- part of the image can be cropped (this is just like cutting out the part you want
- individual colours in the image can be adjusted
- it can be saved in different file formats.

1 DTP stands for:

a Desktop publishing
b Desktop printing
c Desk to publisher
d Dump to printer.

2 Which one of these hardware devices would not be useful when using DTP software?

a digital camera
b scanner
c colour printer
d Magnetic Ink Character Reade.

3 Obtaining material from another file and incorporating it into a document in a DTP package is called:

a importing
b exporting
c emigrating
d deleting.

4 The two formats for graphics files are:

a bitmap and vector
b bitmap and clip art
c vector and clip art
d CAD and CAM.

5 Which one of the following best describes clip art?

a CAD software
b pre-drawn pictures that may be imported into documents
c text from a wordprocessing package
d special art software

6 A salesperson wants to use presentation software to give a talk to customers. Which one of the following will not make the presentation more interesting?

a   a slide show
b   animation
c   colour
d   black and white

7 CAD software can be used by architects. Which one of the following is not an advantage of CAD software?

a   you can produce accurate diagrams
b   drawings can be scaled
c   3D views can be obtained
d   a lot of training is needed before it can be used

8 An engineer wishes to design a component and then look at it in three dimensions. Which software is the most appropriate for this purpose?

a   presentation
b   DTP
c   CAD
d   spreadsheet

9 A company wishes to produce its own newsletter. The newsletter is to contain pictures, photos, text and cartoons in various fonts. The most appropriate software to use for this task would be:

a   desktop publishing
b   wordprocessing
c   presentation
d   spreadsheet.

10 Which one of these best describes presentation software?

a   software for designing buildings
b   an applications package for producing slides
c   software for performing calculations
d   software for checking for viruses

a Name **four** pieces of hardware, other than the computer itself, which would be useful in desktop publishing.

b For each piece of hardware that you have named in part a, say why it would be useful.

2 **a** What do the initials DTP stand for?

b Give the name of a desktop publishing package that you have used or that you have seen.

3 Here are some of the features of a desktop publishing package. Write a sentence to show that you know what each one means and how they are useful.

a columns

b frames

c templates

4 Give **two** advantages of using DTP when preparing a page for a newsletter.

5 DTP software acts as an integrator, bringing lots of different files together in a document.

Give the names of **three** different types of file that can be imported into a DTP package.

F Questions

1 A group of young people at a local tennis club are going to use a DTP (desktop publishing) package to produce a notice to advertise a tennis summer school. Their first attempt is shown here:

Tennis Summer School
Dates – August 4th to August 7th
Time – 10am to 3pm
Chief Coach – Mrs Perry
Clothing – suitable tennis clothing must be worn
Cost – £20 to members, £30 to non-members

This course is open to all age groups – come along and have fun.

They were not very pleased with their first attempt and they have used the DTP (desktop publishing) package t make a number of changes. Their new poster is shown below.

Tennis Summer School

Dates – August 4th to August 7th
Time – 10am to 3pm
Chief Coach – Mrs Perry
Clothing – suitable tennis clothing must be worn
Cost – £20 to members, £30 to non-members
This course is open to all age groups – come along and have fun.

---

a Give **four** features of the DTP (desktop publishing) package that have been used to produce the changes to the new poster.

b Describe **three** different features of the DTP (deskto publishing) package that could be used to further improve the poster. Give a reason why each feature might be used.

(NEAB, Tier F, June 2000, p1, q

---

2 A company which designs and fits bedrooms is planning to buy a graphics package to produce designs that can be printed and given to its customers. Outline **five** features (other than saving and printing) that you would expect the package to have.

(AQA Specification A Tier F full course, specimen paper, q

H Questions

1 For the last ten years a history teacher has used a manua typewriter to produce most of the worksheets. The history department is about to produce a new set of worksheets for Year 7 on the Romans.

a Explain the advantages of using a desktop publishing (DTP) package for this task rather than the typewriter.

b What arguments do you think the teacher could use for continuing to use a typewriter to produce the worksheets?

(AQA Specification A Tier H full course, specimen paper, q10)

2 A company wants to produce its own leaflets, flyers, etc. It decides to produce these using desktop publishing.

a Other than the computer itself, state **three** items of hardware the company should buy for its system.

b For each of the items of hardware you have given in a, say why it is needed.

c The desktop publishing package uses a template. Explain why it is easier to use a template to produce documents than to create them from scratch each time.

Coursework

Coursework is work that you undertake on your own using the computer. It is extremely important, since in all of the GCSE courses (full and short) it will contribute 60% of your final mark.

What you have to do as part of your course is outlined in a lengthy document called a specification. To obtain the relevant specification you need to know whether you are taking the short or full (GCSE) course and also which specification (A or B) you are doing. You can then log onto the website of the exam board, where you will find a lot of useful information, including the specifications. You can then download the documents you need.

Here is a summary of what you need to do for each specification.

AQA Specification A

Full course

Coursework contributes 60% to the final assessment and consists of an assignment and a project.

AQA set assignment   *30% of total marks*

The AQA set assignment consists of a situation in which you have to solve certain problems with the appropriate use of ICT. It is described in a booklet, which you will be given. You will have to produce a report which demonstrates your ability to analyse a problem, identify what is required to solve the problem and to make use of ICT to provide solutions which you will then design, implement, test and evaluate.

Project   *30% of total marks*

Candidates are required to submit a report on the solution to a problem that demonstrates their ICT capabilities. Wherever possible, you should select a problem from your own area of interest.

Short course

Coursework contributes 60% to the final assessment mark and consists of an assignment set by AQA.

AQA set assignment   *60% of total marks*

The AQA set assignment consists of a situation in which you have to solve certain problems with the appropriate use of ICT. It is described in a booklet, which you will be given. You will have to produce a report which demonstrates your ability to analyse a problem, identify what is required to solve the problem and to make use of ICT to provide solutions which you will then design, implement, test and evaluate.

AQA Specification B

Full course

Coursework contributes 60% to the final assessment mark.

Candidates are required to submit reports on two coursework tasks, one from each of the following areas:

- Communicating and handling information
- Controlling, measuring and modelling.

The tasks will:

- involve using ICT to solve a problem
- address a need (e.g. a third party may have asked you to design and implement a solution to a problem).

Short course

Coursework contributes 60% to the final assessment.

Candidates are required to submit a report on one coursework task from either of the two following themes:

- Communicating and handling information
- Controlling, measuring and modelling.

The task will:

- involve using ICT to solve a problem
- address a need (e.g. a third party may have asked you to design and implement a solution to a problem).

Learning about software

Before you start your coursework you should have developed skills in using a range of software. The more you understand the capabilities of the software, the easier you will find the coursework. This is because you will see the solutions to problems more easily.

There are many different ways in which you can build up your expertise and skills in using software. Some of them are listed below.

Experimentation

This is where you have an idea and you see if it works. Try to get into the habit of looking to see what is in each pull-down menu. Don't be afraid to try things out as this is the best way to learn.

Using a computer manual

Sometimes these come with the package but many rely on on-line help to give advice.

Using computer magazines

Computer Active is a cheap computer magazine published every fortnight. It contains step-by-step workshops which show you how to do things using popular software.

Getting your parents, relatives or friends to show you

If someone you know has used a software package, they will probably be only too glad to help you. By sitting down with an experienced user for an hour or two you can learn a lot very quickly.

These people can help you learn the software but they must not help you to do your coursework.

Using the on-line help facility

Most packages come with excellent on-line help. Many people forget that this help is available and are quite amazed at what they can find out once they are shown how to use it. Sometimes there is a complete tutorial in the on-line help which guides you through using the package. Try to get used to using this facility and it will help you not only to improve your skills in using the package, but also to improve the mark you get for the coursework and in the examination.

Figure 16.1 shows how you search for help on a certain topic in Microsoft Word.

Figure 16.1

Searching for help in Microsoft Word

Figure 16.2 is an example of the on-line help provided with Microsoft Word XP. The user wants to know how to put a box around text that has been typed on the screen. In this case they have typed in what they want to do (i.e. putting boxes around text). The help routine then finds the topics nearest to what they want.

Using Figure 16.2, the user has chosen to find out about the difference between a text box and a frame. The following help screen appears:

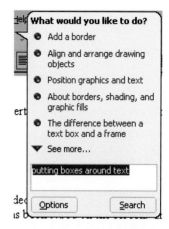

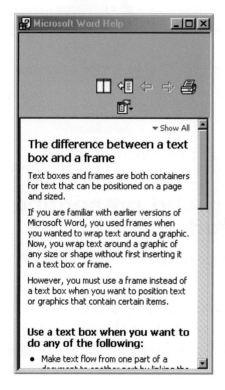

If you get stuck trying to use software, use the on-line help

How much help can my teacher give?

Your teacher can explain how to use the software but they cannot give you any help with work relating to your coursework.

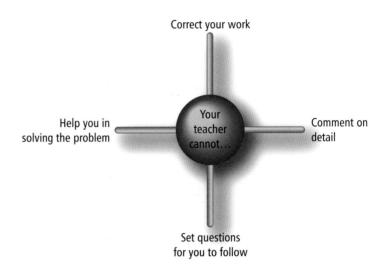

Correct your work

Help you in solving the problem

Your teacher cannot...

Comment on detail

Set questions for you to follow

Figure 16.4

Coursework must be all your own work

Choosing and presenting coursework

Here is some advice on choosing and presenting your coursework:

- Plan your work beforehand and make sure that you have or can obtain the software and hardware necessary for the task.

- Choose your coursework carefully (if you have a choice) and don't be too ambitious. Discuss it with your teacher to make sure that it is not too difficult.

- Wordprocess or desktop publish your work. Since you are following an ICT course, you should make use of all the latest technology.

- To save time, type your work directly into the wordprocessor without writing it out first. If you need to make changes, such as insert text, delete text or shuffle material around, then this can be done easily using the software.

- Make the front cover look attractive but do not spend too much time on it.

- Include diagrams wherever possible. They brighten up the page and by using them you can cut down on the number of words you use. Try to use different types of diagrams such as system flowcharts, structure diagrams, etc., as appropriate.

Hints and tips for coursework

Here are some hints and tips to help you obtain the best mark you can for your coursework.

● Documentation is very important. Do not simply try to solve the problem. It is more important to show that you have carried out the analysis, design and implementation correctly.

● Annotate and explain any work you do. Do not simply produce printouts without any explanation.

● Make your solutions efficient. For example, in a database system, do not duplicate data.

● The user guide should be about using the software rather than how to solve the problem. It is important to mention how the user should perform the day-to-day tasks.

● Always include all your work, even the parts that didn't work. This provides evidence of your solution and must be included to maximise your marks. Remember that before you can find a good solution to a problem, a number of bad solutions have to be rejected.

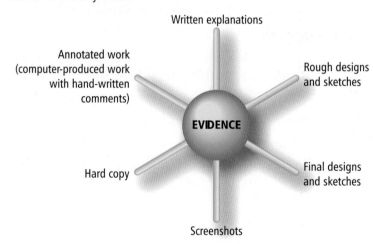

Figure 16.5

Evidence all the way. It is no good just doing it – you must prove that you have done it

Specification A: the project

Your project should be structured in the following way:

Analysis

Your analysis section should include:

● a clear statement of the problem

● an analysis of how the job is presently done (you could find out about the present or proposed system by giving the users questionnaires to fill in)

- identification of the problems with the existing system
- a breakdown of the overall problem into smaller sub-problems
- the different ways of solving the problem
- diagrams to explain how the current system works and also to explain the new system (e.g. flowcharts, structure diagrams and dataflow diagrams)
- forms such as data capture forms
- the performance criteria you will use to evaluate the success of the project (these are lists by which your new system will be judged).

Design

The design looks at how the problem is to be solved. The design stage should include the following:

- the input, processing and output requirements of the new system
- explanations of your choice of hardware/software
- a test plan (i.e. what you intend to test for)
- the design of input screens (include rough designs on paper as well as screenshots of the actual designs)
- the design of output (form designs, screen designs, etc.)
- if a database is used – the tables, relationships, table structure, validation checks, etc.
- if a spreadsheet is used – the design of the worksheet (paper rough as well as on the computer).

Implementation

This is the stage where you start to build your solution to the problem.

You need to provide evidence of doing this, for example:

- screenshots
- printouts
- annotated printouts (these are printouts with your comments handwritten on them)
- photographs (if you have produced a control system)
- text (you need to explain how you made your design a reality).

During the implementation you need to keep records of any changes that you needed to make to your design. Keep records of things that did not work and how you corrected them to make them work.

Testing

Testing should be done against the test plan.

Testing includes:

- comparing the results expected with the results actually obtained and any action that was needed
- comparing the solution with the user specification to ensure that the solution includes everything that the user wanted.

Evaluation

In the evaluation section you need to comment on your solution:

- How effective was it?
- What difficulties did you encounter?
- If you could do it again, what might you do differently?
- What modifications had to be made to get the solution to work?
- What did the user think of the solution to the problem? (You could get the user to fill in a questionnaire.)

User guide

A user guide explains to the user how to use your solution to their problem. It is important that this guide explains how to use the entire system and not just the computer part.

The user guide might contain some or all of the following:

- the hardware and software requirements of the system
- how to load the software
- how to perform certain functions
- how to save
- how to print
- frequently asked questions
- how to deal with error messages and troubleshooting.

Specification B: the two coursework tasks

Both coursework tasks need to contain the following sections:

- description of the task to be attempted
- analysis
- specification
- implementation
- testing
- user documentation
- evaluation.

The implementation stage in the above list is the largest section, carrying the greatest number of marks. This may be further broken down into the following sections:

- hardware resources required
- software resources required
- data collection, data capture and input
- data verification and/or validation
- data and/or program structures
- output format.

Examples of projects

Here are some ideas for projects:

- organising a school fund-raising event
- organising a school trip
- running the annual school/college production – seat bookings, cash flow monitoring, ticket production, etc.
- organising young people's group, e.g. scouts, guides, cadets, youth club, etc. This could include records and finances, letters home, activities, etc.
- running a small business, e.g. a nursery, riding stables, golf club shop, tuck shop, estate agent or charity
- record keeping and stationery for a small business
- running a holiday cottage or flat
- producing a management system for a sports club, e.g. football, hockey, netball or tennis, or for a local club/society

- organising and producing a regular magazine or newsletter, or a range of publicity materials, including production costs and page templates. This could be for any of the organisations mentioned above, or a parish church group

- record keeping for a school or college department – pupil homework/classwork – linked to reminder letters for late submission, missing work, etc.

- lending library or equipment library for a school department

- record system for a school or college store-keeping system, e.g. science, CDT or art department

- booking system for a local leisure centre; this could be linked to an advertising and promotional system for the centre

- keeping records for a local taxi firm, e.g. drivers' hours and availability, mileages for servicing the cabs. Similar idea for a local transport/haulier firm where there is more emphasis on the mileages, service intervals, truck availability, etc.

- used car sales.

Exam preparation

You can be entered for one of two tiers of assessment: the foundation (F) tier or the higher (H) tier. The grades you can get for the two tiers are as follows:

- Tier H – grades A* to D
- Tier F – grades C to G

Spelling, punctuation and grammar

There are a number of marks available for spelling, punctuation and grammar for both the examination and the coursework. You need to make sure that your handwriting is clear and that you use spelling, grammar and punctuation correctly.

How do I revise?

Everyone has their own way of revising but here are a few tips which might help.

- Start your revision early. Remember you will have a lot of other subjects to revise nearer exam time.
- Work at a well-lit table or desk.
- Work somewhere quiet where there will not be any distractions.

- Write out brief notes. You tend to remember more this way.

- Make a plan of how much revision you will do and the times you will do it. Try to stick to this timetable.

- Try to get up early. If you complete your revision early you then have the rest of the day to enjoy yourself.

- Get friends/relatives to test you. You could give them the glossary at the back of this book to test you on definitions of terms.

- Use a copy of the specification to make sure that you have covered everything. Write out a checklist and tick off the material that you have revised.

- Go over past examination papers. You may be able to get these from the exam board's website.

Figure 16.6

You can download a copy of the specification at the AQA website: www.aqa.org.uk

Before the exam

- Collect the necessary equipment: two pens (in case one dries up); two pencils; a sharpener; a rubber; and a ruler. You may be allowed to use a flowchart template but check first. You might not be able to use one with the names of the boxes on it.

- Always take a watch into the exam. There will be a clock in the exam room but if you are at the back you might not be able to see it.

- Go to the toilet before the exam; this avoids the embarrassment of having to leave the room under supervision.
- Check to see if you have to wear school uniform.

The exam

The following list gives some hints on things you should do when actually taking the exam:

- Always read the instructions on the front of the paper carefully. In particular, note the time you are allowed.
- Time yourself. Don't spend too much time on a question that you can answer well at the expense of other questions.
- Try to write neatly. The examiners have hundreds of scripts to mark and it is not worth risking annoying an examiner by making him or her waste time deciphering an untidy script.
- Only do what the question asks. If it asks for two reasons, make sure that you give two; not three or one. Always check that, in an answer to a question with two parts, you have not written similar answers to both parts. If you have, you will only obtain marks for one of them.
- Use the mark scheme at the side of the questions as a guide to how much you should write. If there are, say, two marks, there are likely to be two points you need to mention in order to get both marks.
- After you have answered a question, read it through again to make sure that you have not missed part of it out.

Understanding what the examiner wants

There are certain terms used in questions and it is important to understand what they mean. If you write too much you will waste time. If you write too little you will lose marks. You need to write the correct amount. Here is what each term means:

List, name, give and state
These all require a one-word answer.

Compare
Here you need to look at both the similarities and the differences.

Describe
This means that you need to give a detailed answer. If there are four marks allocated, then make sure that you write a minimum

of four sentences with each covering a different aspect of the answer.

Define

This usually means explain a technical term in language that anyone could undertand.

Explain

Explain means saying why.

"CHEAPER ...

FASTER ...

BETTER ..."

Figure 16.7

Avoid simple answers like this. They will not gain any marks

Using the knowledge you have built up during practical sessions

You will have built up your skills in using IT over a long period of time. You will also have had to demonstrate these skills when doing your coursework. Since many of the questions will be about doing certain tasks using IT, the greater your experience then the more knowledge you will have. You should make sure that you demonstrate the experience you have gained when answering questions.

Even though you may have the knowledge you might have difficulty in answering questions.

Revision websites

There are plenty of websites on the Internet to help you revise. Take a look at the following ones:

http://www.school-resources.co.uk/GCSEITRevisionQuizzes.htm
Find out how well your revision is going. There are lots of multiple-choice questions to test you here.

http://www.dgs.oxon.sch.uk/depts/it/gcse/notes/
There is a good set of revision notes here and some quizzes to test your understanding.

http://www.bbc.co.uk/schools/gcsebitesize/ict/
This is a good on-line revision site produced by the BBC.

http://www.projectgcse.co.uk/it/
This includes some good materials on applications and project work.

Glossary

actuator – a hardware device, such as a motor, which reacts to signals given to it by a computer.

analogue – data represented by a continuously changing quantity.

append – add new data to a table or file.

applications software – software designed to do a particular job.

attachment – a file that is attached to an e-mail.

AutoNumber – a unique number that is given automatically by the computer. It always gives the next number in the sequence.

back-up – a copy of data or software kept in case the original data or software is lost or damaged.

bandwidth – determines how fast data can be passed through a transmission medium.

batch processing – all the inputs needed are batched together and processed in one go.

broadband – a very high-speed Internet connection (usually cable).

bullet point – a line of text or a word that has a symbol placed in front to make it stand out.

capturing – obtaining an image in a form that enables it to be stored or manipulated (sized, cropped, etc.) by the computer.

CD-ROM – a compact disk containing data and programs that can only be read.

CD-RW – a CD that can be used in a similar way to a floppy disk.

cell – an area on a spreadsheet produced by the intersection of a column and a row in which data can be placed.

check digit – a number placed at the end of a string of numbers to check that they have all been correctly input to the computer.

Computer Misuse Act 1990 – a law that covers the misuse of computer equipment.

Copyright, Designs and Patents Act 1989 – a law making it a criminal offence to copy or steal software.

Data – information in a form that can be processed by the computer.

Data capture – the way a computer obtains data for processing.

Data controller – the person in charge of the data in an organisation. They make sure that all the terms of the Data Protection Act are complied with.

Data logger – a device which collects readings from a sensor at a certain rate over a certain period of time.

Data logging – a system that collects data automatically over a certain period of time. Remote weather stations use data logging.

Data Protection Act 1998 – a law that restricts the way personal information is stored and processed on a computer.

Data subjects – the individuals to whom the personal data refers.

Database – a series of files/tables stored in a computer that can be accessed in a variety of different ways.

Desktop publishing – combining text and pictures on a screen to produce posters, newsletters, brochures, etc.

Digital – data represented by groups of the binary digits 0 and 1.

Digital camera – a camera that can be used to take a picture and store it digitally.

Documentation – the paperwork that accompanies a system explaining how the system works.

DVD – digital versatile disk. A disk with a larger storage capacity than a CD-ROM. Set to replace CD-ROMs, recent models allow the user to write data to the disk.

e-commerce – buying and selling goods or services over the internet, as opposed to using traditional methods such as shops or offices.

encryption – the process of encoding sensitive data before it is sent over a network.

expert system – a system that behaves in the same way as a human expert in a specialist field.

fact find – the investigation of a system to understand how it works or should work.

fax machine – a machine capable of sending and receiving te and pictures along telephone lines.

feasibility report – a report/document containing the summarised findings of a feasibility study which the decision makers can use to decide whether or not to go ahead with the new system.

feasibility study – a study carried out by experts to see what type of system is needed before a new system is developed.

feedback – where the output from a system directly affects th input.

field – an item of data or a space for data in a database.

file – a collection of related records.

flaming – emotional, often rude, e-mail messaging.

flowchart – a chart or diagram used to break down a task into smaller parts. It can also show the order of the tasks and any decisions which need to be made.

font – a style of type.

footer – text placed at the bottom of a document.

form – a screen used to enter data into a database. It can also be a paper document that is used to collect data.

Freedom of Information Act 2000 – a law which gives the public access to recorded information held by public bodies that could affect them in some way.

gateway – the device/software that translates between two different kinds of computer networks (e.g. between a WAN and LAN).

GIGO – Garbage In Garbage Out. It means that if you put rubbish into a computer then you get rubbish out.

grammar checker – a program (usually part of a wordprocessing package) that checks a document for grammatical errors and suggests corrections.

hackers – people who try to break into a computer network.

hacking – the process of trying to break into a secure computer system.

hardware – the parts of the computer that you can touch and handle.

header – text placed at the top of a document.

HTML (Hypertext Markup Language) – a language used for the development of websites.

hypertext link – a link that allows you to go from one web page to another.

implementation – the process of converting to a new system.

information – what we get when data is processed.

internet – worldwide network of computer networks. The internet forms the largest connected set of computers in the world.

ISDN (Integrated Services Digital Network) – a communications standard for sending voice, video and data over digital lines. It is much faster than sending data using modems, but not as fast as broadband.

ISP (Internet Service Provider) – a company that provides users with a connection to the Internet.

key field – a field that has a different value in every record.

LAN (local area network) – a network of computers on one site.

log on – to supply your user-ID and password successfully and be allowed to use a network.

logical operator – one of the Boolean operators AND, OR and NOT.

LOGO – a simple programming language which enables a 'turtle' to move according to the instructions given to it.

macro – a program written using applications software to automate a collection of keystrokes or events to save time.

magnetic ink character recognition (MICR) – a method of data input that involves reading magnetic ink characters on certain documents. MICR is used by banks to read information off cheques.

magnetic stripe reader – a device that reads the data contained in magnetic stripes, such as those on the backs of credit cards.

master file – the most important version of a file, since it is th
most complete and up-to-date version.

merge – put two sets of data together to form one larger set c
data.

MP3 – a format for music files that makes use of compression.
is often used when music files are downloaded from the Interne

network – a group of computers which are able to
communicate with each other.

network interface card (NIC) – a card which slots into the
main circuit board of a computer. It is needed to turn the
computer into a terminal.

non-volatile memory – memory which does not lose
programs or data when the power is switched off.

operating system – the software that controls the hardware
and runs the programs.

optical character recognition (OCR) – uses a combination
of software and a scanner to read characters (letters, numbers
and punctuation marks) into a computer.

optical mark recognition (OMR) – the process of reading
marks (such as shaded boxes) made on a specially prepared
document. The marks are read by an optical mark reader.

parity check – a check to see if all the data has been
transferred correctly from one place to another.

password – a group of characters (i.e. letters, numbers and
punctuation marks) that needs to be entered to gain access to a
program or a computer system.

PDA (personal digital assistant) – a small, portable
computer used mainly for organising a busy schedule or sending
and checking e-mail.

physical security – measures to protect computers against
physical harm (usually theft or damage).

presence check – a check to make sure that data is present in
a field.

privacy – being able to decide what information about yourself
can be known by others.

private key – this is kept by the receiver of the encrypted data.
They use it to unscramble the data.

processing – doing something to raw data (e.g. calculating, sorting, etc.).

program – the set of step-by-step instructions that tells the computer hardware what to do.

public key – this is kept by the receiver of the encrypted data. They send it to people who want to communicate with them.

query – used to extract specific information from a database.

RAM – random access memory. A fast, temporary memory area where programs and data are stored only while a computer is switched on.

range check – a data validation technique which checks that the data input to a computer is within a certain range.

real-time processing – the input data is processed as it arrives. The results have a direct effect on the next set of available data.

record – a set of related information about a thing or an individual.

relational database – a database that consists of several files/tables with links between them so that the data can be combined.

relationships – the ways in which tables are related to each other in a relational database.

relative copying – copying a formula so that the formula changes to take account of its new position.

report – the output from software such as a database in which the results are presented in a way that is controlled by the user.

ROM – read-only memory. Computer memory whose contents can be read but not altered.

RSI – repetitive strain injury. A muscular condition caused by repeatedly using certain muscles in the same way. It builds up slowly until every muscle movement can be agony.

scanner – a hardware device used to scan pictures or text into a computer system.

search engine – a program that can be used to search for information on the Internet.

sensors – devices which measure physical quantities such as temperature and pressure.

simulation – an imitation of a system (e.g. aircraft flight) using a computer model. Any phenomenon that can be described mathematically (e.g. how the economy of the country works) can be simulated.

smart card – a plastic card which contains its own 'chip'.

software – the actual programs that allow the hardware to do a useful job.

sort – put into a new order.

spam – unwanted e-mail.

spellchecker – a program, usually found with a wordprocessor which checks the spelling in a document and suggests correctly spelt words.

system life cycle – the series of steps carried out during the creation of a new system.

systems analyst – a person who studies the overall organisation and implementation of an ICT system.

teleworking/telecommuting – working from home by making use of ICT equipment.

templates – electronic files which hold standardised document layouts.

thumbnails – rough, small-scale designs drawn on paper.

top-down design – a way of describing a problem where you start off with the problem and then break it down into a few smaller problems. Each of these smaller problems may then be broken down further. As you break the problem down, you look at it in more and more detail.

topologies – maps of networks showing how the various devices are connected together.

touchscreen – a special type of computer screen that is sensitive to touch. A selection is made from a menu on the screen by touching it.

transaction file – used to hold temporary data which is used to update the master file. It contains the details of changes (transactions) that have occurred since the master file was last updated.

transmission medium – the material through which data travels from one terminal to another.

pe check – a check performed by a computer to see if data is the right type to be put into a field. For example, it would eck that only numbers are entered into numeric fields.

er-ID – a name or number that is used to identify a certain er of the network or system.

er interface – the way that a user interacts with a computer stem.

lidation check – a check performed by a computer program make sure that the data being entered is allowable.

erification – checking the accuracy of data entry.

deoconferencing – using computer equipment to conduct a tual face-to-face meeting.

rus – a program created specifically to do damage to a mputer system.

rus checker – a program that detects and gets rid of mputer viruses which can do damage to a computer system.

oice recognition – the ability of a computer to 'understand' oken words by comparing them with stored data.

olatile memory – memory which loses data and programs hen the power is switched off.

AN (wide area network) – a network in which the rminals/computers are remote from each other and ommunicate using telecommunications.

eb camera – a digital camera used to capture still and video nages.

eb portal – a website where you get redirected to another ebsite.

rap – the process by which a computer automatically starts a ew line.

Index